FRAUDS,
DECEPTIONS
AND SWINDLES

FRAUDS, DECEPTIONS AND SWINDLES

Carl Sifakis

Checkmark Books®

An imprint of Facts On File, Inc.

Frauds, Deceptions and Swindles

Checkmark Books
An imprint of Facts On File, Inc.
11 Penn Plaza
New York NY 10001

Library of Congress Cataloging-in-Publication Data

Sifakis, Carl.
Frauds, deceptions and swindles / Carl Sifakis
p.   cm.
Includes bibliographical references and index.
ISBN 0-8160-4422-8 (alk. paper)
1. Swindlers and swindling—United States. 2. Fraud—United States. I. Title.
HV6695 .S53 2001
364.16'3'0973—dc21   2001017311

Checkmark Books are available at special discounts when purchased in bulk quantities for
businesses, associations, institutions or sales promotions. Please call our
Special Sales Department in New York at (212) 967-8800 or (800) 322-8755.

You can find Facts On File on the World Wide Web at http://www.factsonfile.com

Text design by Cathy Rincon
Cover design by Nora Wertz

Printed in the United States of America

MP FOF 10 9 8 7 6 5 4 3 2 1

This book is printed on acid-free paper.

Contents

Introduction

It was a caper worthy of a Marx Brothers movie, Crazy Eddie's insane fraud. In the 1980s no TV pitch bombarded Easterners more annoyingly than the screaming cry of Crazy Eddie's electronics chain that "our prices are insane." But they weren't the only thing; even more insane was the firm's accounting system, their tax payments and their Wall Street deals.

Wall Street wanted to invest in rapidly growing companies, and when Crazy Eddie's decided to go public, it gave brokers what they wanted, rapidly escalating profits. The firm, headed by Eddie Antar and his cousin Sam, had no trouble coming up with super growth. For years, the Antars had been skimming money from the business—and not just from actual profits, but from sales taxes as well. The boys' attitude on sales tax was that consumers paid them and the company rarely turned them over to the government. It was a simple case of the bucks stopping with the Antars.

Eventually the family skim backlog ran out with the company's profits growing some 40 percent a year, but there was just no more. The boys, taking a leaf out of the Marx Brothers playbook, tried shifting inventories from store to store so that auditors would count the same goods over and over. But the auditors weren't that insane, and jail sentences followed for the Antars. In the end the most insane were the Wall Streeters and investors who believed Crazy Eddie's.

At least the Antars were grown con men. Barry Minkow was only 16 when he started down the road to his great Wall Street stock con. He was hailed in the financial community as a young genius who grew his phantom company, rather amusingly titled ZZZZ Best, until it attained a stock capitalization of $200 million, was favored by lavish newspaper articles and celebrated on the *Oprah* television show. He fooled everyone, including his grandmother, his girlfriend and his parents, whom, it was said, he put on the company payroll just so he could have the pleasure of threatening to fire them.

Minkow's scheme was classic Ponzi, and it matched the Marx Brothers antics of the Brothers Antar: displaying work projects that were not ZZZZ Best's but that conned the auditors. When the bubble burst, the company's assets had shrunk from a capitalization of $200 million to furniture and the like that were auctioned off for a mere $64,000. In its wake, the Minkow rip-off left the usual trail of lost savings and lost dreams by the public.

This is the standard result of all such capers, large or small, since well before the time of Ponzi, allegedly the "man who invented money," and arch swindler Count Victor Lustig, who worked both sides of the Atlantic and managed to "sell" the Eiffel Tower, not once, but twice. In the late 20th century the same could be said of the depredations of big-money hustlers such as Michael Milken, Dennis Levine, Charles H. Keating Jr., Ivan Boesky and Jake Butcher.

Other shady operators find wild ways to impact people's lives, such as Virginia infertility specialist Cecil B. Jacobson, who supplied would-be parents with an "extensive, carefully regulated donor program," taking into consideration the physical, mental and social characteristics that would be most desirable. Dr. Jacobson touted himself as "the baby maker" and boasted that "God doesn't give you babies—I do."

The good doctor had little reason, however, to screen donors or store sperm until the proper time. He simply stepped into his office bathroom and produced the required sperm just before a patient arrived. Fee: as much as $5,000. Jacobson's racket was revealed when parent after parent started noticing how closely their newborns resembled babies of other Jacobson patients. One partial group photo was particularly distressing.

The hallmark of many confidence men and others of that ilk is sheer audacity. Two of the most fabled of American con men to hit the "bunco trail" were Fred Buckminster and Yellow Kid Weil, who frequently worked together but were not above constantly trying to scam one another.

Buckminster went into the con life while still a teenager and remained a swindler the rest of his life. He completed his last prison term at the age of 75, having stolen more than $3 million in an era of very hard money. Like Weil, Buckminster liked to claim that he never cheated the common man. The sad truth was that either would hustle anybody. But it is true that Buckminster enjoyed cheating other thieves, such as gamblers and dishonest businessmen and bankers, mainly because, he said, they were the easiest of pigeons. In the twilight of his career, Buckminster wrote a series of memoirs for a detective magazine. He altered a check given to him for the use of his byline from $100 to $1,000 and cashed it. A rumor never confirmed by the publisher was that he did the same with three other checks. The publishing house took it philosophically and did not prosecute. Sending a dying old man to prison made little sense, and it did seem a little late for Buckminster to mend his ways.

If anything, Weil was even more creative than Buckminster. Whenever possible, he sought to work the government. He came up with a scheme to try and establish a little independent republic on a small island made of fill somewhere in Lake Michigan. The angle, he told Saul Bellow in a magazine interview, was to make himself eligible under the foreign-aid program.

Once, the Kid decided to write his memoirs with Chicago journalist W. T. Brannon, after announcing again that he was going straight. He then sold the movie rights to his autobiography to Brannon as well as to a Hollywood studio. To Weil, the sales were perfectly logical and ethical. After all, hadn't he led a double life?

This volume, drawn from *The Encyclopedia of American Crime* and *Hoaxes and Scams*, covers many of the great deceptions practiced on the gullible. It might be prudent for readers to learn about as many as possible now rather than later—and perhaps more expensively.

Entries A – Z

accident faking   insurance swindle

Over the years faking accidents to swindle insurance companies has developed into a thriving business. There is no way to gauge accurately the extent of this crime since insurance industry figures are themselves suspect; many observers claim that the companies have a vested interest in minimizing the extent of fraud to deter other attempts and to defend their rate structures. Some calculations of accident frauds place the figure between $20 million and $100 million a year, with most estimates falling in the upper range. It was estimated that one insurance gang in Birmingham, Ala. cleared several million dollars over a seven-year period. Such insurance rings sometimes buy duplicates of legitimate X rays from doctors and then use them to bolster phony claims of industrial, auto and personal injuries.

One of the most incredible operations of this kind worked out of Kirksville, Mo. The swindle involved doctors, lawyers, osteopaths, nurses, insurance agents, a county sheriff, farmers and businessmen. Sixty-six of them were eventually convicted and sen-tenced. The racket was run by a crooked insurance agent. He favored realism in staging his phony claims; claimants had their wrists broken with crank handles and their fingers smashed with hammers. An osteopath would be called in to compound such injuries by manipulating the bones of the hand and giving injections designed to cause infections. In some cases miscalculations resulted in amputations, but these only increased the size of the award. The men, women and children who willingly pose as the accident victims in such plots are often of limited intelligence, but they are also usually poor and the pool of these volunteer victims increases dramatically during periods of high unemployment.

Faked pedestrian accidents have long been a mainstay of the racket. Sometimes both the victim and the driver are in collusion, but most fakers prefer to utilize an honest driver who can stand up to rigorous investigation because he really is innocent. "Floppers" and "divers" are used when the motorist is not a willing partner in the swindle. A flopper is a person who is adept at feigning being hit by a car going around a corner. Perpetrators insist this is not as hard to do as it would appear. The flopper simply stands in the street and starts crossing as the car makes its turn. Under such circumstances the car is moving relatively slowly, and the flopper bounces off the front fender and flips his body backward to the ground. As the crowd starts to gather, the flopper moan and groans. The premium flopper is one who has an old fracture, preferably a skull fracture since the break will show up in an X ray no matter how old it is. The flopper is naturally schooled in the art of faking serious injury. Just before the accident he will bite his lip open and dab some of the blood into his ear.

"Divers" are considered finer artists than floppers because their act seems more convincing. They work at night so that witnesses can't really see what is happening. As a car approaches, the diver runs into the street and in a crouching position slams the car door with his hand as hard as he can. The resulting loud noise quickly attracts onlookers as the diver lies on the ground, doing the same moaning and groaning act as the flopper.

One of the most bizarre accident swindles involved a father of identical twins. One child was normal but the other quite retarded. Rather than put the unfortunate child into an institution, the father decided to use him as a prop for a swindle scheme. He would take his normal child into stores and when no one was looking, he'd knock something off a shelf and have the child start screaming as though he had been hit on the head. The father would then create a scene and storm out of the store. Later, he would file suit against the store, charging the accident had permanently damaged his child's brain. As proof, he would produce the retarded twin. Settlements were hastily arranged since no company dared take such a case to a jury. The racket worked a number of times until an investigator making a routine check visited the family's home while the parents were out and saw the normal child playing in the backyard.

Adams, Albert J. (1844–1907) numbers king

A famous and colorful New York City gambler, known as the Policy King, Al Adams was the boss of the most extensive numbers game operation in the city.

Dishonesty has been the keynote of policy games from the time they started in England during the 1700s to the present, but Adams gave them a new wrinkle, not only bilking the public but also swindling other numbers operators in order to take over their businesses.

Adams came to New York from his native Rhode Island in the early 1870s and first worked as a railroad brakeman, a job he found much too taxing. He soon became a runner in a policy game operated by Zachariah Simmons. Duly impressed by Adams' penchant for deviousness, the older man took him in as a partner. Adams developed many ways to rig the game to reduce the winners' payoff. After Simmons died, Adams took over his operation and eventually became the boss of the New York policy racket. At the time, there were scores of independent operators. It was common practice for independent policy men to "lay off" numbers that had been bet too heavily for comfort. They would simply shift part of the action to another operator who had light play on the number, thus spreading the risk. When these operators tried to lay off a heavily played number with Adams, he would note the number and claim he already had too much action on it. He would then lay off the same number around the city, even if he actually had little or no action on it. Thus, a number of operators would become vulnerable to that number. Adams' next move was to fix the results so the heavily played number came out, hitting the owners of many policy shops with devastating losses. To make their payoffs, the operators had to seek loans from Adams, who exacted a partnership as the price of a loan, ultimately kicking the operators out entirely. Some policy operators he simply refused to help, forcing them to make their payoffs (many to Adams' undercover bettors) by dipping into the cash reserved for bribes to politicians and the police. Losing their protection, they were immediately shut down, and Adams simply moved in.

In time, it was estimated that Adams ran between 1,000 and 1,100 policy shops in the city. Over the years his payments to the Tweed Ring totaled in the millions. Even after Tweed fell and reformers came in, Adams was able to operate with the connivance of the police. It was not until 1901 that law enforcement authorities were forced to take action against his nefarious operations, raiding his headquarters. Adams was sent to Sing Sing, where he served more than a year.

When he came out, Adams found that he no longer controlled the New York policy game. The battle for control of the business was turning exceedingly violent, and Adams, who had always operated with bribes and trickery, neither needed nor wanted to be involved in wars to the death. He lived out the next few years in luxury in the Ansonia Hotel and amassed a great fortune through land speculation. However, he was estranged from his family, who was ashamed of his past criminality and blamed him for their inabil-ity to lead normal, respectable lives. On October 1, 1907 Adams committed suicide in his apartment.

Annenberg, Moses L. (1878–1942) gambling information czar

Moe Annenberg rose from Chicago's South Side slums to become, for a time, the possessor of the largest individual income of any person in the nation. Using methods not everyone considered legal, he was able to capitalize on two American traits, the desire to read newspapers and the eagerness to bet. However, like Al Capone, he ended up in prison for income tax evasion. For the year 1932 the government said Annenberg owed $313,000; he had paid $308. For 1936 Annenberg owed an estimated $1,692,000; he had paid $475,000. Together with interest and penalties his unpaid taxes totaled $9.5 million. And just as was true with Capone, Annenberg's income tax problems were merely a logical consequence of his other activities.

Annenberg, who had cut his teeth in the early Chicago circulation wars, was, in the words of William Randolph Hearst, a "circulation genius." That "genius" meant selling newspapers with an army of sluggers, overturning the competition's delivery trucks, burning their newspapers and roughing up dealers who sold papers under the impression that it was a free country. Moe first worked in the circulation department of the *Chicago Tribune* and later switched his allegiance to Hearst's new papers in town, the *American* and the *Examiner*, serving as circulation manager of the latter from 1904 to 1906. The roster of Moe's sluggers read like a future public enemies list. A typical Annenberg hireling was Frank McErlane.

3

Former Chicago newsman George Murray later wrote of the Annenberg-McErlane alliance: "McErlane went on to become the most vicious killer of his time. Moe Annenberg went on to become father of the ambassador to the Court of St. James."

Moving up in the Hearst organization, Annenberg became one of the highest-paid circulation men in the country. His arrangement with Hearst gave him the right to engage in private business dealings on the side, which included his incursion into the racing information field, on both a legal and an illegal basis. In 1922 he bought the *Daily Racing Form,* and by 1926 his various enterprises had become so vast that he quit Hearst and struck out on his own. In a matter of a few years, he had gathered in his domain the *New York Morning Telegraph, Radio Guide, Screen Guide* and the Nation-Wide News Service. He also took over the century-old *Philadelphia Inquirer* and through it became a power in Republican Party politics. According to Annenberg, because these activities occurred during a Democratic era, they got him in trouble with the law. Others said that Nation-Wide News Service gave him his great legal problems, as well as huge profits. The service received its information from telegraph and telephone wires hooked into 29 race tracks and from those tracks into 223 cities in 39 states, where thousands of poolrooms and bookie joints operated in violation of local laws. Annenberg became the fifth largest customer of American Telephone and Telegraph, exceeded only by the three press associations and RCA.

The flow of money simply gushed in, becoming so large that, as the *New York Times* reported, "it apparently did not seem worth while to give the government its share." In 1939 Moe and his only son, Wal-

ter, were indicted. Walter pleaded not guilty and Moe attacked the charges against him as politically motivated. But finally, in what some observers called great paternal devotion, Moe declared: "It's the best gamble. I'll take the rap." Moe was in his sixties, and his lawyers were hopeful that his guilty plea would lead to the dropping of charges against his son. The gamble paid off. Moe Annenberg drew a three-year prison term and made a $9.5 million settlement with the government.

Nation-Wide News folded up and Moe Annenberg was succeeded as the country's racing information czar by James M. Ragen, who founded Continental Press Service. Walter Annenberg remained a great publishing power and society figure and went on to become ambassador to England under President Richard Nixon.

See also: JAMES M. RAGEN.

Further reading: *My Last Million Readers* by Emile Gauvreau.

Ashby, James (c. 1830) riverboat gambler

While the Mississippi was noted for many colorful riverboat gamblers, none was more amazing than old James Ashby, a grizzled sharper skilled at suckering others who superficially seemed much more polished.

Ashby would work with a young confederate, pretending to be father and son returning home after selling off some stock at market. The bumpkin-appearing "son" looked like a perfect victim, easily inveigled into trying his luck at cards, and Ashby pretended to be a fiddle-playing old man teetering on the brink of senility. While the son was gambling, Ashby guzzled white lightning and played snatches of tunes on his fiddle, bemoaning that he no longer remembered how the complete version went. His son proved less dimwitted than he looked, winning hand after hand in defiance of all the odds. "Not for a long time," one historian of the river wrote, "did the gamblers learn that the tunes were signals." Whereupon Ashby retired from Mississippi activities, having grown wealthy by outsharping the sharpers.

badger game sex swindle

The badger game is an ancient con, worked in many variations in every land. The standard modus operandi is simple: man picks up woman; woman takes him to a room; woman's "husband" comes in suddenly, confronts lovers and demands satisfaction. He gets it in the form of the frightened lover's money.

Perhaps the greatest organizer of the badger game was a notorious 19th-century New York City gangster named Shang Draper, who was also an accomplished bank robber. In the 1870s Draper operated a saloon on Sixth Avenue at 29th Street. From it he directed the activities of 30 women and girls in a combined badger and panel game operation headquartered at a house in the vicinity of Prince and Wooster Streets.

In the panel game, a thief would sneak into the room while the woman and her male friend were occupied in bed and steal the man's money and valuables from his discarded clothing. The sneak thief would gain entry to the room through a hidden panel in the wall out of sight from the bed.

However, if the man appeared really prosperous, Draper preferred working the badger game, because the stakes were potentially much higher. Draper added a new wrinkle to the game by using young girls, from age nine to about 14. Instead of an angry husband breaking into the room, the young girl's irate "parents" would burst in. The "mother" would immediately seize the child and smash her face, usually her blows would be hard enough to make the child bleed from the nose or mouth. While this convincing act was taking place, the equally angry "father" would shove his fist under the man's nose and say, "I'm going to put you in prison for a hundred years!"

Men victimized by this technique often could be induced to pay thousands in hush money. Draper himself loved to tell about how he stood in a telegraph office with a quivering out-of-towner waiting for his bank to wire him $9,000 so he could pay off a badger game. It was estimated that Draper's badger game conned 100 or more men each month. The police finally broke up Draper's racket in the early 1880s, but the hardy badger game easily survived the demise of his operation.

Another colorful practitioner was a Philadelphian known as "Raymond the Cleric," who found the pose of a betrayed minister-husband to be more lucrative. While he prayed in a corner for divine forgiveness for his errant spouse and her sinful lover, a couple of "members of his congregation" would appear a bit more threatening, and the sinner usually demonstrated his repentance with a hefty contribution.

To this day, the badger game, in its pure form and in dozens of variations, is one of the country's most widely practiced confidence games, although given the compromising position of the victim, one that rarely comes to the attention of the police.

See also: PANEL HOUSE.

Badman from Bodie   western bogeyman

During the last three decades of the 19th century, western mothers would scare their mischievous children into line by invoking the specter of the "Badman from Bodie," who had to have a victim every day. Unlike the more traditional bogeyman, the Badman from Bodie was rooted in reality. Bodie, Calif. was one of the West's most lawless towns reportedly averaging at least one killing a day for 20 years. Even if that estimation was somewhat off, threatening nasty children with the Badman from Bodie was apparently an effective instrument of parental control.

Baker Estate   great swindle

One of the most lucrative and enduring swindles in American history began just after the Civil War with the establishment of the first of numerous Baker Estate associations. These associations were joined and supported by victims conned into believing they were the rightful heirs to a $300 million fortune in Philadelphia.

The fortune was entirely imaginary, but one association after another roped in suckers with claims that the estate was just about settled. Exactly how much money victims lost to the criminal operators of the fraud is difficult to calculate; the best estimate is that some 40 different Baker Estate associations took at least a half-million persons for a minimum of $25 million in "legal expenses" during the peak years of the fraud, from 1866 to 1936. During that period the estate swindle had very little interference from the law, but finally in 1936 the federal government launched a vigorous effort to stamp it out through many arrests and a massive publicity campaign. Since then similar con games have appeared from time to time, but none has ever been as successful as the Baker Estate swindle was during its early years.

Bakker, Rev. Jim (1940–)   "Praise the Lord for Suckers"

On a par with the bank and Wall Street scoundrels of the 1980s, some in televangelist circles were also grabbing headlines as scamsters. At the top of the list was the Reverend Jim Bakker and his hectic sexual and Ponzi-like shenanigans. Bakker had built up a television network, the PTL (for "Praise the Lord," or "People That Love"), that reached more than 13 million American households.

It was a sexual dalliance that precipitated Bakker's downfall. In December 1980, the youthful-looking Bakker had met a 21-year-old comely brunet named Jessica Hahn, a secretary at a Pentecostal church in Massapequa, N.Y., during a visit to Clearwater, Fla. At the time, Bakker's 19-year marriage to his wife, Tammy Faye, who cohosted his religious television show, was rough going. Bakker and Hahn had sex, and to hear Hahn tell it, she suffered great emotional distress as a result of the encounter. In any event, her pain and suffering were so great that $265,000 was to be paid as compensation for her silence.

Bakker's secret remained safe for a time; the story was eventually broken in the *Charlotte* (N.C.) *Observer,* a newspaper near the headquarters of the PTL ministry. In addition to the television show featuring Jim and Tammy Faye, the PTL empire included Heritage USA, a Christian resort complex and amusement park in Fort Mill, S.C. In the PTL's peak year, the ministry took in $129 million, and in the recent few years, it had garnered $158 million by offering promises of lifetime vocations— which Bakker could not provide. Instead, huge sums were diverted to the couple, which allowed the Bakkers to live in opulence. In March 1987, Bakker was forced to resign his ministry and later was charged with fraud and conspiracy. At his trial (with Tammy Faye—by now regarded as something of an American original—vowing to stand by her man), a former reservation supervisor at Heritage USA said that in the last year of Bakker's regime at PTL, between 1,300 and 3,700 lifetime contributors had been turned away every month from lodgings that had been promised but did not exist.

Bakker was convicted on all 24 counts against him and sentenced to 45 years in prison and fined $500,000. He would not be eligible for parole for 10 years. In passing sentence, U.S. district judge Robert Porter said, "Those of us who do have religion are sick of being saps for money-grubbing preachers and priests. I just feel like there was massive fraud here, and it's going to have to be punished."

Once again, Tammy Faye promised to stand by her man, but she later filed for divorce and planned to marry a businessman who likewise divorced his wife. In the meantime, Hahn had appeared on the cover of *Playboy* magazine and was paid an estimated $750,000 for a photo display and an interview in which she informed readers that "I'm not a bimbo." She later devoted her talents to hosting a late-night show advising viewers via special 800 numbers how to find "love."

After Jim Bakker was freed, he remarried and devoted himself to activities helping the unfortunate, an undertaking that won him considerable accolades from the media.

banco   swindle

A swindle whose name careless writers often misspelled as *bunco,* which was later applied to all types of confidence games.

Banco was based on the old English gambling pastime of eight-dice cloth. Sharpsters who introduced it in America usually converted it into a card game, which could be manipulated more easily than dice. It was very prevalent in the western gold fields during the 1850s until California vigilantes drove out the gamblers using it to swindle miners. About 1860 banco was introduced in New York City, where the two greatest practitioners of the art—George P. Miller, the King of the Banco Men, and Hungry Joe Lewis—amassed fortunes.

In its card game variation, banco was played on a layout of 43 spaces—42 were numbered and 13 of those contained stars.

The remaining space was blank. The 29 unstarred numbers were winning ones, being worth from $2 up to $5,000, depending on the size of the bank. Each player received eight cards numbered from one to six, with the total number in his hand representing the prize. However, if a number with a star came up, he got no prize but could draw again by putting up a certain amount of money. The sucker would generally be allowed to win at first—with no money actually changing hands—until he was ahead a few hundred to a few thousand dollars. Then he would be dealt number 27 which was the so-called conditional prize, meaning he had to stake a sum equal to the amount owed him and draw again or lose all his "winnings." Naturally, he would be dealt a blank or starred card and thereby lose everything.

The pattern of play just described was automatic since the entire banco game was a phony, being played in a "skinning dive" in which all but one of the players were actually confidence operators. The only person not in on the scheme was the sucker who had been steered there.

Miller and Hungry Joe specialized in victimizing bankers, businessmen and other prominent personages. Not only did these victims have plenty of money to lose, they also were likely to be too embarrassed to go to the police. In 1882, Hungry Joe wormed his way into an acquaintanceship with Oscar Wilde, then on a lecture tour of the country. Over several dinners he boasted of the money he had won at banco and then steered the writer to a game. The confidence man later bragged that he had taken Wilde for close to $7,000. Wilde himself, perhaps in a face-saving exercise, later insisted he had lost only $1,500 in cash and had taken care of the rest with a check on which he had stopped pay-

ment once he discovered the play was dishonest. Banco died out not because of a dearth of potential victims but rather because con men found they could attract more suckers to fixed horse races or stock market swindles.

bankruptcy fraud

In recent years bankruptcy scams have become one of the most lucrative activities of organized crime. According to U.S. Justice Department sources, crime syndicates pull off at least 250 such capers every year, each one involving at least $250,000 in goods and materials.

As the racket is generally worked by the New York Mafia crime families, a new company is set up with a "front man" who has no criminal record. "Nut money" of at least $30,000 is deposited in a bank to establish credit, and the company starts ordering supplies that are quickly paid for in full. However, as the orders are increased, the payments slow down a bit until finally a huge order is placed. As soon as these supplies arrive, they are either sold off at extremely low rates or transferred to other business outlets. The nut money is then pulled out of the bank and the operators simply disappear. All the creditors can find is a bankrupt shell of a company.

Perhaps the classic bankruptcy scam was pulled by members of the Vito Genovese crime family, who once took control of a large New York meat wholesale business by advancing the company cash and then insisting on putting in their own president to safeguard the loan. After becoming established, the Mafia operators needed only 10 days to work a $1.3 million swindle. They bought up huge amounts of poultry and meat on credit and sold them off at lowered prices. The mob then pulled out, blithely ordering the cowed management to go into bankruptcy.

Barbe, Warren Gilbert (?–1925)
murder victim

To his neighbors in Berkeley, Calif., Charles Henry Schwartz was a remarkable individual. He was a master chemist and during World War I he'd been a spy in Germany for the Allies. After the war he'd taken an important post in a German chemical plant, where he had discovered a process for the manufacture of artificial silk. He smuggled the process into the United States and set up a hush-hush experimental laboratory, in which he often worked into the night. It sounded impressive, but it was all hogwash. Least of all was he a master chemist. But Schwartz found plenty of people willing to give him money in exchange for a piece of the process. When he produced no silk, however, some of his backers started to grumble and talk of fraud.

In 1925 Schwartz began to take an avid interest in a different science—human anatomy. He cultivated a friendship with a traveling evangelist named Warren Gilbert Barbe. Although the facial features of the two men were very dissimilar, they were of the same overall size. Late in July, Barbe disappeared from his usual haunts, but no one gave it a thought. He most likely got the "call" and had "gone into the wilderness" to preach. Meanwhile, Schwartz was very busy in his laboratory. He said he was almost finished with his process and he worried that some international cartel might try to stop his work. He took out a $200,000 insurance policy on his life and allowed no one to enter the laboratory.

In the lab he was very busy altering the dead evangelist into a stand-in corpse for himself. He burned away a section of the corpse's chest because he had a scar in his own chest. He pulled out two teeth from the upper jaw to match his own dental characteristics. He punctured the eyeballs to solve the problem of different color eyes. But all these he regarded as extra precautions, since he planned to blow up his laboratory in order to really make the corpse unidentifiable. In fact, he believed the entire building would be destroyed in the explosion. He soaked the laboratory with several gallons of benzol which, when detonated, would take care of the building and the evidence. Schwartz set up a timing device and left. He couldn't afford to be seen at the site of the explosion. But he stayed close enough to hear the clanging fire trucks approaching as he stepped into a taxi.

Hiding out in Oakland, Schwartz was shocked to discover he was wanted for murder. The body, hardly singed, had been identified. Even three religious pamphlets bearing Barbe's name had survived the blaze. An incompetent chemist, Schwartz didn't realize that benzol fumes rise very slowly. Several more minutes would have been needed to set off the fire properly. A flop as a chemist, an anatomist and a murderer, Schwartz did better in his final endeavor: suicide.

See also: INSURANCE FRAUDS–FAKED DEATHS.

Barrie, Peter Christian "Paddy"
(1888–1935) horse race fixer

Without doubt the most successful horse race fixer in the United States was Paddy Barrie, a skilled "dyer" who applied his handiwork to swindle bettors out of some $6 million from 1926 to 1934.

Barrie's system was perhaps the simplest ever used to fix races. He would buy two horses, one with a very good record and the other a "dog." Then he would "repaint" the fast horse to look like the slow one and enter it in a race under the latter's name. Based on the past performance record of the slow horse, the ringer would generally command odds of 50 to one or even more; because it really outclassed its opponents, the horse would usually win the race easily. Using stencils, bleaches, special dyes and dental instruments, Barrie changed the identity of a champion horse, Aknahton, and ran it under three less-distinguished names at four tracks—Havre de Grace, Agua Caliente, Bowie and Hialeah. The horse made five killings for a gambling syndicate Barrie was working with. It was a feat that led the gamblers to call him "Rembrandt."

The Pinkerton Detective Agency finally unmasked Barrie following an investigation that was started after a leader in the betting syndicate, Nate Raymond, made a drunken spectacle of himself in Broadway clubs and was heard bragging about a "bagged race" worked by an "artist" from England named Paddy. The Pinkertons queried Scotland Yard and learned that a master dyer named Paddy Barrie had disappeared from the British Isles some years previous. An alert went out for Barrie, but he managed to elude capture for another two years by doing the same thing to himself that he did to horses, adopting disguises and changing his name frequently. One day a Pinkerton operative recognized him at Saratoga race track in New York, and he was bundled off to jail.

Oddly, the laws on horse race gambling and fixing were rather lax and Barrie appeared to have broken no law other than having entered the United States illegally. He was deported back to his native Scotland, where he died less than six month later of a "broken heart," according to a sensational British tabloid, due to constant surveillance aimed at guaranteeing he would never be able to ring another horse.

Because of Barrie's depredations, American tracks adopted such precautions as lip tattoos and other methods of identification to make the ringing in of other horses almost impossible. However, since foreign horses have not been so identified they have been used as ringers in recent years. The disclosure of such fixes has led to close checks on the identification of foreign horses.

Beck, Dave (1894–1993) labor union leader

In the early 1950s David D. Beck was one of the most powerful and respected labor union leaders in the United States. He was president of the country's largest single union, the 1.4 million member International Brotherhood of Teamsters. He was a rich man whose friendship was sought by business executives and statesmen. He boasted that management almost unanimously hailed him as a cooperative labor leader sympathetic to its problems. He was also greedy on a monumental scale.

In his younger years Beck was noted as an aggressive labor leader and an effective bargainer. Founder of the western Conference of Teamsters, he negotiated contracts that became standards for labor settlements throughout the rest of the country. When he became president of the union in 1952, he had seemingly achieved the pinnacle of success, although he had to share his union powers in several areas with tough James R. Hoffa, chairman of the Teamsters Central States Conference. In fact, Hoffa once boasted: "Dave Beck? Hell, I was running it while he was playing big shot. He never knew the score."

Beck knew the score, however, when it came to milking union funds to become a millionaire. He took loans from the union treasury, which he never repaid. With the aid of money from the union, he built for himself an elegant house in the suburbs of Seattle, featuring an artificial waterfall in the backyard and a basement movie theater. He sold it to the Teamsters at twice what it cost to build and then got it back from the union rent-free for his lifetime use. He put the bite on large companies for personal "loans" and gained the reputation of being able to walk off with anything not nailed down.

Beck's downfall came in a confrontation with the Senate Select Committee on Improper Activities in the Labor or Management Field, chaired by Sen. John McClellan of Arkansas with a young Robert F. Kennedy as chief counsel. The McClellan Committee did much to expose the greed of a number of union officials who had often allied themselves with underworld figures and had looted union treasuries for personal gain. Many union officials squirmed under the inquiry, but none more so than the Teamster leadership. Beck, like others, was to infer that the committee and especially the chief counsel were "antilabor," but he came before the investigation declaring: "I have nothing to fear. My record is an open book." He then proceeded to invoke the Fifth Amendment more than 200 times.

In summing up, the committee declared:

The fall of Dave Beck from a position of eminence in the labor-union movement is not without sadness. When named to head this rich and powerful union, he was given an opportunity to do much good for a great seg-

ment of American working men and women. But when temptation faced Dave Beck, he could not turn his back. His thievery in the final analysis became so petty that the committee must wonder at the penuriousness of the man. What would cause a man in such circumstances to succumb to the temptation of using union funds to pay for six pairs of knee drawers for $27.54, or a bow tie for $3.50? In Beck's case, the committee must conclude that he was motivated by an uncontrollable greed.

Exposure of Beck's greed caused him to leave the hearings a broken man. He would soon be imprisoned, although he tried to fend off this fate by refunding huge sums of money to the Teamsters' treasury. By May 1, 1957 he had returned some $370,000, but the next day, with only a few days remaining before the statute of limitations expired, he was indicted on charges of income tax evasion.

Jimmy Hoffa replaced him as president on February 20, 1958, and Beck drew a long prison term. When he came out, he was still worth a considerable amount of money and had intact his $50,000 lifetime pension from the union. Beck still owed the government $1.3 million in back taxes, and the Treasury Department had the right to seize any and all of his assets to satisfy the claim. However, in 1971 John B. Connolly, secretary of the treasury under President Richard Nixon, approved a plan for a moratorium on the payment of the debt. The Teamsters became Nixon's strongest booster in the labor movement.

Beck, Martha (1920–1951) Lonely Hearts Killer
Together with Raymond Martinez Fernandez, 280-pound Martha Beck became infamous in the 1940s as one of the Lonely

Hearts Killers. Although the pair was charged with only three murders, they were suspected of committing 17 others.

Both Fernandez and Beck were social misfits who joined several lonely hearts clubs seeking companionship. In addition to companionship, Fernandez sought money from women he became acquainted with. When Fernandez and Beck met through the auspices of a club, they teamed up to make a business of swindling women. While Fernandez wooed the women, Martha played the role of his sister. They mulcted scores of women and simply killed those who proved uncooperative or troublesome. The murders that tripped the pair up were those of Mrs. Janet Fay, a 60-year-old Albany, N.Y. widow, and Mrs. Delphine Downing, an attractive 41-year-old widow from Grand Rapids, Mich., and her 20-month-old child.

Mrs. Fay traveled as fast as she could to Valley Stream, Long Island to meet her husband-to-be (Fernandez) and his sister (Beck) after selling her home in Albany. Once the pair was sure they had all the woman's money, they beat her to death with a hammer and buried her in the cellar of a rented house. The killers then traveled to Grand Rapids and similarly stripped Mrs. Downing of much of her wealth. After feeding her sleeping pills, Fernandez then shot her to death. A few days later Martha Beck drowned the woman's child in the bathtub. The murderous pair then buried both corpses under cement in the cellar.

That chore completed the couple went off to a movie. When they returned, they found the police inside the Downing home. Suspicious neighbors had not seen the woman around for a few days and notified the authorities. Since the cement in the cellar had not yet dried, the bodies were quickly found. The police also discovered traces of the late Mrs. Fay's belongings in the couples' possession and soon obtained a confession to the New York murder as well. Since New York had a death penalty and Michigan did not, the two were tried for the Fay killing. After a 44-day trial, in which the sexual aberrations of Fernandez and Beck provided a field day for the sensational press, they were sentenced to death. On March 8, 1951—their final day of life—Fernandez received a message from Beck that she still loved him, news he exclaimed, that made him "want to burst with joy." Martha Beck was granted her last request. Before she was executed in Sing Sing's electric chair, she had her hair meticulously curled.

The lonely hearts murders led to the tightening of restrictions on the operations of lonely hearts clubs, but most lawmakers conceded little safeguards could be established to protect foolish and romantic people from being swindled and even killed for love's sake.

begging

The practice, or perhaps more correctly the profession, of begging doubtlessly goes back to prehistoric times. It appeared in America almost with the first settlers and continues to the present day. In New York one resourceful entrepreneur, after years of successful panhandling, opened a school in 1979 to teach the art of begging. (Lesson One: On the subway, pick out one target, stand before him and whine loudly, "Please!" If that doesn't work, get on one knee and continue to plead until he does give.)

There have been many legendary beggars in American history. One of the most successful during the 1920s was New York

City's "Breadline Charlie," who eschewed use of a harness or other equipment to make him appear crippled or helpless. Instead, he carried in his pocket small chunks of stale bread, and when in a crowd, he would drop a piece on the sidewalk. Then he would "discover" it, let out a scream of ecstasy and gobble it down as though he hadn't eaten in days. This pitiful scene always touched the hearts and purses of passersby.

An earlier faker, George Gray, had earned, by his own confession, at least $10,000 a year for many years around the turn of the century thanks to his incredible ability to feign an epileptic fit or a heart attack, usually in front of the residence of a well-to-do Manhattanite. After one of his many arrests, Gray was taken by police to Presbyterian Hospital, where doctors pronounced him "a curiosity of nature in that he possesses the power of accelerating or retarding his heart action at will." A businessman named Jesse L. Strauss gave police a considerable argument when they tried to roust Gray as he lay writhing on the sidewalk. Strauss had his money in hand and was ready to give it to the unfortunate man so that he could seek medical attention. Gray was wanted as the era's most professional "fit-thrower" by police in a dozen Eastern cities.

Robert I. Ingles was an energetic beggar who toured the country for years on a regular begging beat until his death in a charity ward in New York during the 1950s. On his person was found a pass book showing he had $2,500 in a Manhattan bank. In due course, it was found he had 42 other savings accounts with a total value of well over $100,000.

Rose Dym (born Anna Dym), a nightmarishly homely daughter of a retired Brooklyn pushcart peddler, hit the bright-light district in 1929. She was 17 then, a stage-struck little autograph hunter. Almost immediately, she developed a knack for making a pest of herself, and people gave her whatever she asked for just to get rid of her. Soon, she was asking for money. Her technique worked so well that after a while, she would accept folding money only. Celebrities quailed at Rose's glance. Jack Dempsey once fled his own restaurant when she walked in to put the touch on his customers. In time, Broadway Rose prospered to the extent that she could refuse donations from nobodies with the admonition, "Go get yourself a reputation, jerk, before I'll take your scratch."

Probably the most profitable approach used today is a beggar in a business suit who embarrassedly tells victims he has lost his wallet and needs commuter fare home. Since home is a far way off, a minimum bite is $5. While such a routine can be most remunerative, it probably will never earn the profits attained by a New York beggar who used to pose as a leper. He was a tall, gaunt, olive-skinned man who'd haunt shadowy alleys and emerge only when he saw a prospective sucker coming along. "Mister . . . I'm a leper. . . . Will you drop some money on the sidewalk for me? . . . Will you, please? . . . For a poor leper?" All this time, the "leper" would keep moving toward his quarry, his arms outstretched—and many a poor soul was known to have reacted by dropping his entire wallet and then racing out of harm's way.

Benson family murders a not-so-ideal son
During the 1980s—the decade of greed—it was inevitable that scandals and homicides among the rich and famous received a great deal of attention. The Benson family murders in Florida were a case in point.

Mrs. Margaret Benson, a 58-year-old widow and heiress to a $10 million tobacco fortune after the death of her wealthy husband in 1980, moved herself and her grown children to a life of self-indulgent ease in Naples, Fla. She supported her children: a married daughter, Carol Lynn Benson Kendall; her older son, Steven; and her young adopted son, Scott. Of the boys, Steven—seemingly the ideal son—was by far the more responsible and dependable and had taken charge of managing the family's affairs. Twenty-one-year-old Scott, by contrast, was always a problem, prone to violence and the use of drugs, snorting cocaine and inhaling nitrous oxide (laughing gas). Given to expensive clothes and flashy sports cars, Scott had difficulty living within a $7,000-a-month allowance. On occasion, he beat his mother and sister, and once the police had to haul him away to a drug-treatment center. Still, the members of the Benson family remained loyal and loving toward him.

In 1985, Steven bought a $215,000 home complete with tennis court and swimming pool, which aroused his mother's suspicions about how he could afford to do so. She began to realize he had been skimming money from a company the family owned. She made plans to have an audit conducted and hinted at disinheriting Steven. One summer day in 1985, the family climbed into their Chrevolet Suburban van for a drive when Steven said he had forgotten something and reentered the Benson mansion. While he was gone, two pipe bombs sent off in the van. Mrs. Benson, now 63, and young Scott died instantly, and Carol was badly injured.

After recovering, Carol told investigators that Steven had made no effort to aid her after the explosion and had shown little emotion at the scene. He was eventually charged

with murder. At Steven's trial in 1986, Carol shocked the court by revealing that Scott Benson was actually her son and that her mother—actually Scott's grandmother—had adopted him.

Steven Benson's defense was that the pipe bombs had probably been made by the drug-crazed Scott, who was seeking to destroy the family. The pipe bombs, the defense argued, must have gone off sooner than Scott had anticipated. However, prosecution witnesses contradicted that line of reasoning; one of them testified that Steven had once declared he had learned how to make pipe bombs years before. A purchase order for materials used for such devices was found to bear Steven's finger- and palm prints.

While no one had actually seen Steven plant the bombs, the circumstantial evidence was strong enough for the jury to quickly bring in a guilty verdict. Steven, then 35, was sentenced to two consecutive terms of life imprisonment with no parole for at least 50 years.

Berman, Otto "Abbadabba" (1889–1935)
policy game fixer

Few rackets have ever produced as much money for underworld coffers as the numbers game, and although the profit slice is 40 percent or more, crime bosses have always searched for ways to give the suckers even less of a break.

Otto "Abbadabba" Berman was for a time a magician at this, as his nickname indicates. During the 1930s Berman devised a system for rigging the results of the game so that only a lesser-played number would win. He worked for Dutch Schultz, the crime czar who controlled the bulk of the numbers game in New York, including most of the action in black Harlem. At the time, the winning number was derived from the betting statistics at various race tracks. The underworld could not control the figures at the New York tracks, but during the periods when those courses were closed, the number was based on the results from tracks that the underworld had successfully infiltrated, such as New Orleans' Fair Grounds, Chicago's Hawthorne and Cincinnati's Coney Island. Berman was able to figure out how much money to put into the mutual machines to have a low-played number come out. It was estimated that Abbadabba's magic added 10 percent to every million dollars a day the underworld took in.

In 1935 Dutch Schultz was assassinated by vote of the Luciano-Lansky national crime syndicate, allegedly because Schultz had announced he intended to kill Thomas E. Dewey, whose racket-busting activities were hampering underworld operations. Luciano especially was concerned about the ramifications of killing a man of Dewey's stature. His concern, however, was no doubt heightened by the opportunity he saw to take over the Schultz numbers racket. Schultz and three of his favorite underlings were cut down at the Palace Chophouse in Newark while having dinner. Unfortunately for the mob, one of those shot with Schultz was Berman. His loss was to cost the mob literally millions of dollars a year, for while others tried to imitate the technique of what Luciano's aide, Vito Genovese, called "the Yid adding machine," few approached even a fraction of his results.

bigamy

Few crimes are as welcome to newspaper editors as bigamy, the act of ceremonially marrying another person when already legally married. Although the typical state statute exacts up to five years imprisonment for the offense, few bigamists are ever punished, usually getting off with a stern lecture provided they make amends by speedily annulling the illegitimate marriage. Meanwhile, the newspapers have their human interest story, especially when, as often happens, the bigamist's spouses violently denounce or attack one another.

One such case involved two women who went at each other in a Chicago courthouse corridor, pulling hair, gouging and biting. "I'm still in love with him," wife number one announced to reporters, after the two battling women were separated. "I'll help him all I can." Which is how things turned out. Since he was her husband first, she got him while the second wife got only an annulment. Triumphantly, in fact, wife number one paid the $500 fine her errant husband faced for his misdeeds.

It is not unusual to find a bigamist with six or eight spouses who still does not end up with a prison sentence, unless he or she is also guilty of stealing his or her spouses' money or defrauding them of their fortunes. Few prosecuting attorneys will expend much energy on bigamy complaints because as many as a dozen investigators would have to be put on a single bigamy case full time to clear the tangled web. Another discouraging factor is that bigamists often have wives and families in different states. As a result, for every bigamist finally hauled into court, possibly as many as a hundred or more go free and undetected.

Many bigamists have bizarre or zany reasons for committing the crime. Often, they have concocted and sold their spouses wildly improbable tales to sustain their deception. This was the case of a Washington woman who married two Canadian navy seamen, assuring each that she had a twin sister who had married the other. When it was discovered that both "twins" had identical cuts on a finger, her double life was exposed.

Courting exposure, indeed, seems very common among bigamists. A gray-haired 52-year-old night watchman was clapped in the county jail in New Haven, Conn. for having two wives—living a mere block from each other. He was exposed when a long distance call for one wife mistakenly went to the other. One Michigan bigamist got caught when his wife went by a photographer's shop and spotted a picture of her husband and a stunning young bride. A Massachusetts man's bigamy was revealed when two of his wives met in court while both were bringing action against him for nonsupport.

Harried bigamists often find themselves mired deep in serious crime before long. The "flying lothario" of Memphis made the headlines from coast to coast after it was found he kept one wife in Tennessee and another in California, commuting back and forth each week by plane in order to spend weekdays in Memphis and weekends in Los Angeles. Travel costs murdered him, and he finally confessed to stealing $19,000 from the Memphis firm where he worked as a cashier.

Few bigamists are exceptionally attractive. In fact, some of the country's most successful bigamists are bald and fortyish, both in age and waistline. Master swindler and bigamist Sigmund Engel was only coming into his prime when he was arrested at the age of 73. At the other end of the scale was a 17-year-old schoolboy who had already walked up the aisle three times, evidently incapable of saying no to older women.

Probably the only way to end bigamy would be to enact a proposal made in recent years by several district attorneys that a central national office be established to receive notice of and record every marriage made anywhere in the country. In addition, every person being married would have to be fingerprinted. Obviously, while this would effectively stop the bigamists, the proposal's disregard for American concepts of civil liberties outweighs its usefulness as a measure to eliminate bigamy.

Big Store   major confidence game operation
Prior to 1900, swindles were pretty much "short cons" in which the victim was cheated for a few dollars, perhaps a few hundred and occasionally a few thousand. It was difficult to keep the sucker in tow long enough to make a really big killing. Buck Boatright, an ingenious gambler and the originator of a little con game called the smack, solved this problem by devising the most elaborate and successful confidence racket ever invented.

Boatright's plan was to set up a permanent base of operations, either an office or a store with seemingly respectable or authentic trimmings as well as many employees and "customers." Here the sucker could be skinned with near-scientific precision. Boatright set up his operation with the backing of a number of con men who became his partners. The first requirement was to establish a protected territory in which police and politicians would cooperate for either a flat payoff or a percentage of the take. Boatright's selection was Webb City, Mo., where in 1900 he opened what was to become known as the Big Store.

Boatright's operation was a fake gambling club, featuring among other things fixed sporting events (generally foot races or fights). So convincing was the atmosphere in Boatright's establishment, which soon spawned a branch in Council Bluffs, Iowa, that a sucker almost never suspected he was losing his money in a completely play-act arena where everyone except the victim was a member of the gang.

After the sucker was roped in by being allowed to win a few small bets, he then was informed of a big fix and induced to bet thousands, only to watch as something unforeseen went wrong. In a footrace or fight the participant the victim was betting on might suddenly "drop dead," triggering a false panic since such sporting events were illegal. In other cases the victim would be kissed off when the two operators who suckered him in, and who allegedly lost their money with his, got into an argument that would end with one pulling a gun and "killing" the other. In this play-acted "sting" the shot con man would slump to the floor with blood gushing from his mouth. This would really be chicken blood secreted in a pouch in the man's mouth and bitten open at the right moment. It was an act well calculated to put the sucker "on the run" since, while he had intended only to break the law against illegal betting, he now believed he was an accessory to murder.

Although the Big Store would seem to be an operation that could fleece only the most gullible, it was carried off with such convincing performances that many men of business and wealth were easily taken, never for a moment suspecting a swindle. Perhaps the greatest of all big store operators was Lou Blonger, a master fixer, who for four decades made Denver, Colo. the "con man's capital of America."

See also: DOLLAR STORE, SMACK GAME.

Black Hand extortion racket

"The Society of the Black Hand" was one of the sillier journalistic hoaxes of its time. Contrary to what newspapers of the era published, there was no such Society of the Black Hand, but that was undoubtedly of little comfort to Black Hand victims.

Recalcitrant victims of this extortion racket were shot, poisoned, dynamited or maimed; more pliant targets willingly turned over their funds after receiving a demand for money usually outlined at the bottom with a hand that had been dipped in black ink, a menacing sight sure to produce an icy feeling around a victim's heart. Actually, there once had been a Society of the Black Hand—not in New York, not in Italy, not even in Sicily, but in Spain. It originated in the days of the Inquisition, when like such genuine Italian secret societies as the Camorra and Mafia, it was organized as a force for good, trying to fight the oppression of its day. In later centuries the Mafia and the Camorra turned into criminal bodies, while the Society of the Black Hand in Spain simply withered away. But for New York City newspapermen, La Mano Nera, or the Black Hand, had a nice ring to it; it was easy to remember and lurid. Thus was reborn the Black Hand. Reporters and some detectives wasted their time trying to trace suspects' family trees to tie them to some Black Hand Society. In reality, the Black Hand was simply an extortion racket practiced in the Little Italy sections of numerous American cities. The senders would threaten the recipient or his family and would warn that they would kill or maim a family member as a starter. Usually, the letter was signed with some sort of ominous symbol, such as a skull and crossbones or knives, hatchets or sabers dripping blood. Once the newspapers publicized the symbol of a black hand, that symbol became standard.

Certainly, Black Handers, many of whom were Mafia and Camorra gangsters, often killed if they did not receive their payoff, although more often they might at first catch a victim's child and cut off a finger as a convincer. A typical victim of a Black Hand operation was a wealthy Brooklyn butcher named Gaetano Costa, who in 1905 got a Black Hand letter that read: "You have more money than we have. We know of your wealth and that you are alone in this country. We want $1,000, which you are to put in a loaf of bread and hand to a man who comes in to buy meat and pulls out a red handkerchief." Costa, unlike his neighbors, refused to pay and was shot dead one morning as he worked behind his counter. His killers were never caught, although it was suspected that gangsters working for Lupo the Wolf, a Black Hand chieftain in Italian Harlem, were behind it.

Lupo was regarded as the biggest Black Hander in New York City, and years later, an infamous Murder Stable, which he owned on East 107th Street in Manhattan, was discovered to be the burial place for at least 60 victims, many of them individuals who had refused to pay Black Hand extortion demands. Lupo's power sprang from his shrewd use of terror. Strutting around Italian Harlem, the man exuded cruelty, and it was the custom for residents, at the very mention of his name, to cross themselves and extend their fingers in an effort to ward off his spell.

Within Italian-American society almost anyone could be a Black Hand victim. While on a triumphal engagement at the Metropolitan Opera shortly before World War I, tenor Enrico Caruso got a Black Hand demand for $2,000, which he paid, regarding an appeal to the police as useless if not foolhardy. However, his payment of the money led to a new demand for $15,000 more. This time the tenor notified the authorities because he realized paying the money would only lead to further, even greater demands. Under police direction, Caruso left the money beneath the steps of a factory as the extortionists had ordered. When two prominent Italian businessmen tried to retrieve the loot, they were arrested. Both went to prison in one of the few successful prosecutions of Black Hand criminals. Caruso was kept under guard for a number of years thereafter on the theory that he faced Black Hand retribution, but it never came, because his extortioners were no more than independent operators who had no connection with a crime family or the nonexistent Society of the Black Hand.

A New Orleans Black Hander, Paul Di Cristina, considered himself so immune from interference by the law that he delivered his Black Hand notes in person. His victims always quaked and paid—all except Pietro Pepitone, a grocer. He informed Di Cristina's strong-arm men that he would not pay. So the boss came around personally to collect. When Di Cristina alighted from his wagon in front of the grocer's store, Pepitone picked up a shotgun, stepped out on the sidewalk and blasted the Black Hander to death.

It has been estimated that at least 80 different Black Hand gangs operated in Chicago, totally unrelated to one another except that their messages to their victims were always the same, "Pay or Die."

Virtually all the Black Hand gangs were wiped out or disappeared around 1920. The leaders of the Cardinelli Black Handers were executed in Chicago; the DiGiovanni mob leaders were convicted in Kansas City, Lupo the Wolf got 30 years in New York, albeit for counterfeiting rather than Black Hand crimes. Some observers of the crime scene have attributed the decline of the Black Hand racket to the rise of the big-money rackets under the scourge of Prohibition; there was so much more money available in bootlegging, rumrunning and hijacking that the extortionists couldn't be bothered anymore with what was by comparison a penny-ante racket. However, that was hardly the whole answer. The fact was that Prohibition brought the Italian immigrants into close contact with the feared police for the first time. Most Little Italy sections around the country turned alcohol making into a "cottage industry," with its attendant odors, smoke and fumes. That meant the neighborhood policeman had to be paid off. And when you paid off a man, you had the right to ask him for a favor, such as taking care of this Black Hander who was bothering you.

blackmail

Blackmail, the extortion of money from a victim by threats of public disclosure, censure or exposure to ridicule, is not a frequent crime, if judged by the numbers reported to the police. In one year the New York district attorney reported only four cases had reached his office. However, during that same period three of the larger detective agencies in the city handled more than 50 cases, none of which had been reported to the authorities—and at the time, there were also 300 private detectives in the city. Since even a small agency will get eight or 10 blackmail cases a year, it is evident that police statistics on the crime are meaningless, with perhaps only one in 20 or 50 cases

reported. Furthermore, there is no way of measuring how many other victims are too frightened even to enlist the service of a private agency and instead pay off.

Most blackmail cases are based on modern versions of the badger game and involve the sexual misadventures of the victim, complete with pictures. The second largest category is probably homosexual cases, and many of the remainder relate to business shenanigans. A classic example of the latter involved a Brooklyn businessman who faked company expenses to beat the Internal Revenue Service on his income. Unfortunately for him, the businessman let his secretary help with the doctoring, and shortly afterward, the secretary decided she would work only from 11:30 A.M. until 3:00 P.M., with two hours or so for lunch. She doubled her own salary, the balance being off the books. Ironically, the secretary ran afoul of the tax men, and the blackmail case came to light.

Many blackmailers are freelancers such as a brother and sister team who blackmailed a university professor in Massachusetts for $21,000 by claiming that he had fathered the woman's son or a prostitute who milked the son of a former governor for $40,000. However, there have been a number of organized blackmail rings. The most successful of these was the Forcier-Gaffney gang, which extracted at least $2 million from wealthy homosexuals over a period of 15 years. The ring was smashed when one victim finally had the courage to go to the police. Organized crime often uses blackmail in its bankruptcy scams, first getting something on a businessman and using it as a wedge to become his "partner." At the petty end of professional blackmailers was a Midwestern ring that concentrated on housewives who shopped in supermarkets. They spied on the women until they spotted one slipping small items into her purse or coat pocket. Outside the store they would confront her under the guise of being police detectives. They would settle for all the money the woman had on her plus, of course, the groceries.

Blackmail is a crime with a long history. According to the Greek historian Xenophon, blackmailing was so pervasive some 2,300 years ago that many prominent and wealthy citizens of Athens went into exile to escape the exactions of its perpetrators. He also tells us of another victim who subsequently lost all his money in a commercial venture and thus, happily, no longer was compelled to live in fear of the blackmailers. Even today that is probably the most foolproof protection.

Black Sox Scandal baseball betting coup

Before 1919 the fixing of baseball games for betting purposes was by no means unheard of. But in that year it went too far; the "unthinkable" happened: a World Series was fixed by eight star players for the Chicago White Sox who managed to lose the series to the underdog Cincinnati Redlegs five games to three (the series that year was being played in an experimental nine-game set).

All the details of what was to be called the Black Sox Scandal were never fully exposed, primarily because there was an attempted cover-up by the baseball establishment, in general, and White Sox owner Charles A. Comiskey, in particular. The offending players were not even suspended until there were only three games left to play in the following season, when confessions by three players to the grand jury forced Comiskey to act.

The throwing of the series appears to have been thought of initially by Chicago first baseman Charles Arnold "Chick" Gandil,

who passed the word to Boston gamblers that he could line up several teammates for a lucrative killing. The other players involved were Eddie Cicotte and Claude Williams, star pitchers who between them had won 52 games during the season; left fielder Shoeless Joe Jackson; center fielder Oscar Felsch; third baseman George "Buck" Weaver; shortstop Charles "Swede" Risbergand; and utility infielder Fred McMullin. The gamblers first approached were Joseph "Sport" Sullivan of Boston and William "Sleepy Bill" Burns of New York. Because they felt they needed more capital to finance a gigantic killing, they approached the country's leading gambler, Arnold "the Brain" Rothstein. It is debatable whether or not Rothstein entered the plot or turned them down and then simply went ahead and bet at least $60,000 on Cincinnati (and collected $270,000) because he knew the fix was in and saw no need to pay out any bribe money himself. In any event, the main operator behind the fix became Abe Attell, the ex-featherweight boxing champion. A caller to Attell's hotel suite in Cincinnati later told of seeing money stacked on every horizontal surface in the room, on tables, dresser tops and chair seats, after the Reds won the first game.

In the first two games Cicotte's invincible "shine ball" failed him, and he was knocked out in the fourth inning; Williams was uncharacteristically wild and lost 4–2. By the end of the second game, rumors of the fix were rampant, and the Reds were big favorites to take the series. It was impossible to find a professional bookmaker who would bet on Chicago, that action being played strictly by amateur bettors. It took a yearlong grand jury investigation to crack the case, with confessions coming from Jackson, Cicotte and Williams. Comiskey was forced to fire all the players except Gandil, who had already "retired."

Testimony showed that most of the players had gotten $5,000 for their parts in the fix, while Gandil had kept $35,000 for himself. How many hundreds of thousands the gamblers made was never really determined. When several of the players left the grand jury room, a group of small boys awaited them. One said to Shoeless Joe Jackson: "It ain't true, is it, Joe?"

"Yes, boys," the outfielder replied, "I'm afraid it is."

The conversation has come down in folklore as the boy wailing plaintively, "Say it ain't so, Joe."

Another bit of folklore is that the baseball establishment excised this cancer as quickly as possible. In fact, the baseball magnates provided legal aid to the players, and indeed, the jury acquitted them and carried some of the defendants out of the courtroom on their shoulders. However, Judge Kenesaw Mountain Landis, appointed commissioner to oversee the integrity of "the Game," was not satisfied. He never let any of the players don a Comiskey uniform again.

blue-sky laws

In 1911 the state of Kansas passed the first law to protect the public from the marketing of deceitful stock or shares in worthless, often imaginary enterprises. The "blue-sky" nickname was given to them by a state legislator who demanded that the rules placed on investment concerns "should be as far reaching as the blue sky." The Kansas law and those enacted by other states were vigorously challenged by investment and banking interests until the Supreme Court upheld them in a 1917 ruling. The High Court bolstered the

nickname by denouncing fraudulent investment schemes "which have no more basis than so many feet of 'blue sky.'"

Boesky, Ivan (1937–) "Ivan the Terrible" of stock deals

Until the mid-1980s Ivan Boesky was regarded as the most controversial high-rolling stock speculator on Wall Street. Few such operators were more feared than "Ivan the Terrible," as he was called. Boesky gambled tens of millions on risky securities deals. Later, when the secrets of his methods were uncovered, he was regarded as one of the biggest crooks in the financial world.

The son of a Russian immigrant in Detroit, Boesky was graduated from law school in 1962 and moved to New York four years later. He did stints in an investment firm and then a brokerage house, and then was attracted to the wild world of risk arbitrage—risking huge sums buying and selling stocks of companies that appeared to be likely to merge or be taken over by other firms.

Boesky launched his own arbitrage firm with $700,000 in capital, and 11 years later had a financial empire worth some $2 billion. He lived with his wife and four children in a 10-bedroom mansion on a 200-acre estate in suburban Westchester County and maintained a lavish river-view apartment in Manhattan. Corporations competed to get him on their boards, and he gave huge sums to charities while making increasing profits on his stock dealings.

Unfortunately, Boesky didn't do this on the up-and-up. He sought out insider tips and paid generously for such illegal information. In May 1986, Dennis Levine, one of Boesky's key illegal sources and a wheeler-dealer in his own right, was

"Ivan the Terrible" Boesky's wealth skyrocketed to $2 billion in a little over a decade—very little of it acquired legally.

trapped by government investigators and started to "sing." The man he gave to the government was Boesky, and Boesky in November of that year made an agreement to pay $100 million in penalties for violating securities laws. To cut his potential prison time, Boesky started to outwarble Levine and turned in his fellow lawbreakers. He even agreed to let investigators tape his phone conversations as he carried out his stock deals. Numerous heads rolled as a result, and Drexel Burnham Lambert, one of the giant financial institutions on Wall Street, plunged to near collapse, turning into a shell of its former self.

In a plea bargain Boesky got off with a three-year sentence, saying he was "deeply ashamed" of his past actions. Many observers thought he had paid a very tiny price for the ruined financial fortunes of so many shareholders. Even his $100 million penalty—the largest of its type in history— left him a most wealthy man. When he left prison, Boesky did, however, face a host of legal actions undertaken by ex-partners and victimized shareholders.

See also: DENNIS LEVINE.

Bolber-Petrillo murder ring

The Bolber-Petrillo murder ring, which reaped a fortune from insurance killings in the Italian community of Philadelphia during the 1930s, is an excellent example of why murder statistics are not to be trusted. The ring disposed of an estimated 30 to 50 victims before police suspicions over just one or two brought about the killers' downfall. From a statistical viewpoint, the case is often cited as an indication that the generally accepted figure of 20,000 murder victims a year may be greatly understated and that a truer figure would be 20,000 known homicides a year and 20,000 undiscovered ones.

Neither Dr. Morris Bolber nor his two cousins, Paul and Herman Petrillo, were much interested in such a statistical overview, being content to rake in a goodly income from the occupation of murder during the Depression, a period when most forms of business were hardly rewarding.

The original murder scheme was hatched by Dr. Bolber and Paul Petrillo in 1932, when they decided to have Petrillo seduce Mrs. Anthony Giscobbe, the wife of one of the doctor's patients. The woman had often complained to Dr. Bolber of her husband's infidelities. When she fell in love with Petrillo, she also rather enthusiastically agreed to a plan to kill her husband for the $10,000 insurance on his life. Since the errant Mr. Giscobbe often staggered home dead drunk, it was a relatively simple matter to undress him and leave him all night by an open window in the dead of winter. Eventually, the husband succumbed to pneumonia, and the grieving widow and Dr. Bolber each netted $5,000. Perhaps the only sad development for the widow was that immediately upon completion of this financial transaction, Paul Petrillo lost all amorous interest in her. The slick-haired Petrillo had moved on to conquer new lonely wives, all of whom had husbands not long for this world.

Since the plotters found that few Italian husbands carried much, if any, insurance, they decided to add a new wrinkle to the operation by recruiting Petrillo's cousin, Herman Petrillo, an actor of some accomplishment with church groups, to impersonate the husbands and apply for insurance. Naturally, the wives were required to screen their husbands' mail and weed out all insurance correspondence. After a few premium payments were made, the husbands were efficiently dispatched. A roofer named Lorenzo was heaved off an eight-story building by the Petrillos in an on-the-job accident that doubled the payment on his life. To make the death more convincing, the Petrillos gave the roofer some French postcards before shoving him off the roof, making it rather obvious that the victim had been distracted by them when he misstepped.

After a dozen or so murders, the plotters recruited a valuable new accomplice, Carino Favato, a faith healer known as the Witch in her own bailiwick. The Witch had murdered three of her own husbands and apparently been consulted by female clients who wished to be rid of their spouses. The Witch poisoned them for a price. However, when Dr. Bolber pointed out that she had erred grievously by not adding the insurance wrinkle to the operation, the Witch was duly impressed, readily agreed to a liaison and was able to supply the names of quite a few potential victims.

The ring went busily about committing murder, most often by poison or by Dr. Bolber's favorite method, "natural means," a canvas bag filled with sand that, when artfully applied, caused a fatal cerebral hemorrhage without any telltale marks. By 1937 the ring's death toll may easily have approached 50, at least 30 of which were rather well documented later on.

A recently released convict in need of money called on Herman Petrillo with a scheme by which they could both make money. Herman was not impressed, mainly because he already had a very good thing going. "Dig up somebody we can murder for some insurance and you can make some dough with us," he told the ex-convict earnestly. The ex-con was frightened of murder and informed the police. The ring's members were rounded up, and with unseemly eagerness, each agreed to inform on all the others in the hope of gaining leniency. Although some wives went to prison, others were permitted to turn state's evidence. Dr. Bolber and the Witch were sentenced to life imprisonment and the Petrillos were executed.

bounty jumping Civil War racket
During the Civil War enterprising individuals and organized gangs reaped a fortune collecting bounties for enlisting in the Union Army and then immediately deserting. The cycle would then be repeated, generally in another congressional district or state, for

amounts that varied from $100 to as much as $1,000.

One specialist in this racket was caught after 32 enlistments and desertions, a record that drew him a four-year prison term. A notorious Chicago underworld character named Mike McDonald operated a bounty racket on an organized basis, recruiting hoodlums to sign up for service. McDonald collected a commission each time and shuttled the men around to different areas for repeat tries, keeping track of his "campaigns" on a large war map with tacks indicating where each hoodlum was assigned. Profits from this racket provided McDonald with the capital to set up several gambling houses after the war.

There are some estimates that perhaps nearly half of all desertions from the Union Army, which totaled 268,000, were really cases of bounty jumping. While such figures are most likely too high, considering the large number of draftee desertions, they are at least indicative of how widespread the crime was.

See also: MICHAEL CASSIUS "MIKE" MCDON-ALD.

Buckminster, Fred (1863–1943) con man

One of the most fabled of American con men, Fred Buckminster started on the "bunco trail" while still a teenager. He was to be a swindler the rest of his life, completing his last prison term at the age of 75. In an era of hard money, he stole a minimum of $3 million.

He worked for 20 years with another fabulous fraud, Artist Yellow Kid Weil, together developing and pulling off some of the most famous con games of all time. They worked variations of the "fixed" prize fight and

horse race swindles, utilizing a "big store," or phony betting shop, to trim the suckers. Everyone in the establishment other than the victim was a fake, betting and collecting on phony races. On some occasions Buckminster and Weil would turn things around and swindle a genuine betting parlor; one of them would get the results of a race at the Western Union office while the other placed a bet before the hotel bookie joint received the results. They swindled "Palmer House" Ryan, operator of the Stockade, a horse-betting establishment in the woods outside Chicago, by having a railroad engineer toot out the winner in code as his train passed the Stockade.

Buckminster discovered early in his career that the easiest person to cheat was another thief, amateur or professional. He victimized dishonest bankers, seeking out those who had been accused of cheating customers. He would pose as a depositor with some stocks that he would leave for safekeeping and then would permit himself to be "swindled" out of them after the banker was fed false information that the stock had suddenly ballooned in value.

As Buckminster once put it, "When I see a crook, I see nothing but dollar signs."

Buckminster's greatest swindle of other swindlers was a racket he worked with Kid Dimes, a leading gimmick man who fixed roulette wheels for crooked gambling houses. Buckminster was probably the first man to "fix" a fixed roulette wheel. In 1918 the Kid was busy rigging a wheel for the King George Club, a crooked gambling joint in Chicago's Loop area populated by con men who steered suckers there nightly.

The wheel Kid Dimes constructed allowed the croupier to let the ball stop in any of three numbers he desired, giving him complete control in picking red or black, odd or even or the winning set of numbers. On Buckminster's instructions, Kid Dimes added another button at the customer's end of the table that would cancel out the croupier's choice and magnetize the ball into the number 8 slot.

Outfitting himself in a 10-gallon hat, Buckminster posed as a Texan looking for some gambling action and soon was steered into the King George. With a con man at each elbow, he began playing the wheel. Despite their egging and his swagger about being a Texas oilman, he made only small bets. The house let him win a few while the con men kept working on him to set up a killing. Finally, Fred rose to the bait. He plunked down a roll of $10,000 on a bet covering numbers 7 through 12. The odds against Fred winning were 5-to-1. But of course there was no danger of that. Then just before the croupier rolled his roll, Fred tossed a fat $1,000 bill on number 8 "for good luck."

As the wheel spun, the croupier hit the secret button that guaranteed the ball would stop in a safe number in the 30s. At the same time, Fred pushed his button, canceling out the croupier's action. The little ball came to rest on number 8.

A loud cry went up in the place. Nobody had seen a hit like that. Five-to-1 on the combination bet and 35-to-1 on the number bet paid a total profit of $85,000. The croupier was stunned. A hurried conference was held, but Buckminster was relaxed. With so many suckers in the place, the house could do nothing but pay off. Others pounded on his back, congratulating him. Fred announced he hadn't had enough and continued to play further until he lost back $5,000. In the process, he also removed the secret button

from under the table. Then he walked out, promising the con men to return the next evening. Naturally, he did not come back.

The gambling house owners were furious and sent for Kid Dimes to explain what went wrong. Kid Dimes was a picture of innocence as he inspected the table. He emerged from under the table holding a dead battery. Shaking his head in disdain, he said: "Why don't you people change batteries at least once a week to be safe? At a dime a throw you ought to even be able to afford to change batteries every night."

Over the next decade, whenever things cooled down, Buckminster and Kid Dimes worked that racket on several gambling houses. Buckminster once estimated it netted close to $750,000.

Despite his successes, Buckminster spent a great many of his adult years in prison. He was acutely aware of how greatly the odds favored the police over the crook. "A copper can make a thousand mistakes but a crook only one to get put away," he said sadly when he got out of prison the last time. At the age of 76, Buckminster retired from the rackets. In 1941 he did a series of memoirs for a detective magazine. He raised one of the checks given him for the use of his byline from $100 to $1,000 and cashed it. The publishing house took it philosophically and did not prosecute. Sending a dying old man back to prison made little sense, and it did seem a little late for Buckminster to alter his ways.

See also: JOSEPH "YELLOW KID" WEIL.

Burton, Mary (?–?) false informer

An 18th-century prostitute and thief named Mary Burton had a more chilling record as an informer than even the girls involved in the Salem witchcraft hysteria. Finding herself in prison in 1741, Burton, also known as Margaret Kelly, sought and won her freedom by concocting a story about an imaginary "Negro criminal plot" in New York City. Because blacks, slave and free, comprised a large segment of the population, any talk of concerted action by them provoked fears on the part of the whites. Given that climate, the general rule was that any testimony by a white woman, regardless of her character or motive, was sufficient to convict a black. Mary Burton also found that every new accusation she made added to her prestige. As a result, 71 blacks were transported away, 20 were hanged and 14 others were burned at the stake. As was the case in the Salem executions, the general dignity with which many of the condemned died finally sparked doubt in the public's mind, and Mary Burton's charges were later simply ignored.

Butcher, Jake (1937–) the $700-million bank man

Of all the high finance scam operators whose depredations came to the fore in what came to be known in financial circles as the "Greedy 1980s," Jake Butcher had the distinction of being the most punished by the law, ending up with much more prison time than such offenders as Ivan Boesky, Michael Milken, and Charles Keating, Jr., among others.

Jacob "Jake" Franklin Butcher was a former Democratic candidate for governor of Tennessee and organizer of the 1982 World's Fair in Knoxville. Considered a respected figure in Tennessee banking circles, Butcher defrauded his own banks (he controlled 26 in Tennessee and Kentucky) of millions of dollars so that many of them failed and went bankrupt. Butcher's depredations, which financed his flamboyant lifestyle—such as the purchase of such "toys" as a 60-foot yacht for a mere $400,000—ended up costing the Federal Deposit Insurance Corporation (FDIC) well over $700 million, with Butcher and his wife having personal debts of more than $200 million.

It was said at the time that by his actions alone, Butcher had destroyed the deep-held faith that people had put in their banks since the reforms of the 1930s. The public grasped clearly the threats to their banks and savings and that they would have to pay for FDIC losses through their taxes. As a result, there was universal praise for the sentence imposed on Butcher—two 20-year concurrent terms, the maximum allowed.

Butterworth, Mary (1686–1775) counterfeiter

One of the first successful counterfeiting rings in America was masterminded by a woman, probably the first of her sex to practice the art in the New World. In 1716 30-year-old Mary Butterworth started her monumental fraud right in her own kitchen in the Plymouth colony, copying the Rhode Island pound "bills of credit." Using a hot iron and some starched muslin, she simply reproduced the image onto a blank paper. With several confederates of artistic bent, she filled in the images with quill pens and then passed them on through a pipeline, which included a local justice who was above suspicion.

It is impossible to establish any firm money figure on the scope of the profits realized, but the bills reportedly caused considerable financial havoc in Rhode Island, and the operation must have been extensive. The so-called kitchen counterfeiters stayed in existence for seven years before Mary Butterworth was arrested along with a half-dozen others. However, while a number of bogus bills were found and the counterfeiter's tools located in the woman's kitchen, no hard evidence could be produced proving the bills had been there. Eventually, Butterworth and the others were released for lack of evidence. She was closely watched for many years thereafter to prevent any resumption of the counterfeiting. Thus, tranquility was restored to the New England financial scene.

cackle-bladder   con man's trick

Probably the most efficient method ever devised by confidence men to "blow the mark off," i.e., to get rid of a victim after fleecing him is the use of a "cackle-bladder." The victim is lured into a supposedly sure thing such as betting on what he is assured to be a fixed horse race. He is steered to a phony betting parlor where everyone is an actor playing a role, from the supposed tellers to the bettors winning and losing fortunes. Naturally, the horse he bets on loses, but before the mark can remonstrate another supposed loser, who is actually in on the scheme, turns on the con man playing the role of the chief conspirator. He screams he has been ruined, pulls a gun and shoots the con man dead. There seems no doubt the man is dead as blood literally gushes from his mouth. Everyone starts to scatter, and so does the bilked victim. Not only has he lost his money, but even worse, he's now involved in a homicide. Sometimes the supposed murderer will flee with the mark, even conning the sucker into leaving the city with him. Eventually, of course, the mark decides he is better off to part company with a man who has committed murder and who could now drag him into prison as an accessory.

This type of scam is made convincing through the use of a cackle-bladder, a tiny bag of chicken blood concealed in the mouth and bitten open at the appropriate moment. The gimmick was also used in the last century at fixed running races and boxing matches as well, where the "sure thing" runner or boxer whom the sucker had bet on seemed to drop dead. Since gambling on such races or fights was illegal and all the bettors were therefore liable to imprisonment, everyone, including the gullible victim, fled when the faking runner or boxer dropped.

While the cackle-bladder is only used on rare occasions in contemporary confidence games, it remains a favorite with insurance accident fakers, who use the dramatic spurt of blood to convince witnesses that they have really been injured.

Calico Jim (?–1897?) shanghai operator

Shanghaiing of men was an old San Francisco custom and one of its most proficient practitioners, along with the infamous Shanghai Kelly, was Calico Jim. A Chilean whose real name was said to be Reuben, Jim ran a saloon and crimping joint at Battery Point, from which a great many men were sent on long sea voyages. During the 1890s the San Francisco police received so many complaints against Jim that they began paying him close attention. Evidently not close enough, however, because a policeman sent to arrest him didn't come back. Another tried and also never returned. A total of six police officers went to the saloon and disappeared; all had taken a sea cruise, compliments of Calico Jim. Feeling now that his days in the business were limited, Jim sold out and returned to his native Chile.

It was many months before the policemen made their way back to home port. It has been said that they pooled their money, drew lots and sent one of their number off to Chile to hunt down Calico Jim. After many months of hunting, according to the story, the policeman found Jim on a street corner in Callao, Chile and shot him six times, one for each officer he had shanghaied. There is some doubt about the truth of this account, although it gained a great deal of currency. For years the police department insisted there was no record of six officers being shanghaied. But jaded citizens of San Francisco contended they knew a cover-up when they heard one.

See also: SHANGHAI KELLY.

Cardiff Giant scientific hoax

The Cardiff Giant, allegedly the fossilized remains of an authentic giant who in ancient times walked the earth in the area of what has become New York State, was one of the most lucrative hoaxes in history.

George Hull, a former cigar maker from Binghampton, N.Y., conceived the plot to create the the giant. In 1868 he obtained a five-ton block of gypsum in Iowa and had it fashioned into the shape of a huge man by a stonecutter in Chicago. He then shipped the statue to the farm of a cousin, William Newell, near Cardiff, N.Y., where after a year the latter duly "discovered" it. It is not clear whether the pair had first concocted their plot as a swindle or if, as he would later state, Hull had had the giant built to ridicule clergymen who were always quoting from Genesis about a supersized race—"There were giants in the earth in those days."

A Syracuse newspaper headlined the find as "A Wonderful Discovery," and the pair pitched a tent and began exhibiting the giant, charging 5¢ for a view. News of the find flashed across the country and indeed around the world. Thousands swarmed to see it and admission was raised to 50¢ and then to $1. Meanwhile, most experts were convinced the Cardiff Giant was genuine. Two Yale professors, a paleontologist and a chemist, agreed it was a true fossil. The director of the New York State Museum thought the giant was really a statue but indeed most ancient and the "the most remarkable object yet brought to light in this country." Others, including Oliver Wendell Holmes and Ralph Waldo Emerson, concurred. Still, a few were doubtful; the president of Cornell University felt the giant was made of gypsum and thought there were hints of a sculptor's chisel. But the crowds, now arriving by special trains, continued to grow, and P. T. Barnum, the great showman, offered $60,000 to lease the object from Newell for three months. The farmer refused. Undeterred, Barnum hired a sculptor, Professor Carl C. F. Otto, to make an exact copy of the giant.

When Hull and Newell brought their giant to New York in 1871 for exhibit, they discovered Barnum was already displaying his version in Brooklyn. While they hauled Barnum into court, newspapermen were tracing Hull's activities and uncovered his purchase of gypsum in Iowa. They located the stonecutter in Chicago, one Edward Salle, who admitted to carving the giant, aging it with sand, ink and sulfuric acid, and punching pores into it with darning needles. Faced with the growing evidence of fraud, Hull confessed. Barnum now was able to avoid prosecution by claiming all he had done was show the hoax of a hoax.

Thanks to their fraud, Hull and Newell netted about $33,000 after building expenses of $2,200. Barnum, who continued showing his version for years, made much more. Today, the Cardiff Giant, Hull's authentic fake, is on display at the Farmers' Museum in Cooperstown, N.Y.

carnival gyps

Probably half the people in this country visit a carnival or fair of some kind during the course of a year; yet the so-called games of skill or chance they play are obviously among the most lucrative gyps practiced today. None of the games played are susceptible to being beaten, either by skill or chance. All of them are or can be rigged. The television program *60 Minutes* once devoted an entire segment to the exposure of just one gyp game, "razzle," an involved form of gambling in which the customer can never win.

The "gaff," or fix, is applied to every game or built right into it, as is the case with various coin-pitch games in which a player wins a prize if his coin lands inside a square or circle without touching a line. In this game valuable prizes can theoretically be won, but the house percentage has been mathematically worked out as 80 percent—compared to a little over 1 percent for casino dice, 2.5 to 5 percent for roulette and 15 percent or so for one-armed bandits.

Milk bottle toss is a notorious gaff game, although the proprietor or a shill, or phony player, will always be seen winning. The object of the game is to knock six imitation milk bottles off a podium with three baseballs. Knocking them down is not sufficient—they must be knocked completely off the table. The key to the gyp is that three of the six bottles arranged in pyramid form are lead-weighted at the bottom. When these three are placed at the bottom row, or base, they will do no more than fall over even when hit directly, and the player loses. Yet it's relatively simple for the operator of the game to demonstrate how easy it is to win. He throws the three baseballs and the six bottles topple to the floor, but his assistant has simply stacked the six bottles so that three non-lead-weighted bottles are on the bottom row and the weighted ones are on top. A mere brushing will topple the weighted bottles to the floor.

Even games with a guaranteed prize are gaffed. The most common variation of this is the "string game," in which all prizes are attached to strings that feed into a crossbar, or collar. The player pulls a tab for one of the strings on the opposite side of the collar and wins whatever prize pops up. The operator demonstrates the honesty of the game by grabbing all the strings on the other side of the collar and pulling them so that every prize, including very valuable ones, jump up to tempt the public. The trick: the strings attached to the valuable ones are "dead-enders," reaching the collar but not extending to any of the tabs on the other side.

One of the most exotic gaffed games, and a very popular one at big carnivals because it seemingly can't be fixed, is the "mouse game." The public bets on which of 60 numbered holes a mouse will enter, and the prize is quite a good one. A mouse is placed on a wheel, covered with a tin can and spun around vigorously so that when liberated, it is weaving almost drunkenly. Then completely unrehearsed, the mouse heads for the numbered holes. Meanwhile, the operator of the game has made a quick survey of the board and judged whether more money is bet on odd or even numbers. With a foot pedal, he simply closes either the odd or even holes, thereby greatly increasing the house's winnings, especially if the mouse enters an unplayed number. If the mouse, staggering around the holes, butts his head against a closed-off hole, it simply backs off and heads for another opening. This does not look suspicious to the public because the mouse has been moving erratically all along. Finally, the creature enters a hole. Whether or not there is money bet on it, the house almost always wins much more than it loses.

Carson, Ann (1790–1838) counterfeiter

A strange set of circumstances turned Ann Carson into one of early America's most notorious female criminals. The daughter of a naval officer, she was the lovely and vivacious wife of Capt. John Carson of the U.S. Army, who disappeared in 1810 on a mission in the West against the Indians. Carson was listed as presumed dead. In 1812 Ann Carson met Lt. Richard Smith, who was stationed near her home in Philadelphia. After a short courtship they were married and lived happily until January 20, 1816, when her first husband arrived at his home and banged loudly on the door. He told Smith who he was. Smith, who later insisted he had been confused, drew a revolver and shot Carson dead. Within days Smith was brought to trial, and it was soon evident that everyone assumed he had killed Carson rather than give up his wife.

While the trial was going on, Ann Carson made a desperate attempt to kidnap the governor of Pennsylvania, Simon Snyder, and hold him as a hostage to gain her second husband's release. She failed, and Smith was convicted and, on February 4, 1816, hanged. Ann Carson lost all respect for law and order and became the head of a band of hardened criminals. Drawing on her military background, she organized the gang under strict regulations that made them most effective. While they engaged in some violent crimes, Ann Carson's gang were most competent at counterfeiting, passing notes for six years with brilliant efficiency. After they were finally rounded up, all were given long prison terms in 1823. Ann Carson died in Philadelphia Prison in 1838 while working on her memoirs.

cash machine rackets

The explosive growth in bank and store cash machines in recent years has inevitably fostered various criminal means of exploiting them. While there have been occasional murders resulting from crooks forcing victims to hand over their personal codes so as to allow them to extract money from the machines, this is not a frequent occurrence since banks generally limit the amount of money that can be withdrawn in any one day from any one account. As a result nonviolent but ingenious scam artists represent the more common cash machine predators.

Not long ago in New York City, a bankcard customer approached a cash machine during evening hours and found a handwritten sign reading: "Sorry for the inconvenience. Minimum withdrawal $300." This happened to be the maximum withdrawal permitted from the machine.

The customer wanted much less cash but given the alternative opted to withdraw $300. He inserted the card, punched out his code and saw the bills drop into a withdrawal slot. However, the man soon discovered he could not raise the slot cover to retrieve his money. Puzzled for a time, he finally noticed two tiny screws inserted on either side of the slot cover that effectively sealed it. The man left the outer bank lobby in search of a policeman. After going only one block in an unsuccessful search, he returned to find the screws removed and his $300 gone.

Bankcard machines are designed to thwart theft, but with every new safety technique, thieves refine their methods. In this case the bank announced it would alter the slot cover design, but experts regarded this as an unsatisfactory solution. The slot covers on some machines had replaced certain types of money dispensers that dropped the cash through an open slot. These were plugged by thieves using various wax sprays and the like. Money could be cleared out by the thieves at their leisure after a customer attempting to make a withdrawal left. Most cash machines have a special telephone connection to the bank machine's main office, enabling a customer to call on the spot when such a caper is suspected. To counter this, crooks simply put the communication system out of service.

Security experts and police advise bankcard customers to be wary when using cash machines, and to walk away from any machine that seems to have any sort of unusual problem. It is recommended that a card user frequent only a machine that has been observed to be in good working order from use by a previous customer.

Chadwick, Cassie (1857–1907) swindler

One of the most audacious swindles ever worked in this country was accomplished in the 1890s by a Canadian woman and incorrigible thief, Mrs. Cassie Chadwick, who married into Cleveland society. She was, she hinted, the illegitimate daughter of Andrew Carnegie, the steel magnate. In fact, she did more than hint—she flashed all sorts of promissory notes supposedly signed by Carnegie and then deposited some $7 million worth of allegedly valid securities in a Cleveland bank. She told the banker to keep her secret, which meant, of course, that the news spread like wildfire throughout the banking community and soon among the city's social set. Clearly, Mrs. Chadwick was somebody, and she was invited to the best functions. Bankers too volunteered their services without asking. Yes, Mrs. Chadwick acknowledged, she might be able to use a little loan or two against future payments from her tycoon father. She took a few small loans, all under $100,000, and repaid them promptly by taking out other loans from different banks and private lenders. She then went whole hog, borrowing millions. Mrs. Chadwick paid high interest, but with all that Carnegie money behind her, she seemed good for it.

The hoax was simplicity itself, being so outrageous that it was never questioned. Certainly, no one was going to approach Carnegie for confirmation. The Chadwicks now traveled frequently to Europe and, when they were in Cleveland, entertained lavishly. Mrs. Chadwick was also a leading public benefactor. In less than a decade, it was later estimated, she took banks and private lenders for upwards of $20 million.

The bubble burst in 1904, when the *Cleveland Press* heard of a Boston creditor who had become dubious about getting his money back. The newspaper checked on Mrs. Chadwick's background and found out her real name was Elizabeth Bigley, a convicted forger who had been pardoned in 1893 by Gov. William McKinley of Ohio. When the news came out, Charles T. Beckwith, president of the Citizens National Bank of Oberlin, to whose institution Mrs. Chadwick owed $1.25 million, promptly keeled over from heart failure. There was a run on the bank and on scores of others that were found to have made loans to the woman.

Mrs. Chadwick, who was in New York on a spending spree when the unpleasantness surfaced, was arrested and extradited back to Cleveland, where she was tried and sentenced to 10 years in prison. She died there in 1907. It was believed at the time of her death that many of her victims had still not come forth, some individuals hoping to avoid ridicule and the banks to avoid runs. Remarkably, there were still those who firmly believed that Mrs. Chadwick was indeed Carnegie's daughter and that he would in due course make good on her debts. All of which made Cassie Chadwick's swindle among the most enduring ever concocted.

check passing

Not long ago a professional check passer, a forger who writes worthless checks, in New York, was asked why he only passed his rubbery works of art in bars and taverns. Paraphrasing Willie Sutton, who supposedly said one robs banks "because that's where the money is," the check passer declared, "Because that's where the crooks are." The check passer's technique was simple enough, relying as it did on human greed. He would enter a saloon, appearing well bombed, and hoist a few. Then he would produce what appeared to be his paycheck drawn on the account of a well-known local firm and in an apparent stupor, ask the bartender to cash it. Normally, the barkeep would be reluctant to cash a check for an unknown party, but since in this case the customer could barely stand erect, he would find it too appetizing to pass up. The bartender would cash the check and invariably shortchange the purported drunk $10 or $20, figuring he was too far gone to notice. The check passer would hoist one more and stagger out of the place, heading for another bar to repeat his routine.

The check passer stated he generally could cash eight to 10 bad checks an evening and get turned down in no more than two or three places. He had found a new wrinkle to make one of this country's most common and easiest crimes even easier.

Check forgery is so common, in fact, that no one really knows how extensive it is. Spokesmen for surety companies have put the losses at $400 million to $1 billion, and those estimates are probably too low, since a great many businesses have one to a dozen bad checks tucked away unreported. With the value of checks written annually now totaling a few trillion dollars, the bogus-check business is currently the most lucrative field available to a smooth-mannered con man, or even to people with a lot less finesse.

In Washington, D.C. a few years ago, a 14-year-old boy walked into a small store and made a few inexpensive purchases with a government check that eventually bounced. It had been stolen, but the shopkeeper had no one to blame but himself. The rightful recipient was an 83-year-old woman, and the check had been clearly marked "Old Age and Survivor's Insurance."

Once, in Cleveland, Ohio, the story goes, a bad-check artist handed a bank clerk a check to cash after signing it "Santa Claus." He got his money.

Another comic check passer liked to sign his phony masterpieces, "N. O. Good." No one ever caught on—in time. And a Bedford, Ind. grocer, who was not too quick, accepted a check signed "U. R. Hooked." Fun-loving check passers have used bum checks drawn on such institutions as the East Bank of the Mississippi.

The interesting fact about all these cases is the ridiculous chances the bad-check writer will take, so sure is he that the sucker will bite at his bait. Not all forgers are so cocky and contemptuous of their victims, but these incidents do point out what check passers have learned: with the proper approach and in many cases, without, a person can have far less trouble cashing a bad check than a good one.

The professional operator runs into absolutely no trouble 95 percent of the time as long as he has a gimmick to distract suspicion. A California forger cashed 200 bad checks by pretending to be a physician. He found that by passing checks that carried such corner notations as "In Payment for Tonsils" or "Balance over Blue Cross," he was seldom questioned. In big cities he often

entered a store dressed in a doctor's white coat in order to give the impression that he had just stepped out of his office in a nearby building to get a check cashed.

One of the most prolific bogus-check passers was Courtney Townsend Taylor, who was most active in the 1940s and 1950s. In Chicago he once went down a certain street and cashed a check in every other store the whole length of the street. On the return trip he hit all the stores he had missed. Caught once in Mobile, Ala., he pulled a fountain pen from his pocket while he was being frisked for a weapon and said: "This is the only gun I need. I can get all the money I want with it."

Nobody knows how many rubber-check artists are operating, but one estimate placed the figure at around 2,500 full timers. Roughly two-thirds of all phony checks sent to the FBI are quickly identified as the work of known forgers by examining a file of about 60,000 current fraudulent check signatures. The rest are the product of amateurs.

Check passing is the type of crime that gets into a practitioner's blood. Rapists and muggers may slow down over the years and quit by the time they start graying at the temples. Check passers simply mellow. Their dignified look turns into a plus. Although in his seventies, Joseph W. Martin had no trouble separating thousands of dollars from gullible check cashers until his arrest in 1952 by the FBI. An actor, Martin had actually played in more than 500 motion pictures during more honest times, including a 1932 film in which he portrayed President Warren Harding. As a check passer, he simply carried on acting. His favorite technique was turning up at bar association meetings and cashing checks with his "colleagues." He was arrested in New York while posing as a lawyer from Nebraska attending a meeting of the American Bar Association in the Waldorf-Astoria.

Experts consider the late Alexander Thiel the most accomplished forger of modern times. Also high on the list is Frederick Emerson Peters. However, the great-granddaddy of all check chiselers clearly was Jim the Penman, who was born Alonzo James Whitman in 1854. He dissipated an inherited fortune, amassed an illegal million, became a state senator in Minnesota, received an honorary degree from Hamilton College and was almost elected to its board of trustees. He also passed thousands of bad checks. During his career, Jim the Penman was arrested 43 times, indicted 27, convicted 11. Once while doing a stretch in Auburn Prison, he was assigned to teach in the prison school—until it was discovered he was teaching forgery.

See also: FREDERICK EMERSON PETERS, ALEXANDER THIEL.

Chicago May (1876–1935) Queen of the Badger Game

May Churchill Sharpe did not invent the badger game, whereby a gentleman is invited to a lady's room to be "done for" and ends up being "done out" of his money through blackmail or simple robbery, but she was its most accomplished practitioner in the 1890s.

Born in Dublin, Ireland in 1876, May Sharpe spent six years in a convent school before running off to America, with 60 pounds from her father's strongbox as traveling money. Within a year after arriving in New York in the spring of 1889, she was living the fast life as the mistress of Dal Churchill. Churchill eventually married her and took her west. He was "a robber, highwayman, safecracker, cattle rustler and general all-round crook," according to May, and also a member of the Dalton gang. May was sublimely happy for an exciting year. Then Dal fouled up a train robbery and ended up hanging from vigilantes' rope near Phoenix, Ariz.

Widowed at 15, May went to Chicago, where with her looks she became the Queen of the Badger Game. At first, she operated as a loner, choosing her victims from hotels, night spots and other places where good-time Charlies congregated. Because of the publicity involved and the resultant effect on their families, most of the men who took her to a hotel wouldn't dream of going to the police after she had robbed them. May would also steal a sucker's valuable papers and write him, asking if he remembered the gay time they almost had together and wondering if he wanted his papers back. She would threaten, if ignored, to take the matter up with the wives. The tactic got results, and the errant husbands would give the money to an underworld pickup man sent by May. She would then deliver the papers. She never double-crossed a sucker a second time. She took him in the badger game and then once with a spot of blackmail, but then she let him off the hook.

Later, May took to using male accomplices and an older woman posing as her mother. The "mother" would catch May and her gentleman and shriek for help, which would come in the form of a hulking relative or neighbor. There would be no escape for the unfortunate victim until he paid. By her 16th birthday Chicago May had made $100,000, and by 17 she had run that up to $300,000.

Deciding the really big money was in New York, May transferred her operations there in the early 1890s. She frequented a famous criminal hangout, Considine's, which was also a slumming spot for sportsmen and literary and theatrical personalities. One evening she spotted a bushy-haired man with a drooping mustache. Thinking of him as a likely victim, she inquired about his identity and learned he was the celebrated author Mark Twain. May immediately started boning up on her Tom Sawyer and Huck Finn, and one night, done up in finery, she strolled over to Twain and introduced herself as Lady May Avery of England. She said she so admired Twain's work and had to meet him. The next evening Lady Avery dined with Twain and amused him greatly. It was well known that Twain was highly appreciative of the spicier things in life, and May expected him to jump at the bait when she invited him to visit her in Connecticut. Twain's eyes twinkled, but he shook his head.

"I'm sorry, dear lady," he said, "but I'm off to Washington in the morning and then am going West for an extended period."

Chicago May was crushed. However, the real crusher came when Twain got up to leave. He kissed her hand and whispered to her: "May I thank you, my dear lady, for a most amusing time. Of course, I don't believe a word of your story that you are an English noblewoman."

Such defeats were rare for May, especially after she formed a business relationship with Sgt. Charles Becker, New York's notorious cop-crook who was to die in the electric chair for murder. Becker fed May victims and took a 25 percent cut of the revenues.

A few years after the turn of the century, Becker advised Chicago May to pull out of New York because of an impending reform wave, and she moved to London, where she met the accomplished bank robber Eddie Guerin. She helped him rob some $250,000 from the Paris branch of the American Express Co. However, the couple had a falling out and were eventually caught by

French police. Eddie Guerin was sent to Devil's Island, from which he later made a sensational escape. May did a short stint in an English jail for transporting the American Express loot to London and then was kicked out of the country. She returned to the United States, but she was pushing 40. Hard-living had left her with wrinkles, puffs and rheumy eyes. There was no way she could be the Chicago May of the badger game.

The road the rest of the way was down. There were a number of arrests and convictions for various thefts, even petty larceny. For a time, May's fortunes picked up. She ran what she called a "nice house" in Philadelphia, where she used to entertain the prostitutes with tales of her exploits as Chicago May. However, a reform movement put her out of business.

Rather belatedly, May came to the conclusion that crime did not pay and wrote her autobiography in 1928. In an amused air, she noted: "My old friends, in the police write me letters of encouragement. Christians feel called upon to send me platitudes. Reformers insist upon drawing their pet theories to my attention. Professional crooks berate and praise me. Beggars importune me. Sycophants lather me with adulation. The rich . . . and others . . . patronize me."

But May was actually trying to live in her past. Her real life was nothing like that. The last newspaper clipping about her tells the whole story. She was arrested in Detroit during the early 1930s for soliciting male pedestrians, asking the bargain price of $2. She died a few years later.

Choctaw legacy, the con game

Fleecing Indians became a major sport for con men during the 1930s. Most of these swindles were based on telling the victims that under old treaties Indians were entitled to $1,000 each for their deceased relatives and that the only thing needed was to get an enabling act through Congress. The Indians could finance the lobbying necessary to pass the act for a mere $5 apiece.

A notorious sharper, Odie Moore, worked the scheme to perfection in Neshoba County, Miss., promising the Indians great rewards due them because of the breaking of the Dancing Rabbit Treaty of 1839. Since there had been wide intermarriage between whites and Choctaws over the decades, thousands of white suckers added their $5 contributions. Moore's fanciful association managed to come up with a slogan, promising "$1,000 for every dollar." A number of young whites even sought out girls with traces of Choctaw blood in them to get on the promised gravy train.

Moore's victims gave and gave from the time he started his swindle in 1930 until his death in 1945, and even after that, many remained sure their promised windfall would soon be forthcoming.

circus grifting

Compared to circuses in other countries, the American version has relied much more on criminal enterprises and fake exhibits and less on talented performers. A prime source of revenue in 19th-century circuses was gambling, particularly such crooked pastimes as the shell game, three-card monte and eight-dice cloth. Some seemingly ran independently of the circus management, but all paid a certain percentage of their take for the right to operate on the circus grounds. For these circus cons to thrive required four basic ingredients: grifters, victims, a dishonest circus management and public officials open to bribes. None were ever hard to come by.

The arrival of a circus in a community meant that within the next day or two many residents would find themselves swindled out of much of their ready cash, just as several church sermons the previous Sunday had warned. What the gambling grifters didn't take, circus shortchangers and pickpockets would. As late as 1900, many of the small circuses that traveled about the country still made each ticket seller pay up to $35 a week for the job because shortchanging the excited "rubes" on ticket sales was so easy and profitable. The pickpocketing franchise was sold to professional thieves, and to assist them in their chores, the master of ceremonies would make it a point to warn patrons about pickpockets. As a result, most men would quickly feel their wallets and thus reveal to the watchful crooks in which pocket they carried their cash. When a circus pulled up stakes, the grifters would ride out in the "privilege car," one lined with steel to protect them from angered rubes taken by the gambling grifts.

Criminologists have attributed the dishonest inclinations of the American circus to its more mobile existence compared to its European counterparts, especially the English circus, which stayed rooted in one place for much longer periods of time. The footloose lifestyle of American circuses encouraged a criminal business thrust. Many circuses in early years were ideal fences for stolen horses. Knowing they would be gone from an area the next day, circus employees became notorious for stealing from farms, barns and clotheslines.

Any one-shot method for improving profits would do. Balloon sellers typically hired an assistant to blow tacks at balloons in order to create an instant demand by howling children for a second or third sale. Many of the exhibits were outright frauds, particularly in small circuses, which used grifters because they could be paid far less than, for example, talented acrobats. Thus, the "Siamese twins" were simply two individuals held together by a flesh-colored belt while on display. As soon as that exhibit closed, the twins could hurry off, one to be perhaps a clown and the other to work, say, at the refreshment stand.

Circus grifting was an accepted practice in virtually all circuses until the 1880s and in all except Ringling's up to 1900. By as late as 1930, only the large circuses were free of grifting. The change did not come about as a result of a sudden reformation of the circuses or because public officials were less willing to take bribes or due to any growing sophistication among the customers. In earlier years a circus changed its name frequently so that it could return the following year to a community that it had angered on a previous trip. But as circuses grew, their very name became more of an asset than the revenues brought in by grifting. Faced with the necessity of making a choice, the bigger outfits, reluctantly, gave up grifting.

See also: CARNIVAL GYPS, SHELL GAME, THREE-CARD MONTE.

Civil War gold hoax

Perhaps the most audacious illegal money scheme of the Civil War period was perpetrated by a professional newspaperman, Joseph Howard, city editor of the *Brooklyn Eagle*, who concocted a false proclamation by President Abraham Lincoln. The hoax, in the words of one witness, "angered Lincoln more than almost any other occurrence of the war period."

Working with a reporter named Francis A. Mallison, Howard forged an Associated Press dispatch of the supposed proclamation that began, "In all seasons of exigency it becomes a nation carefully to scrutinize its line of conduct, humbly to approach the Throne of Grace, and meekly to improve forgiveness, wisdom, and guidance." The document, recounting the military stalemate in Virginia and disastrous news from Louisiana, called for a national day of "fasting, humiliation and prayer" eight days hence, on May 26, 1864. The real crushing news in the proclamation was the drafting of an additional 400,000 men.

Howard realized such a doleful pronouncement would shake the financial community to its roots, upset the stock market and undoubtedly cause a rise in price of gold. Days before he and Mallison unleashed their hoax, Howard bought a considerable amount of gold on margins, much of it apparently under other names, so that the best estimate of his profits could only be put at "many, many thousands of dollars."

The schemers used young boys to deliver the bogus AP dispatch to various New York newspapers. The news was so startling that several of the publications decided to confirm the facts before printing the story. However, two papers, the *World* and the *Journal of Commerce,* were pressed by deadlines and tore down their makeup at the last moment to get the story out. Quite as Howard had expected, the stock exchange "was thrown into a violent fever." The price of gold instantly shot up 10 percent. Fortunes were made and lost before the hoax was exposed.

Incensed by the false story, President Lincoln, Secretary of State William H. Seward and Secretary of War Edwin M. Stanton ordered the two newspapers seized. Only two days later, on May 20, the trail led to Howard and Mallison when it became apparent that the newspapers had been the victims rather than the perpetrators of an act that in Stanton's words "distinguished [them] by the violence of their opposition to the Administration."

The clearing of the newspapers led to a firestorm of protest against President Lincoln's initial seizure of them. Lincoln, locked in a battle for renomination and reelection, found the charges of suppression of the free press particularly embarrassing. Almost forgotten in the controversy were the culprits, Howard and Mallison, who were confined in Fort Lafayette. Finally, Howard's father, an elder of Henry Ward Beecher's church, prevailed upon the famous minister to petition Lincoln for mercy. Beecher told Lincoln that the 35-year-old Howard was "the only spotted child of a large family" and his only guilt was "the hope of making some *money*." Finally, after the culprits had been confined for less than three months, Lincoln ordered their release.

The freeing of the gold hoaxers many not have been as magnanimous as it appeared on the surface. Ironically, when the report of the phony proclamation was published, an as yet unreleased proclamation lay on Lincoln's desk. It called for the draft of 300,000 more men. When Lincoln saw the adverse effect of the bogus report on the people and on the financial markets, he postponed all call-up plans for an additional two months.

coffin, double-decker   Mafia body disposal method

From the time of its first appearance in America during the 19th century, the Mafia has been most inventive in the ways it disposes of the bodies of murder victims; a great many are finally listed in official records as missing, instead of dead. Some victims have been fitted with "concrete overcoats" or ground up in garbage shredders. Top New York mafioso Tony Bender is believed now to be either part of a large Manhattan skyscraper or of the recently crumbling West Side Highway (an in-joke in certain Mafia circles is that "dagos make lousy roads").

Perhaps the quaintest of all body disposal devices is the "double-decker coffin." A murder victim is taken to one of the mob's cooperative undertakers who constructs a special panel in a coffin he has ready for an about-to-be-buried corpse. The unwanted murder victim is placed in the bottom of the coffin and a panel is put over the body. Then the right corpse is placed on top. After a properly mournful funeral, the two corpses are buried together. No undertaker has ever been convicted as a result of this method because he can always claim the mob must have dug open the grave after burial and put in the extra corpse. The undertaker cooperating with the mob on such a matter is assured of the proper financial reward because the crime family will see to it that he gets a good deal of their regular business thrown his way.

Collins, Dapper Don (1880–1950)   confidence man

The archetypal smooth operator who uses his charms to seduce women and defraud them of their wealth, Dapper Don Collins was a notorious rogue who, by his own admission, "could never pass up a score," large or small. He swindled women by reversing the old badger game, so that they were extorted when he was "arrested" by confederates posing as law officers. The police impersonators would say he was a Mann Act violator or suspected procurer for white slavers. To protect the honor of the woman, usually upper class and perhaps married, he would give the bogus officers all his cash, only to be visibly shaken when they announced it was not enough. The panicky woman, facing sure ruin if the case was publicized, could be counted on to contribute her money, jewelry and furs.

Born in Atlanta, Ga. as Robert Arthur Tourbillon, he affected a number of aliases for his various cons but became best known as Dapper Don Collins, because according to his confederates, he was a dandy who could "sweet talk a lady" or anyone else for that matter. He often used a phony police badge and pretended to be a police officer, one who, of course, was always open to a bribe. Dapper Don first arrived in New York around the turn of the century after an unrewarding circus career riding a bicycle around in a cage full of lions. He gravitated to the notorious Broadway poolroom of Curly Bennett, where he befriended most of the metropolitan underworld.

Dapper Don soon became a gang leader, forming the first of his blackmail rings for extorting money from women. Besides his various confidence games, he masterminded train robberies and drug-smuggling and alien-smuggling operations and later, with the onset of Prohibition, was a top bootlegger and rumrunner. Collins often used a luxury yacht for rumrunning and bringing in aliens. In one of his more audacious exploits, he once entrapped a society woman aboard the yacht by having phony law enforcement raiders seize him on Mann Act violation for transporting the woman from Connecticut for "illicit purposes." They shook the woman down for $7,000 in cash and diamonds. Before the raiders left the yacht, they seized three aliens Collins had brought into the country from a ship offshore. Dapper Don had already collected $1,000 from each of them, but now the "law officers" confiscated the rest of their personal fortunes as a payoff for not taking them into custody. Because Collins was fearful of overlooking some of their money, he even had his men take all the victims' luggage with them to search at their leisure.

While he bossed many of these grandiose schemes, Collins could not pass up even the smallest take. For a time, he headed a "punch mob" on Manhattan's West Side that specialized in looting nickels from pay telephones. One of his extraordinary cons occurred in 1920 during the hunt for a Railway Express agent who had skipped out of his job with $6,000. While police hunted the agent, Dapper Don came across him first. He immediately turned copper and swindled the thief out of his haul in return for letting him go free, appropriating as well the man's watch, ring and tiepin.

While Collins occasionally did time for various capers, he usually beat the rap for his blackmail exploits because his victims refused to testify against him. He retained the Great Mouthpiece, Bill Fallon, to defend him on a number of charges and usually went free. The pair were constant companions on Broadway.

According to Gene Fowler in *The Great Mouthpiece*, when Fallon was asked why he chummed with such a notorious individual, he replied: "Because he is a philosopher as well as the Chesterfield of crime. He performs in a gentlemanly manner. This first bit of philosophy he ever dropped in my company made me laugh and made me like him.

We were discussing whether any man is normal; precisely sane; and what sanity consists of. Collins said: 'Between the ages of sixteen and sixty, no man is entirely sane. The only time any man between those ages is sane is during the first ten minutes after he has concluded the supreme love gesture. Fifteen minutes after, and the old insanity creeps back again'!"

Part of his success with the ladies stemmed from his reputation as the biggest spender and fashion plate on Broadway. It cost him plenty. What Collins netted from one gullible but adoring lady one day he might blow the next on another lady. Once Collins set up a Maryland matron and took off to Atlantic City with her. He was then to guide her to Washington for the kill. Instead, he stayed in Atlantic City for a week with her. At the end of that week of bliss, he kissed her good-bye and went to Washington alone. He had four confederates in this operation and had to pay them $350 apiece for a caper that was intended to net a $10,000 profit.

In 1924, with the police hunting him for a number of capers, Dapper Don transferred his operations to Europe and seduced several women in Berlin and Paris. In the French capital, he took up with Mrs. Helen Petterson, former wife of Otto Young Heyworth, and extracted money from her under a number of ruses. Moreover, during a New Year's party at the Hotel Majestic, he flipped her out of a third-floor window. She broke her leg in the fall, and Collins was hustled off to prison for that offense and failure to pay his hotel bill. Undaunted, Mrs. Petterson limped from her hospital room at Neuilly to visit Collins, announcing, "We are going to be married." However, some New York police officers were in France to pick up a suspect in another case and spotted Collins in the prison. They promptly arranged for his extradition to the States on a robbery charge. Dapper Don was brought home in grand style aboard the steamship *Paris,* sharing a fine stateroom with a New York detective. Passengers knew that one of the two was a crook, but most believed the detective was the guilty party.

Back home, Collins beat the rap but later did short stretches on a couple of other charges. Dapper Don then got involved in a liquor-smuggling operation with another top confidence operator, Count Victor Lustig, supplying the notorious Legs Diamond with booze. They worked a label-switching dodge that enabled them to cheat the gangster out of thousands of dollars. Eventually, Diamond found out about the swindle, and the pair had to go into hiding. For a time, Collins left the country again, but in 1929 he came back and was caught swindling a New Jersey farmer out of $30,000. He was sent to prison for three years. When he came out, a lot of the old Dapper Don was gone, as indeed was the pre-Depression era that nurtured him. He was over 50, paunchy around the waist and looking tired, perhaps having lost some of his self-confidence. He told the press he was reforming.

That was impossible; he was plain tired. In 1939 Dapper Don, then a drug addict, was far gone, and his swindles were petty. Long ago, Collins had learned the danger of going after small potatoes. Unlike big people, little victims scream. He swindled an immigrant woman out of a few hundred dollars by pretending to be an immigration official and threatening to deport her husband. For this unimportant caper Collins drew the longest sentence of his career, 15 to 30 years.

The newspapers reported that Dapper Don started off on his train ride up the river as light hearted and debonair as ever. But that was newspaper hyperbole. Collins was old and beat. "The only way I'll ever come out again," he told the officer escorting him, "is feet first."

He was right. He died in Attica Prison in June 1950 and was buried in a pauper's grave. No one attended the funeral.

computer crime

Computer crime is the least understood of all illegal activities because it is so new and steeped in a technology not as yet fully developed. The difficulty of detecting computer fraud has attracted many criminal minds. Some known swindles are monumental, such as the 64,000 fake insurance policies created between 1964 and 1973 on the Equity Funding Corp.'s computer. That operation involved $2 billion.

The main weakness in a computer system is that a criminal can perpetrate a fraud once he or she has learned the code or password that will activate the system. In one case a bank employee simply programmed the firm's computer to divert over $120,000 from various customers' accounts to those of two friends. A clever scheme was pulled off by a programmer who ordered a computer to deduct sums from many accounts and credit them to dummy accounts, which he then emptied. In another case a bank employee embezzled more than $1 million to finance his betting on horse racing and basketball games. Ironically, his computer-based system for handicapping the horses proved nowhere near as efficient as his money diversion scheme.

With the discovery of each new method, computer practices are changed to prevent such fraud. Some sophisticated systems use fingerprints or voiceprints as a method of insuring their integrity, and the FBI has computer fraud experts who conduct training seminars for police officers and businessmen to combat this new type of crime. But it is obvious that computer fraud is itself a growth industry.

See also: INTERNET CRIME.

confessions, false

In Chicago during the 1950s a pregnant woman was viciously slain and her body dumped in a snowbank. Almost immediately a factory worker came forth and confessed. He stood a good chance of becoming a modern-day lynching victim since a spirit of vengeance dominated the woman's neighborhood. That sentiment dissipated, however, when a 19-year-old sailor at the Great Lakes Naval Station also confessed to the slaying. This second confession turned out to be the real one.

In 1961 a young widow in New York tearfully told police she had killed her husband several years earlier. His death had been attributed to natural causes. The body was exhumed and an autopsy performed. The man had died of natural causes, and psychiatrists found the woman was merely suffering from delusions that stemmed from a guilt complex that she had failed to be a good wife to her late husband.

Both of these persons could easily have been convicted of the crimes to which they so eagerly confessed. Throughout hundreds of years of legal history, the confession has been viewed by the courts and society as the "queen of proofs" of criminal guilt. Yet, each year probably thousands of persons in this country confess to crimes that they did not, and could not, have committed. Why do they do it? Some are neurotics who will confess to any crime just for the excitement of being the center of attention; for example, more than 200 persons confessed to the Lindbergh baby kidnapping. Others are motivated by bizarre guilt feelings for some other incident, often trivial; they seek punishment, consciously or subconsciously, for a crime they did not commit.

Whenever legal experts discuss false confessions, the subject of the mutiny of the *Hermione* is raised. The *Hermione* was a British frigate captained by a harsh disciplinarian named Pigot. In September 1797 the seething anger of the crew erupted against Pigot and his officers. The men of the *Hermione* not only murdered the captain and the officers, they butchered them. The crew then sailed to an enemy port, but one young midshipman escaped and got back to England. He identified many of the offenders, and some of them were run down and hanged.

Many innocent sailors confessed to taking part in the *Hermione* mutiny. One admiralty officer later wrote:

In my own experience, I have known, on separate occasions, more than six sailors who voluntarily confessed to having struck the first blow at Captain Pigot. These men detailed all the horrid circumstances of the mutiny with extreme minuteness and perfect accuracy. Nevertheless, not one of them had even been in the ship, nor had so much as seen Captain Pigot in their lives. They had obtained from their messmates the particulars of the story. When long on a foreign station, hungering and thirsting for home, their minds became enfeebled. At length, they actually believed themselves guilty of the crime over which they had so long brooded, and submitted with a gloomy

pleasure to being sent to England in irons for judgment. At the Admiralty, we were always able to detect and establish their innocence.

The last sentiment was, of course, self-serving and perhaps not shared by all. Sir Samuel Romilly related the fate of another seaman who confessed to taking part in the same incident. He was executed. Later, Sir Samuel learned that when the mutiny had taken place on the *Hermione*, the sailor was at Portsmouth aboard the *Marlborough*.

American criminal history is replete with persons confessing to crimes and indeed to noncrimes. The classic case of the latter occurred in Vermont during the 19th century, when two brothers, Stephen and Jesse Boorn, confessed in colorful detail the slaying of Russell Colvin, their brother-in-law. They were both sentenced to death, but Jesse, in recognition of the fact that he had confessed first, had his sentence commuted to life. Stephen's hanging was only postponed when Colvin fortuitously returned home after an absence of seven years, during which time he had had no idea that he had been "murdered."

Probably the great-granddaddy of all cases involving false confessions was the Los Angeles murder of Elizabeth Short in 1947. The case was to become famous as the Black Dahlia murder. The police took full written confessions from at least 38 suspects, and after more than 200 others had telephoned their admissions of guilt and offers to surrender, the police stopped keeping count of confessions.

In the Black Dahlia case the number of confessions was attributable to the sadistic nature of the crime. Such vile crimes invariably produce great numbers of confessions, as though the neurotic confessors literally beg for the spotlight of revulsion and contempt. Many, experts say, are made by persons propelled by a death wish and eager to find the most spectacular method of committing suicide, e.g., in the Black Dahlia case, going to the gas chamber. Others have different motivations. When a girl named Selma Graff was bludgeoned to death by a burglar in Brooklyn during the 1950s, the police got the usual rash of phony confessions. One of them came from a young ex-con out on probation for auto theft. He carried within him a vicious hatred for his mother, who was always so embarrassed by his criminal traits and who at the moment was threatening to notify his parole officer that he had been visiting bars. So he walked into police headquarters and gave himself up for the Graff killing. His story proved to be a hoax when he was unable to supply the murder weapon and could not describe the Graff home accurately. Finally admitting his falsehood, he said he gladly would have gotten himself convicted of the murder, even gone to the chair, in order to torment his mother.

Privately, even some former prosecutors say all confessions should be suspect, that it is illogical to expect that a police officer who has worked hard to extract a confession from a suspect will be just as diligent in his efforts to test whether the confession is true or not. More often, the police and prosecutors have clung to discredited confessions in an effort to convict someone who later proved to be an innocent man. A case in point was George Whitmore, Jr., the man who was wrongly accused of the notorious "career girl" sex slayings of Janice Wylie and Emily Hoffert in their Manhattan apartment in 1963. Whitmore-type incidents, especially repudiated confessions, were cited by the Supreme Court

in the landmark Miranda decision, which led to curbs on police powers to interrogate suspects. Some attorneys, such as O. John Rogge, a former assistant attorney general of the United States and author of the book *Why Men Confess,* hold to the theory that no repudiated confession should ever be used in court. They believe that the Supreme Court is gradually moving, perhaps with some steps backward from time to time, in that direction. Quite naturally, prosecuting attorneys claim that such action will make convictions next to impossible to obtain.

Cook, Dr. Frederick A. (1865–1940) explorer and land fraud conspirator

Dr. Frederick A. Cook is most famous for his dispute with Commodore Robert E. Peary over who was the first to reach the North Pole. For a brief time, Dr. Cook was hailed throughout the world after announcing he had reached the North Pole. However, shortly thereafter, Peary made the same claim and labeled all of Cook's claims false. In the controversy that followed, Peary clearly gained the upper hand, and Cook was to keep only a few believers. He returned home disheartened and in disgrace, and things were to get worse for him. In the 1920s Cook's name was used to promote a Texas oil-land sale that was branded fraudulent. While there was much reason to believe that Cook was not an active member of the fraud, he had a famous name and thus made an excellent target. He was convicted of using the mails to defraud and sentenced to 14 years. After working as a prison doctor in Leavenworth, he was released in 1931. Considering that the lands in question were now selling at prices well above the so-called fraud figure, it would indeed have been unseemly to hold him longer. President Franklin D. Roosevelt granted Dr. Cook a presidential pardon shortly before the latter's death in 1940.

counterfeiting

Throughout American history there have always been people who have thought the best way to make money is, simply, to make money.

Mary Butterworth, the kitchen counterfeiter, may have been the first. This housewife with seven children operated a highly successful counterfeiting ring in Plymouth colony during the early 1700s.

The comparatively crude paper money used in colonial times, "Continental currency," was so frequently and successfully faked that it gave rise to the saying, "Not worth a Continental." During the Civil War, it was estimated that a good third of the currency in circulation was "funny money." The counterfeiter's chore was made much easier because some 11,600 state banks across the nation designed and printed their own currency. Finally, in 1863 the nation adopted a uniform currency.

Counterfeiting today is hardly a lost art, but few stay successful at it for very long. In 1976 the Secret Service made a record haul in the Bronx, New York City, arresting six suspects who had run off $20 million in what was characterized as "highly passable" bills. This followed on the heels of raids in Los Angeles that netted four men with more than $8 million worth of bogus bills. The main worry of the government today is that sophisticated new photographic and printing equipment will permit counterfeiters, as never before, to approximate the intricate whorls, loops and crosshatching that makes American paper money just about the most difficult in the world to imitate. In recent years, the government has introduced new bills said to be even more counterfeit-proof, but that must be tested over time, while understanding that all moneys have always been duplicated.

In a typical counterfeiting operation, distribution is handled by an army of wholesalers, distributors and passers. The standard breakdown calls for the counterfeiters to sell their output to wholesalers for 12 percent of face value. The wholesaler then has the job of reselling the bills to distributors for 25 percent. The distributors turn it over to street-level passers for 35 percent.

Although counterfeiting is punishable by up to 15 years in prison and a $10,000 fine and Treasury officials estimate that almost 90 percent of all bad-money makers are jailed in less than a year, counterfeiters, big and small, still keep trying their luck. There are those who will print fake $1 bills despite the rather high overhead involved. It took the Secret Service 10 years to catch up with a lone operator who passed fake $1 bills in New York. He was an elderly former janitor who circulated only eight or 10 ones every few days, making it a point never to pass them twice at the same place. He explained later that he "didn't want to stick anybody for more than a dollar."

Some even try their hand at counterfeiting coins, even though breaking even is nearly impossible in these inflationary times. In the past, however, coin counterfeiting was big business. In 1883 a deaf-mute named Joshua Tatum made a small fortune by slightly altering the original liberty head nickel and passing it for 100 times its real value. On the face of the nickel was a woman's head wearing a liberty headpiece. On the other side was the motto *E. Pluribus Unum* and a large *V*. The

V, the Roman numeral five, was the only indication of the coin's value to be found on the nickel. Tatum noted that the liberty head nickel closely resembled in design and size the half eagle, or $5 gold piece, which was then in general circulation. The face of the latter also displayed a woman's head with a liberty headpiece. On the reverse side was the sign of value, Five D., indicating $5. About the only difference was the color: the nickel had a silvery appearance, and the half eagle, gold. Tatum began gold-plating nickels by the thousand and then buying 5¢ items all over the East Coast. Invariably, he got $4.95 in change. On occasion, a merchant would flip the coin over, note the V for five and assume it was a newly issued $5 gold piece. He couldn't prove it by Tatum, who was a deaf-mute. When Tatum was finally caught, the courts freed him because he was a deaf-mute. The authorities could never prove Tatum had ever asked for change, and there were no laws on the book prohibiting a person from gold-plating a nickel. The law was changed accordingly and an emergency session of Congress was called to alter the design of the nickel.

Students of the fine art of counterfeiting contend that the true craftsmen are all in their graves. There were, for example, artists like Baldwin Bredell and Arthur Taylor, who in the late 1890s turned out such perfect $100 bills that the government had to withdraw from circulation the entire issue of $26 million in Monroe-head bills. Sent to Moyamensing Prison, Bredell and Taylor astounded the experts by pulling off a moneymaking caper so amazing that Treasury Department experts at first refused to concede it possible. Within several months of their arrival in the prison, Bredell and Taylor began turning out counterfeit $20 bills at night in their cell. To do this, they needed to have supplies smuggled in. One of Taylor's relatives brought books and magazines on his weekly visits. These hid engraving tools, steel plates, files and vials of acids. Another smuggled in a kerosene lamp piece by piece and some magnifying glasses hidden in a basket of cookies. The printing press they needed was made to specifications the counterfeiters drew up and had smuggled out. Getting the press in was easy because it was the size of a cigar box. Since Bredell's wife was pregnant, she became just a bit more expecting. Inks were a different problem. With their former workshop under government padlock, there was no way to get the special bleaches and inks that were needed. One couldn't buy the proper ink legitimately without the government knowing about it, so the pair stole the bleaches they needed from the prison laundry and then their relatives started bringing fruits and flowers. From the dried fruits and berries and the green leaves of the flowers, they made their own ink.

Soon the Bredell-Taylor $20s—virtually as good as Uncle Sam's—started turning up. What the pair hadn't counted on was that John E. Wilkie, the chief of the U.S. Secret Service, would spot the work as being too good to be anybody's but theirs. Naturally, Wilkie assumed the plates had been prepared by the pair before their arrest and they were just being used now, so he put a watch on relatives of Taylor and Bredell, and after one was caught passing some of the fake $20s, Wilkie uncovered the whole story. The experts called in by the Secret Service scoffed at the possibility that Bredell and Taylor could have produced such work in prison. They insisted it could not have been done without a camera, a huge workroom and an

8-ton press. Only when the prisoners reenacted their feat were the experts convinced.

In recognition of their extraordinary talents, Chief Wilkie decided to help the pair get a new start in life when they were released. He got financial backing for a mechanical engraving machine Taylor had perfected, starting the ex-counterfeiter on the way to becoming a prosperous manufacturer. Bredell went on to establish a leading engraving and lithography plant and also became rich. The two master counterfeiters were lured away from their illicit activities the only way the government could think of—by making them rich, legally.

Today, there are no counterfeiting geniuses such as Taylor and Bredell or Jim the Penman, perhaps the only counterfeiter in history to make top-grade notes simply by drawing them. Using a fine camel's hair brush, he made phony bills by tracing them from genuine notes that he placed before a strong light. Criminal craftsmen of such caliber, to the U.S. government's relief, are a dying breed.

See also: MARY BUTTERWORTH, "COUNT" VICTOR LUSTIG.

Further reading: *Money of Their Own* by Murray Teign Bloom.

Crazy Eddie's insane fraud their prices and their stock offerings were truly insane

In the 1980s few television pitches bombarded Easterners more than of Crazy Eddie's, an appliance and hi-fi chain that declared ad nauseum "our prices are insane." And they were—and so was their accounting system, their tax payments and their Wall Street deals.

Crazy Eddie's went public at a time when Wall Street was mad about rapidly growing companies. In effect, proprietor Eddie Antar and his cousin Sam were telling the best brains in the financial community: "You want super growth, we got super growth."

The Antars realized that super growth thanks to Sam Antar's creative accounting. As the law was later to determine, the Antars had been skimming money from the business for years. In fact, they were making money not only from actual profits but just as lucratively from avoiding sales taxes. It was as near to a Marx Brothers operation as possible. But then an even more insane inspiration hit the Antars:

"Why don't we go public?" Why not indeed.

Of course, to be a super growth company they had to show explosive profits. Nothing was easier for the boys. All that had to be done was to cut back on the family skimming. With the abrupt reduction in the skim, profits seemingly ballooned from $1.7 million to $4.6 million. That figure for 1984 truly astounded Wall Street brokers, and a public stock offering was a resounding success. The Antars had barely warmed up.

In the quest for more imaginary profits, the family bought up imaginary merchandise so that gross profits by 1986 had soared to the level of 40 percent. For a second time Wall Street put out a stock issue that was even more successful than the first.

Alas for the Antars and their investors, there was no way Sam Antar could produce more bogus profits. Hungry Wall Streeters now were expecting an additional $20–$30 million for 1987.

"My pencil is only so long," Sam informed Eddie. The boys tried to move inventories from store to store so that auditors would count the same goods time after time. Unfortunately, that was the end of the road. Auditors were not that insane.

Jail sentences followed, but this did not end the Antar saga. In later years Sam Antar made speeches to such groups as the National Association of Fraud Examiners, outlining the crookedness of Crazy Eddie's. His theme to the experts and to credulous investors was that fraud is so easy—insanely so.

creep joint   crooked brothel

Much of the prostitution activity in San Francisco during the 19th century was conducted in what were called cribs or cowyard cubicles. When business was brisk, a customer was not permitted time to undress, even to remove his footwear. Instead, a piece of oilcloth was spread along the bottom of the bed to keep the man's boots from soiling the bedding. Of course, all customers were required to remove their hats, since no self-respecting prostitute would consider entertaining a man with his hat on.

One type of crib that never forbade the removal of clothing by customers was the so-called creep joint. Here men were encouraged to hang everything in a closet that was attached to the back wall of the crib. The back walls, however, were really doors, and while the customer was otherwise occupied, an accomplice of the woman would open the door and steal all the man's money and valuables.

Creep joints may or may not have originated first in San Francisco, but at least in that city the rip-off was carried out with a certain amount of style and a touch of sympathy; a dime was always left in the man's clothing for his carfare home. Few men ever taken in creep joints attempted to put up a fight. It was common knowledge that such cribs had a push-button alarm attached to a nearby barroom which, if activated, would bring the saloon bouncer and several other toughs over to manhandle the protesting victim.

See also: BADGER GAME, PANEL HOUSE.

Dannan, Emmanuel (1843–1851)

murder victim, folk hero

Known as the "boy who wouldn't lie," eight-year-old Emmanuel Dannan became an instant Wisconsin folk hero when he was killed by his adopted parents, Samuel Norton and his wife, in 1851. Both of Emmanuel's English-immigrant parents died before he was five years old, and he was saved from the poorhouse by an uncle, who unfortunately died a year later. The Samuel Nortons then adopted the child.

Emmanuel was eight when he happened to see his stepparents murder a peddler. The Nortons ordered the boy to lie to the police, but he said he would not. He was hanged by his wrists from the rafters of the family's log cabin deep in the woods and beaten with willow switches for two hours. During his ordeal the only thing the boy would say was, "Pa, I will not lie!" After two hours the boy's spirit was still unbroken, but his body was and he died. The facts came out in an investigation, and the Nortons were both sent to prison for seven years, while Emmanuel's tale spread throughout the area.

There was talk of erecting a monument to his memory, and a total of $1,099.94 was collected, only to be siphoned off by a fund-raiser. Over the years the story of Emmanuel Dannan's bravery became part of the state's folklore, and finally, on May 2, 1954 a monument was erected in his memory at Montello, Wis. The inscription read, "Blessed are they which are persecuted for righteousness sake, for theirs is the kingdom of Heaven." Since then, Truth Day in Montello has been celebrated every May 2.

Demara, Ferdinand Waldo, Jr. (1921–1982)

impostor

Known as the greatest impostor in 20th-century America, Ferdinand Waldo Demara, Jr. had a compulsion to impersonate people. A high school dropout, he was nonetheless able in the 1940s to masquerade successfully as a doctor of philosophy named Robert L. French and to teach college psychology classes. He also passed himself off as Cecil Boyce Haman, a zoology Ph.D.; a Trappist monk in a Kentucky monastery; a biologist

Perhaps the most active and frequently charming imposter in American history, Fred Demara was a successful naval surgeon, a Trappist monk, a cancer researcher, a law student, a college psychology teacher, a soldier, a sailor, a hospital orderly, a deputy sheriff, a prison guidance counselor, among other careers. Why did he do it? "Rascality, pure rascality," he said.

doing cancer research in a Seattle, Wash. institution; a law student; a hospital orderly; an American soldier; an American sailor; a recreational officer at a maximum security prison in Texas; a two-time "convert" to Catholicism (although he was born a Roman Catholic); and a deputy sheriff.

Demara's greatest impersonation occurred during the Korean War, when he assumed the role of a lieutenant-surgeon with the Canadian navy and successfully performed a number of major operations under severe battle conditions. Demara would bone up on medical books aboard ship and then remove tonsils, pull teeth and amputate limbs. In his most accomplished operation, he successfully

removed a bullet from within a fraction of an inch of the heart of a wounded South Korean soldier. When he finished the skillful operation, a small cheer went up from fascinated spectators.

However, news stories about the amazing medical lieutenant wired back to Canada finally resulted in Demara's exposure, and he was ordered back to Victoria. Incredibly, the Canadian navy decided that Demara had enlisted under a false name; it didn't occur to them that he was not actually a doctor. As a result, he was merely discharged with all pay due him and asked to leave the country.

In 1956 Demara was caught posing as an accredited teacher at a school in Maine. He served a few months in jail for "cheating by false premises." His longest prison term for any offense was 18 months. Demara was the subject of a book and then a Hollywood movie starring Tony Curtis. When asked why he engaged in a lifetime of impersonations, Demara said, "Rascality, pure rascality."

Devol, George (1829–1902) riverboat gambler

With Canada Bill Jones, George Devol was probably the most talented of the riverboat gamblers, an expert not only at three-card monte but also at poker, seven-up and other card games, especially faro, in which he was the bank and could control the flimflamming. By his own estimate in his 1887 autobiography, *Forty Years a Gambler on the Mississippi,* he made more than $2 million but, like most others in his profession, could not hold on to it, losing most of it in casino faro games. He described himself as "a cabin boy in 1839; could steal cards and cheat the boys at eleven; stack a deck at fourteen . . .

fought more rough-and-tumble fights than any man in America, and was the most daring gambler in the world." And the amount of exaggeration was not too great.

Devol's most constant partner was Canada Bill Jones, and the pair made a perfect team. Devol dressed like a fashion plate while Canada Bill acted and dressed like a lout with an intelligence level somewhere below that of moron. Together with Canada Bill and two others, Devol formed a riverboat combine that netted each of the participants $200,000 a year by the time the group broke up. While he was not, and most likely no one was, as great a manipulator at three-card monte as Canada Bill, Devol was nonetheless a master at card skullduggery. On one occasion, in a friendly poker game with four other gamblers he rang in four cold decks on the same hand and dealt each of the other players a set of four aces. He then sat back and watched the fireworks. Each of the gamblers felt he had been hit with a hand that comes once in a lifetime, and soon, everything the gamblers owned was in the pot. When the hilarious showdown came, it took them hours to sort out who owned what.

Like all cardsharps, Devol appreciated a sucker who lost magnanimously, but not surprisingly, he often met the opposite kind. A sore loser once pulled a gun on Devol, who extricated himself from the dilemma by "using my head." He butted his foe unconscious. Devol was probably correct when he said he engaged in more rough-and-tumble fights than any other man in America. He usually did so as a "butter." Devol was the proud possessor of a massive, dome-shaped cranium that made an awesome weapon. Besides using it against sore-losing gamblers, he won many a bet in butting contests against various strongmen and circus performers, including the famed Billy Carroll of Robinson's Circus, billed as "the man with the thick skull, or the great butter." When Carroll recovered consciousness, he placed his hand on the gambler's head and said, "Gentlemen, I have found my papa at last."

After more than 40 years of gambling on the great rivers and in the Wild West, Devol married late in life. Between his wife and a militant mother-in-law, he was pressured to give up gambling and settle down in Cincinnati. In 1887 he published his memoirs. More or less retired from gambling, he sneaked away for an occasional poker game and allegedly slipped into Kentucky now and then to trim the racetrack suckers at monte. He celebrated his 60th birthday by winning a bet that he could batter an oak whiskey cast to splinters with his hard head. When Devol cashed in his chips in 1902, the *Cincinnati Enquirer* reported that he had won and lost more money than any other gambler in American history. Whether that was true or not, George Devol typified his lusty era.

See also: THREE-CARD MONTE.

diamond switch   confidence theft game
Considered to be superstars of shoplifters, diamond switch experts, often women, victimize top jewelry stores by feigning interest in the purchase of a diamond. The thief will examine the stone and, when the salesperson's attention is distracted, substitute a worthless or inferior stone for the genuine article. The thief then makes a hasty exit before the switch is discovered.

The prowess of these operators was pointed out not long ago by a woman who had cheated two leading jewelry stores on New York's Fifth Avenue. Handsomely dressed in a fur coat, the woman considered the purchase of an $18,000 ring but after some thought decided it was too expensive. She handed the clerk back a cheaper diamond, one worth only about $7,500. Since the two stones were cut alike and determination of the full quality of the costlier diamond required more than examination by the naked eye, no suspicions were aroused until some time after the supposed customer had departed. Meanwhile, the same thief had entered a second store to inspect a $35,000 diamond, for which she neatly substituted the $18,000 stone. By the time both stores discovered their losses, the woman was long gone from Fifth Avenue.

Dillinger, John Herbert—double

The death of John Dillinger in July 1934 marked the end of crime's greatest folk hero of the 20th century, and it was therefore hardly surprising that his death was not accepted by many. This has been a common behavioral reaction. For decades there were people who believed Jesse James had not been shot by Bob Ford, that a substitute corpse had been used. And for decades one "real Jesse James" after another turned up. In the cases of the Apache Kid and Butch Cassidy, the weight of opinion seems to favor the theory that they survived their alleged demises, but the identification of their corpses was far more controversial.

The disbelief about John Dillinger started instantly after his death and continued for years. In a book entitled *Dillinger: Dead or Alive?* (1970), Jay Robert Nash and Ron Offen made perhaps the most complete case that the great public enemy had not been killed by FBI agents. Their basic premise was that the FBI had been duped into thinking the dead man was Dillinger, and when the agency discovered otherwise, it could do nothing but develop a massive cover-up.

What makes this case less than totally acceptable is the number of people such a plot would have required. Certainly Anna Sage, "the woman in red," and her East Chicago police contact or contacts. And someone would have had to have planted a phony Dillinger fingerprint card days before the killing. According to this theory, "Jimmy Lawrence" was not a Dillinger alias but the name of a real minor hoodlum whose career was rather hazy.

Proponents of the fake Dillinger theory make much of glaring discrepancies found in Dillinger's autopsy report, which was allegedly lost for more than 30 years. For instance, in the report the dead man's eyes were listed as brown, Dillinger's were blue. But this was an autopsy performed in Cook County during the 1930s, a time when coroners' findings nationwide were notorious for being replete with errors. The autopsy was performed in a "looney bin" atmosphere. A reporter for the *Chicago Tribune* appeared in news photos propping up Dillinger's head and was identified as the "coroner." Even after the autopsy was performed, Dillinger's brain was actually "mislaid" for a time. If all errors made in autopsies of that period were taken seriously, probably just half the victims of violent deaths could really have been considered dead.

Another question that must be raised is how John Dillinger lived happily ever after and on what. By all accounts, he had less than $10,000 available to him for a final, permanent escape. Could he stay away from crime forever? And if he could not, would he not have been identified sooner or later? And what of Anna Sage? Despite promises made to her by the FBI, she was deported back to her native Romania. She could undoubtedly have bought a reprieve from that fate had she come forward with the true facts about a Dillinger hoax.

In sum, the "Dillinger lives" theory appears to be a case of wishful thinking, one fostered by the fact that John Dillinger was too good—or too bad—to be allowed to die.

Dollar Store first "Big Store" swindle

In 1867 a stocky, red-whiskered, friendly man named Ben Marks opened the Dollar Store in Cheyenne, Wyo., where everything in stock sold for that price. Marks, however, was not interested in merchandising but in confidence games, and what he started would develop into the "Big Store," the grift that was to become the technique used in most great confidence rackets for the next 100 years.

In the windows of his store, Marks featured all sorts of useful price-worthy items, but sales proved few and far between since the pitch was used merely to draw gullible travelers and immigrants into the store. A pioneer exponent of three-card monte and other swindles, Marks had confederates operating several games complete with shills who appeared to be winning. Many a wagon train settler stepped into the store to buy a sturdy shovel and left minus most of his stake for a new life in the West. Ben Marks' cheating Dollar Store in time graduated into the Big Store concept, the phony gambling club, horse parlor or fake brokerage and other "stings" in which the gullible were separated from thousands of dollars. Ironically, among the scores of dollar stores that sprang up to imitate Ben Marks' pioneer venture was one in Chicago that grew into a great modern department store. Its founder had originally leased the building for a monte operation but discovered he could actually sell cheap and flashy goods at a dollar and make more profits than he could at monte.

See also: BIG STORE, THREE-CARD MONTE.

drop swindle

A notorious con game employing a variety of techniques is the drop swindle. A "dropper" drops a wallet at the heels of a likely victim and then pretends to find it. The wallet is stuffed with counterfeit money. Pleading that he is in a hurry, the dropper offers to sell the wallet to the victim, saying something like: "There's a couple of hundred bucks in there. The guy who lost it will probably give half the dough as a reward just to get the rest of it and his IDs back. Tell you what, give me fifty and you can take care of returning the wallet to him and get the rest of the reward." Naturally, like most cons, this racket appeals to a victim's larcenous streak since he has the option of simply keeping the wallet. One of the most famous practitioners of this swindle was Nathan Kaplan, better known as Kid Dropper, who, after earning his nickname practicing the swindle in his youth, went on to become the most famous gangster in New York City during the early 1920s.

While the drop swindle is well worn, it remains viable. Almost any big city police force will handle a few dozen complaints of the scam annually, and of course, the unreported cases are undoubtedly far more numerous.

Edwards Heirs Association   swindle

As much as any of the incredible "heirs swindle," the one involving the so-called Edwards estate was among the most durable. Its operation was handed down from father to son and lasted for decades.

The swindle was the brainchild of Dr. Herbert H. Edwards of Cleveland, Ohio, who in the 1880s maintained with much fervor that he was a descendant of Robert Edwards, a colonial merchant who had willed to his heirs 65 acres of Manhattan Island, right in the middle of which eventually had been erected the Woolworth Building. It was obvious that this bit of real estate had become one of the most valuable in the world. The Edwards estate was apparently worth not millions, but billions.

Dr. Edwards formed the Edwards Heirs Association, which was passed down from father to son, taking in $26 annually from each of thousands of people named Edwards as dues to fight for their legal rights. Naturally, every member of the association believed he would receive at least a thousand times what he had put in when a set-tlement was reached, an event that was always just about to be achieved. The association was also noted for having a great fete each year, which members attended by the hundreds, to celebrate the profits soon to come. The suckers even had their own anthem, which they sang with leather-lunged joy:

We have rallied here in blissful state
Our jubilee to celebrate.
When fortune kindly on us smiled,
The Edwards Heirs now reconciled.
Our president deserves our praise,
For strenuous work through dreary days,
In consummating our affairs
and rounding up the Edwards heirs.

We're Robert Edward's legal heirs,
And cheerfully we take our shares.
Then let us shout with joy and glee
And celebrate the jubilee.

Finally, after several decades of successful operation, the great swindle was smashed by the post office. The members of the association never saw any of the promised rewards, but they could at least recall their annual hangovers, perhaps still with some measure of fondness.

embezzlement

The most enduring crime magazine article is probably the embezzlement story. There is something so eternal about the crime, probably because its root causes are deeply related to basic human failings. At times a writer will explain the motive for embezzlement in terms of the "three W's" or the "three R's"—it's all the same whether one speaks of wine, women and wagering or rum, redheads and race horses. The fact is that sex and greed can drive many people to steal large amounts of money, and they frequently do. Recent estimates place embezzlement losses at more than $4 billion a year.

Typical embezzlers work at a bank or other business institution for years or even decades before they are finally exposed—if ever. As a cashier, John F. Wagner, was able to skim somewhat more than $1.1 million from the First National Bank of Cecil, Pa., by juggling the bank's books for at least a score of years until he committed suicide in 1950. The vice president of a bank in Baton Rouge, La. kept up his looting for a dozen years. When he was finally caught, he said: "I'm glad it's finally over. These past twelve years of living under the constant strain of wondering when I'd eventually get caught have cost me more than any amount of money could be worth."

Some embezzlers don't like the strain of wondering if and when the Federal Deposit Insurance Corporation auditors will come calling. Richard H. Crowe, an assistant branch manager of a New York bank, was that type. So he simply went to the vault one Friday in the late 1940s, stuffed $883,000

into a bag and went home to dinner. The following Monday he was nowhere to be found. However, such runaways are generally not difficult to find, and often all the FBI has to do is determine where a man with a lot of extra spending money is most likely to turn up. Agents found Crowe in a plush bar in Daytona Beach, Fla.

Perhaps the classic bank embezzlement, with certainly the brashest motive of all, was that committed by bank president Ludwig R. Schlekat. Out of the $719,000 in cash supposedly on hand at the Parnassus National Bank of New Kensington, Pa., Schlekat managed to appropriate no less than $600,000, accumulating the sum over a 23-year period. When the shortage was found by bank examiners in 1947, it was determined that Schlekat had used $100,000 for his own better living. What had happened to the rest? Well, when Schlekat started working for the bank as an apprentice clerk at the age of 17 he had had only one ambition: to rise to bank president. After the bank's owner became eager to retire, Schlekat used the bulk of the $600,000 to purchase the bank through two nonexistent individuals who supposedly lived in Cleveland. Schlekat had simply used the bank's own money to buy the institution for himself. Then he had the bogus owners make him president. He was caught, tried and given a prison term of 10 years.

Generally, bankers and other business officials insist that people continue to embezzle because of the light sentences that are often imposed. It would be a somewhat more telling argument if all banks paid employees decent wages. In a classic case of that sort some years ago, federal judge Frank L. Kloeb refused to sentence a cashier of an Ohio bank who had been convicted of embezzling $7,500 over a 10-year period ending in 1941.

The judge hit the ceiling when he learned that the man had started as a cashier in 1920 at an annual salary of $1,080 and 22 years later he had been earning no more than $1,900 a year. The cashier had stopped his embezzlements as his salary started to rise faster, and he was not found out until many years later.

The judge simply deferred sentencing indefinitely and refused even to put the cashier on probation, because that would have made him a criminal. "If I had the authority," the judge said, "I would sentence the bank officers and the Board of Directors to read the story of Scrooge at Christmas and think of the defendant."

Experts say women are just as likely to become embezzlers as men are. Bankers claim it is very common for middle-aged spinsters to resort to juggling the books. Having gone through life with perhaps little or no romance, such women may be desperate for companionship at this stage. In their eagerness to cement new friendships, they bestow gifts with reckless abandon. That old cliché of a shocked banker asking a trusted employee-turned-embezzler—"Was it a woman?"—definitely has its reverse—"Was it a man?"

As a rule, women are more generous with their loot than men. One trusted bookkeeper who stole $30,000 with the aid of some skillful record doctoring gave most of it to fellow employees in the form of salary increases.

The boom in computers in recent years has opened up new vistas for embezzlers. One bank employee developed a computerized money-diversion scheme to steal more than $1 million, which he used to finance his gambling. It seemed he also had a computer system for handicapping the horses, but unfortunately for him, it was less efficient than his embezzlement operation.

Computer embezzlement has even become a problem within the Internal Revenue Service. One IRS computer programmer set up a system that funneled unclaimed tax credits into a relative's account, and another IRS programmer computer-transferred to his own account checks being held for taxpayers whose mailing addresses could not be determined.

In the precomputer era it was estimated that there were at least 200 ways to embezzle money from a bank without danger of immediate exposure. Now, in an era of advancing technology, the ways cannot be counted. According to John Rankine, IBM's director of data security, "The data security job will never be done—after all, there will never be a bank that absolutely can't be robbed."

See also: COMPUTER CRIME, JOHN F. WAGNER.

Emma Mine fraud

In the West's great scramble for the riches of silver ore from the 1870s to the end of the 19th century, there was scant exploitation by legitimate mining interests of Utah's silver deposits. The origin of this strange diffidence toward a profitable opportunity was the notorious Emma Silver Mining Co. bubble, which had caused investors to lose millions, some in this country and even more in England.

With the first sign of a silver strike in Little Cottonwood Canyon in 1868, a mining speculator, James E. Lyon of New York, moved in to take effective control. He in turn had to yield a good deal of it to San Francisco mining interests, and they then brought in Trevor W. Park of Vermont and Gen. H. Henry Baxter of New York. To protect his interests, Lyon introduced Sen. William M.

Stewart of Nevada into the combine, which by then had decided to sell stock in the mine in England. Important names were added to the operation. Professor Benjamin Silliman, Jr. of Yale, for a fee of $25,000, issued a favorable report on the mine's ore deposits. The board of directors of the British company included three members of Parliament, the U.S. minister to the Court of St. James and a former president of the New York Central Railroad, among others. Marketing of the company's stock was handled by Baron Albert Grant, a London financier of dubious ethical standards but a brilliant salesman, who was paid a fee of £170,000 for his troubles. It was a small price since the income from floating the stock was something like £600,000. All the American operators did extremely well, with the possible exception of the original investor, James Lyon. His supposed protector, Sen. Stewart, was able to buy him out for £50,000, half of what Lyon had been promised.

For a time, even the English investors did well, as the stock in the Emma Silver Mining Company, Ltd., quickly moved from £20 to £50. Then a rival firm, the Illinois Tunnel Co., announced the Emma claim had not been recorded correctly and that the English company was mining the ore from the claim to pay the dividends on its stock. Even more shocking was the revelation that the owner of Illinois Tunnel was Trevor W. Park, who was also a member of the board of Emma Mining and who had made one of the biggest profits in the entire deal. All sorts of suits were then filed, especially after 1872, when Emma Mining announced its ore deposits had run out. In the end, everyone who had been in the original combine made and kept money and all the shareholders in Emma Mining lost their money

except for a total of $150,000, which Park offered in 1877 for all outstanding shares. Park continued to mine Emma for a number of years and is believed to have made that money back easily. In any event, the Emma Mine scandal was to frighten off virtually all investment in Utah mines by outsiders for some three decades, and the fraud was often cited as an example of "Yankee ingenuity."

Estes, Billie Sol (1925–) con man

In the 1960s Billie Sol Estes, a flamboyant Texas "salesman" and political supporter of President Lyndon Johnson, became famous as a prototypical big-time swindler after being convicted of inducing farmers to invest in fertilizer tanks that never existed. He was sentenced to 15 years and paroled in 1971 after serving six years. Under the terms of his parole, Estes was not allowed to engage in promotional schemes, but almost immediately, he was implicated in some financial dealings that involved allegations of fraud. In August 1979 Estes was sentenced to two five-year federal prison terms to be served consecutively following his conviction for bilking investors by borrowing money and using as collateral oil field cleaning equipment that was nonexistent. One of his victims, J. H. Burkett, an Abilene used-car dealer who lent Estes his life savings of $50,000 shortly after meeting him in 1975, said: "I met him in church, in Bible study in Abilene, and he struck me as a very nice guy. He seemed very humble, very earnest, remorseful. I was very impressed by him, and I still am, but in a different way. The man is the world's best salesman. Just go and meet him, and you'll find out. He'll sell you something."

Following his 1979 conviction Estes told the judge: "I love this country. I'd rather be in prison here than free anywhere else in the world." He said that whether or not he went to jail, he would pay the money he owed, including $10 million in back taxes, to the government. Estes claimed he had more than a million friends and could raise $10 from each of them. There were those who said he probably could.

Estes was always a spellbinder. In a 1961 interview he once outlined his personal philosophy, which apparently won him devoted followers. "You win by losing, hold on by letting go, increase by diminishing, and multiply by dividing. These are the principles that have brought me success."

fake murder fakes   deadly insurance fraud

A particularly deadly scam that insurance companies constantly guard against is what may be called "fake murder fakes." Swindler-murderers have attempted many such capers in every country in the world and undoubtedly have succeeded on numerous occasions. The theory behind the scam is to kill off someone after he or she has taken out a large insurance policy to the plotters' benefit. Of course, few victims see any reason to cooperate in a plot that requires their actual murder. The plotters solve this dilemma by concocting a scheme in which the victim becomes a willing partner after being assured a substitute corpse will be used. The insurance policy is purchased with the victim's eager participation and then the plot is put into operation. But there is one catch: Substituting another corpse is no easy matter. The obvious solution: Use the real thing.

Perhaps the classic example of this involves a beautuul but dumb 21-year old Chicago model named Marie Defenbach (1879–1900) who was inveigled into such a conspiracy by one of the plotters, who pre-tended to be in love with her, and a murderous doctor, August M. Unger. Marie was to take out $70,000 in various life insurance policies, naming her lover and another conspirator as beneficiaries. Dr. Unger assured Marie he would personally handle her "demise" in a most careful manner. He would give her a special medicine of his own concoction that would induce a deathlike sleep. Later, the doctor told her, she would be revived in the back room of the funeral home and spirited away while an unclaimed body of another female would be cremated in her stead. For her cooperation in the plot, the conspirators thought it eminently fair that Marie should get half the loot.

Marie swallowed the story, never realizing to her the men could save themselves a lot of effort and add $35,000 to their profit by simply feeding her some real poison. This was precisely what occurred on the night of August 25, 1900, with poor Marie dying in terrible agony after 15 minutes of suffering. Dr. Unger signed the death certificate, and the body was cremated forthwith. The conspirators claimed all the insurance money but eventually were caught by private investigators hired by the girl's uncle to find out what had happened to her. Ironically, they could not be convicted of murder because there was no body left to be examined. However, one of the trio turned state's evidence and Dr. Unger and one accomplice, Frank Brown, were sentenced to five years in prison for fraud.

Feejee Mermaid   Barnum's fabulous find

Of all the hoaxes perpetrated by that master showman, P. T. Barnum, the one that catapulted both him and his American Museum into national prominence was the Feejee Mermaid. Barnum obtained the so-called mermaid in 1842 and used a massive mailing to the New York press from various locations reporting the incredible discovery of a mermaid in the Feejee [sic] Islands and that it was then being preserved in China. By the time Barnum announced he would have the Feejee Mermaid on display in his American Museum in New York, the public was more than prepared to pay almost any price, including Barnum's then hefty 25-cents for admission.

What they saw, however, was a dried, ugly specimen that had some fish and some humanlike characteristics. In later years, Barnum admitted the Feejee Mermaid was a hoax, having been constructed by combining the upper portion of a monkey with the lower half of a fish.

In 1842 P.T. Barnum astounded New Yorkers with his Feejee Mermaid, which was actually a combination of the upper portion of a monkey with the lower half of a fish.

flaking   police slang for frame-up

This is the term used by policemen and private detectives to describe the framing of an individual. When it is done, the police officers usually justify it as being a service to society; since the victim has committed so many other crimes, it hardly matters if the facts of a crime he is actually charged with are a fabrication.

Naturally, not all law enforcement officials engage in the practice. Deputy Chief Fire Marshal John Barracato of New York relates in a book called *Arson!* about how he was urged to participate in a flaking by another fire marshal and refused. He says, "To me flaking was the most heinous violation of a cop's honor."

Flaking was heavily practiced in the heyday of union organizing in this country, when private detectives framed unionists, often based on the belief that unionism did a worker more harm than good, and that even if a unionist was not actually guilty of a certain act of labor violence, he was undoubtedly responsible for others.

Flamingo Hotel

Known as the casino that made Las Vegas, the Flamingo was the brainchild of mobster Bugsy Siegel. Siegel had come to the West Coast in the late 1930s to handle the mob's betting empire. During the war years he began envisaging a new gambling empire, one that could turn the Nevada sands into gold dust. Gambling was legal in Nevada, where the main attraction was Reno, offering diversion to passing tourists and individuals waiting for their divorce decrees. Siegel saw Las Vegas, then no more than a highway rest stop with some diners, gas stations and a sprinkling of slot machines, as a lavish new gambling oasis.

Bugsy had little trouble convincing Meyer Lansky, treasurer of the national crime syndicate, that his vision was a great idea, and several big city mobs laid out money to build a new casino-hotel, which was to be called the Flamingo, the nickname of Virginia Hill, Siegel's girlfriend and the former bedmate of a number of top mobsters.

During the construction of the Flamingo, Siegel assured building contractor Del E. Webb, who had become nervous about the mob's involvement, that he had nothing to fear because "we only kill each other." At the time Bugsy didn't realize how accurate his statement would prove to be. In the short run, the Flamingo was a disaster, mainly because in the immediate postwar years it was an idea ahead of its time. It would take considerable patience to make it a success, but Siegel had no time. Not only had he failed to produce the profits the mob expected on its $6 million investment, but it appeared he had been skimming off the construction funds. When Siegel refused to make good, indeed could not make good, he was rubbed out.

After Siegel's execution the mob continued to support the Flamingo and eventually saw it grow and prosper. The syndicate poured millions more into Las Vegas, building one successful casino after another.

See also: LAS VEGAS, BENJAMIN "BUGSY" SIEGEL.

floppers and divers   faked car accident specialists

The elite among car insurance swmdlers are "floppers" and "divers" who give vivid performances as supposed victims of automobile accidents. A flopper can be quite acrobatic, moving in front of a car coming around a corner and faking being hit by it. This appears quite frightening but for an expert it is not a difficult maneuver. The flopper stands in the street and starts across just as he sees a car make its turn.

The car is moving relatively slowly at the time and the flopper simply bounces off the front fender and flips backward to the ground. As a crowd gathers, the flopper groans and some blood comes from his ear. (Just before beginning his act, the flopper bites his lips and dabs some blood in his ear.) A prize flopper is a person who has an old skull fracture. No matter how old the fracture, it will always show up on an X ray. In due course, it's time to collect.

"Divers" do a much more impressive performance than even the most adept flopper. The diver prefers to work at night, since witnesses are far less likely to spot his act as a phony. As a car approaches, the diver moves into the street and while crouching slams his hand against the car door as hard as he can. The bang quickly attracts passersby who are actually sure they have seen more than really happened.

At times the driver is in on the scam but usually the floppers and divers pick on innocent motorists so that insurance investigators cannot prove any collusion. Sometimes freelance floppers work near parking lots of roadside cafes, and fake being hit by patrons driving away. Since such motorists will often test positive for alcohol, the flopper has a sure-fire case. Sometimes, instead of waiting for an insurance settlement, the driver is shaken down on the spot and pays rather than face arrest for hitting a pedestrian while driving intoxicated.

Usually, however, it is better for the flopper or diver to go through the lawsuit process and take a settlement from the insurance company. While the floppers and divers are the "elite" of the racket, they are seldom well paid. Usually they work for a "manager" who arranges to get a shady lawyer and doctor to handle deals with the insurance companies. One such manager admitted after he was caught that he swindled his own floppers and divers, giving them only a paltry few hundred dollars per caper and insisting he had to make huge payoffs to the lawyers, doctors and dishonest insurance adjustors. For every $100 his floppers and divers got, he netted $2,000 or $3,000.

Florida land boom   America's greatest real estate swindle

The great Florida land boom of the 1920s remains the greatest real estate swindle in U.S. history. At the height of its frenzy in 1925-1926 it was estimated that more than $7 billion worth of real estate changed hands, the major portion of which property sadly happened to be underwater. Whole communities in "America's tropical paradise" sold out while still on the drawing boards, and were never built.

The key word common to all the swindles was "proposed." Whatever it was, once it was proposed it sold. Why not have the Grand Canal of Venice, complete with Rialtos, lavish landings and electronically driven gondolas? This was Florida and any magic was possible. However, the "proposed" blue-watered Grand Canal never got beyond being an ugly, muddy stream. Still, the proposals came forth. Kenneth Roberts tells of a group of hustlers who hired a painter to do a sign reading: "A MILLION-DOLLAR HOTEL WILL BE ERECTED HERE." This was a surefire way of peddling surrounding lots for supporting businesses. The only trouble was the fledgling capitalists could not come up with the $18 to pay for the sign, so the painter sold it to another group of capitalists to use in their proposed deal.

Charley Ort, one of the most brilliant hustlers of the boom, arrived broke in Miami and promptly took options on a city dump. He covered the refuse, ashes, broken bottles, tin cans and furniture pieces with blazing tropical flowers and unloaded this enchanted oasis for millions. He headed for his Key Largo City, where he would earn the swindler sobriquet the "King of the Keys."

Not that Ort was not rooked himself. A shrewd realtor unloaded a tract on Key Largo without mentioning that it had been a quarry and was gutted with deep holes. Ort surveyed his atrocious buy and suddenly danced a jig of joy, crying, "Sunken Gardens! Sunken Gardens!" He blithely doubled the prices on the deepest lots and palmed them off to suckers and investors.

The hustlers who peddled Wyldewood Park, near Fort Lauderdale, had little in the way of natural features to boost their subdivision. But there was one large tree, a banyan, which had branches rooted to the ground and thus resembled a mini-forest. The hustlers erected a huge sign that said "$2,000,000 Tree," the claim being that one banyan-crazy Northerner had once offered $2 million for the tree if it were moved to his home up North. The suckers snapped up the extra-large homesites just to have a banyan tree of their own.

The suckers swallowed almost everything, even when rational voices were raised in opposition. Humorist Will Rogers weighed in with an imaginary world capital to be built in Florida. "All of these here lots," he propounded, tongue very much in cheek, "are by our Proposed Ocean."

Perhaps the grandiose dream of all was El Camino Real, or "the King's Highway," which was at least partly built by two grand real estate swindlers, Addison and Wilson Mizner. It was to be the broadest highway in the world, with 20 traffic lanes—219 feet wide in all—allegedly leading to the Mizner principality of Boca Raton. The highway would have indirect illumination with concealed curb lights instead of lampposts. And El Camino Real was waterscaped as well as landscaped; down the middle was that celebrated Grand Canal of Venice. Unfortunately, El Camino Real ran only a half-mile before petering down to a mere two lanes and disappearing as a lost trail in the sand. But of course on proposed blue prints and maps El Camino Real would run past a series of magnificent, if nonexistent, cities. In real life, the highway simply died in swamps and brambles.

And while investors awaited the completion of El Camino Real, they bid up the prices of corner lots in Boca Raton to dizzying levels. Operating on the greater fool theory, Wilson Mizner himself offered Lytle Hull, the well-known society figure, $50,000 for a choice Boca Raton lot, certain he could get double the price on a resale. Hull was insulted by the offer and refused to talk to Wilson for some time thereafter. Hull held on to the lot through the entire boom, not selling for $50,000 or $100,000. After the bubble burst, he got only $200.

The great boom had victimized upper-middle- and higher-income people. After that it took some decades before land prices picked up and swindlers came back as well, now to zero in on lower-income folks and retirees seeking to find the rewards of Ponce de Leon country. Many were victimized by these new-breed "swamp swindlers."

See also FLORIDA'S PIRATE GOLD COINS.

Florida's pirate gold coins

Are there pirate gold treasure troves still to be unearthed? Quite possibly, but the real money to be made in pirate gold comes not in finding it but rather in talking about it. Tales of pirate gold especially abound in Florida, most tracing their origins to the Florida swindlers who promoted the fraudulent land boom of the 1920s.

Besides buying a retirement and vacation paradise homesite, buyers were assured they could very well end up finding a few odd millions of pirate treasure on their property. Two of the grandest hustlers of the state's land boom, Addison and Wilson Mizner, blatantly claimed that Captain Edward Teach (better known as Blackbeard) had headquartered around their Boca Raton development and littered the sands with buried treasure (always having the chest buried with a dead pirate).

Later on, Wilson Mizner and the celebrated publicist-hoaxer Harry Reichenbach buried some doubloons and some phony Blackbeard relics in Boca Raton inlet, and had them disinterred with much public excitement. Nobody noticed there were never any confirming skeletons. Other land promoters planted stories, if not buried treasure, to promote their subdivisions. A Portuguese fisherman gave a boost to Miami real estate by claiming he'd hauled up an iron chest weighing 200 pounds, but his fishing line had broken and he hadn't been able to latch on to the chest ever since. And over at Grassy Key a large trove of ancient Mexican money was allegedly found.

Public relations men roped in Captain Kidd, Sir Henry Morgan, Black Caesar, the Laffite boys, Gasparilla, and Sir Francis Drake to hype up sales. The greatest center of pirate gold yarns was Key Largo. One press agent alone successfully sunk 17 Spanish galleons jammed with gold, jewels and coins of Key Largo with a single inspired sentence on his magic typewriter.

The Key Largo City subdivisions being peddled by the audacious Charley Ort—one of the boom's grandest scam artists—excited the public the most about finds of pirate gold all over the property. Ort got the best of the PR men he could find—Broadway author J. P. McEvoy and novelist Ben Hecht. This sterling pair managed to have two ancient crocks filled with doubloons turn up in the Key Largo sands, found by a fisherman worthy named Captain Chester, who had to be led by his nose to what he truly believed was an honest find. Hecht wired accounts of the Chester find to hundreds of newspapers. Pulitzer Prize–winner Herbert Bayard Swope of the *New York World* wired Hecht that he intended to come down to report on the fabulous finds, but first insisted that Hecht personally guarantee that the tale was not a hoax. Hecht most ethically pretended he never got the telegram.

Meanwhile scores, then hundreds of treasure hunters descended on Key Largo to dig and dive for treasure. Some with the true fever even bought homesites so they could hunt for the treasures well into their golden years. The real pirate fever lasted right up to the end of the high point of the land boom in 1926. By then most of the treasure hunters gave up and headed home. The prize victim of all—Captain Chester—kept right at it with his 13 grandchildren for a long time. The lucky ones were treasure hunters who had departed. Those who bought homesites did not get either gold or homes.

football hoaxes   scoring the easy way

Back in the 1920s the Providence Steamroller won the 1928 championship of the fledgling National Football League. A star performer of that team was a brilliant lineman named Perry Jackson-but he was not Perry Jackson. In 1927 the Steamroller had invited the real Perry Jackson, a college star in Oklahoma, to try out. Jackson, however, was badly ill and sent his friend Arnold Schockley to pretend to be him. The masquerade worked; Schockley made the team as Perry Jackson. When the real Perry Jackson regained his health, he tried out for the Steamroller as Arnold Schockley. He was cut from the squad.

If the unreal Perry Jackson enjoyed an illustrious career, it was nothing compared with that of the redoubtable Johnny Chung, the half-Chinese "Celestial Comet" who in 1941 led New Jersey's Plainfield Teachers to victory after victory, renewing his amazing strength at halftime by wolfing down wild rice. With Chung in the lineup, the little-known Plainfield Teachers were fast becoming a small-college powerhouse, their victories duly reported in such newspapers as the *New York Herald Tribune* and the *New York Times*.

There was a good reason the school was so little known until that time. It didn't exist. Neither did the Celestial Comet. The hoax was concocted by a group of Wall Street brokers who telephoned in mythical scores of the Teachers' seven straight wins and deluged the papers with press releases of the never-ending heroics of Johnny Chung. The pranksters' grand plan was to take their creation through an undefeated season so that they would get an invitation to the first annual—and fictitious—Blackboard Bowl.

Unfortunately, a traitor tipped off *Time* magazine, and it prepared an expose of the Celestial Comet. The chief culprit, stockbroker Morris Newburger of Newburger, Loeb & Company (one Morris Newburger played right tackle for the Teachers), rushed to the magazine's office to plead desperately that the team be allowed to complete its undefeated season. As an inducement he even offered *Time* the scores of the remaining games in advance.

Time waited not. Determined to have the last word, the pranksters sought to outflank the newsweekly by firing off one final press release: Johnny Chung and a number of other players had flunked their exams and lost their playing eligibility. Plainfield Teachers had to cancel the rest of its season. Not even the most trusting of newspaper sports desks could swallow that one, and the *Trib* dispatched sportswriter Caswell Adams to New Jersey, where he found the real city of Plainfield and its real Chamber of Commerce ignorant of any learning institution called Plainfield Teachers. Adams checked telephone lines and found his way back to Newburger's office (Plainfield Teachers maintained a one-way telephone that made outgoing calls but received none), and the real father of the unreal Johnny Chung was unmasked at the very moment Time hit the newstands with its scoop to an astonished and amused public.

The *Trib* took the hoax with good grace and joined in the general laughter, but the *Times* maintained an icy silence.

gambler's belt

Employed by crooked gamblers in the 19th century, the so-called gambler's belt was a lethal body device of considerable firepower used to discourage any attempt by a victim to recover his losses forcibly.

The belt appeared in gambling dens in Philadelphia, Cincinnati and Chicago and proved popular on the Mississippi and in the West. In a typical version, a body belt was fitted with three small-caliber revolvers that could be fired simultaneously by operating a trigger mechanism hidden on the wearer's right side. Naturally, when fired, the device destroyed the wearer's trousers but did far worse damage to his foe, who would be struck by three shots in the abdomen. According to one account, an unnamed gambler in Nevada used such a belt to kill a miner objecting to his method of dealing, and the other miners gathered around, expressing wonder at the device's design. On reflection, they decided it gave the gambler an unfair advantage in the gunfight, so they marched him out to the street and hanged him.

Garfield portrait swindle

Shortly after the assassination of President James A. Garfield in 1881, some 200 newspapers carried an advertisement that was to become a minor classic swindle. The ad offered the grieving public what seemed to be a rare portrait of the dead president, stating:

I have secured the authorized steel engravings of the late President Garfield, executed by the United States Government, approved by the President of the United States, by Congress and by every member of the President's family as the most faithful of all portraits of the President. It was executed by the Government's most expert steel engravers, and I will send a copy from the original plate, in full colors approved by the Government, postpaid, for one dollar each.

To every eager person sending a dollar, the swindler fulfilled his promises to the letter by mailing back an engraving of President Garfield on a 5¢ postage stamp.

Following the Garfield portrait swindle, con men went on to pull the same racket countless times in endless variations involving other notable persons and subjects that have appeared on commemorative stamps, sometimes also promising "suitable mounting," which meant putting the stamp on an index card.

gold accumulator swindle

A monumental fraud perpetrated on hardheaded New Englanders in 1897 involved a so-called gold accumulator, which allegedly mined gold from the ocean. The scheme was the work of a veteran English con man named Charles E. Fisher and a Connecticut Baptist minister named Prescott Ford Jernegan. Jernegan may well have been a dupe at the beginning of the operation, but by the time it reached fruition, he proved just as adept as Fisher at holding on to his ill-gotten gains.

Fisher, it seemed, had a secret invention to extract the gold eddying about in Passamaquoddy Bay near the town of Lubec, Maine. Fisher's gold accumulator was painted with mercury and another "secret compound" and lowered into the water. When the device was raised the following day, it was crusted with thin flakes of gold. Fisher and Jernegan demonstrated the device on several occasions to some extremely dubious Yankee businessmen, who insisted on guarding the scene of the demonstration all night to prevent any tampering. However, they were unaware that Fisher, who had been a deep-sea diver back in England, would swim to the accumulator during the night and plant the grains of gold.

Eventually, shares in the Electrolytic Marine Salts Co. were sold to a gullible public. The value of the initial issue of 350,000 shares at $1 a share soon climbed to $50 a share as New Englanders rushed to get in on a good thing. In addition, a grateful board of directors voted to give Fisher and Jernegan $200,000 each for their services. All this took place on the basis of $25,000 having been "mined," but it was apparent that the process could just go on forever. It went on only until Fisher quietly disposed of his shares of stock, added that money to his $200,000 and left for Boston "to get more supplies." He didn't return and suddenly the gold accumulator didn't accumulate any more gold.

Rev. Jernegan announced he was off in search of Fisher and disappeared with his $200,000-plus as well. His search apparently took him to France, where he was later found living in luxury with his family. The irate board of directors of the marine salts company demanded the French government take him into custody. It did, but the minister was soon released. It was obvious that the $200,000 had been legally voted him and there was no way to force him to return it. All that appeared to have gone wrong was that an apparent gold-mining procedure had run dry.

Jernegan finally came back to America and actually returned $175,000 to the swindled stockholders. This represented what he said was left of the $200,000. He continued to live well thereafter in the Philippines and Hawaii, undoubtedly on the revenues from the sale of his bloated stockholdings. When Jernegan died in 1942, there was a report circulated that Charlie Fisher had been living in the South Seas as a rich American. According to the story, Fisher had been caught fooling around with the wife of a tribal chieftain and that he and she had been killed according to tribal custom. Apparently, the still-living investors in the Electrolytic Marine Salts Co. were determined to have their revenge, real or fancied.

gold brick swindle confidence game

The gold brick swindle is a hardy perennial that just will not die. The victim buys what he thinks are gold brick ingots and ends up with worthless lead or brass. Most big-city bunco squads handle several such cases each year.

The origin of the gold brick swindle is unknown but probably started in the California gold fields during the 1850s. Wyatt Earp and Mysterious Dave Mather got involved in the game in Mobeetie, Tex. in 1878, after Earp learned how well the racket worked in Kansas. A fabulous young swindler, Reed Waddell, brought the racket to New York in 1880 and trimmed some rather bright and supposedly sharp business-men with it. Waddell's bricks certainly looked real, being triple goldplated and marked in the manner of a regulation brick from the United States Assayer's Office, with the letters "U.S." at one end and, below that, the name of the assayer and the weight and fineness of the bullion. Waddell's operation included a phony assayer's office where the brick was supposedly tested. If the sucker hesitated, Waddell would get angry, pull a slug from the brick and insist the victim take it to any jeweler of his choice. As part of the ruse, Waddell had sunk a slug of pure gold into the center of the lead brick, but the trick always worked and his victim would become eager to buy. In all, he took in some $350,000 over the next dozen years. Another

ring, headed by Tom O'Brien, netted $100,000 in just five months working the World's Fair in Chicago in 1893. Waddell and O'Brien then joined forces and took the scam to Europe, where O'Brien killed Wad-dell in an argument over the division of the proceeds from one of their swindles.

Perhaps the greatest swindle of this nature occurred in Texas, where from 1932 to 1935 two crooks, one posing as a minister, victim-ized a wealthy widow. They told her that gold had been buried in various spots on her vast ranch about 100 years earlier and that ancient maps to the locations could be bought from an old man in Mexico. The widow gave them enough money to buy one map, and sure enough, they came back with some gold bricks. Over the next three years the widow gave them $300,000 and they dug up what was allegedly $4 million in gold. Since at this time the hoarding of gold was illegal, the woman didn't dare attempt to cash in the bricks and therefore never learned they were fake. The con men's downfall came about because of their wild spending, which caused a government agent to investigate the source of their money. The swindle was thus uncovered, and the two crooks were sent to prison.

See also: REED WADDELL.

Gordon-Gordon, Lord (?–1873) swindler

One of America's most audacious confidence operators was a Scotsman who, masquerad-ing as Lord Gordon-Gordon, swindled some of America's greatest robber barons, includ-ing Jay Gould, out of $1 million in negotiable securities. Gordon-Gordon never revealed his real identity. Instead, he spread the word through intermediaries that he was the heir of the great Earl of Gordon, cousin of the

Campbells, collateral relative of Lord Byron and proud descendant of the Lochinvar and the ancient kings of the Highlanders.

Gordon-Gordon's first known peccadillo occurred in 1868 in Edinburgh, where, under the equally fanciful name of Lord Glencairn, he swindled a jeweler out of £25,000. Then in 1871, as Lord Gordon-Gordon, he appeared in Minneapolis and opened a bank account with $40,000 from his jewelry swindle. He set up representatives of the Northern Pacific Railroad for a swindle by declaring he was in search of immense areas of good lands on which to settle his over-populated Scottish tenantry. He suggested he could use upwards of a half-million acres, the very answer to the railroad's dreams. Since the company in its push westward was sorely pressed for capital, it did all it could to woo several millions from Gordon-Gordon. He was wined, dined and taken on lavish hunting expeditions. How much hard cash Gordon-Gordon managed to pocket was never known, but the "trinkets" given him in one instance were worth $40,000. After some three months Gordon-Gordon had picked out all the land he wished to buy, and he told the railroad executives he was returning to New York to arrange for the transfer of funds from Scotland to make the purchase. He left Minneapolis not only with fond farewells but also with special letters of introduction from Col. John S. Loomis, the line's land commissioner, to Jay Gould, then fighting for control of the Erie Railroad, and Horace Greeley, a stockholder in the Erie and a business associate of Gould.

Lord Gordon-Gordon portrayed himself as a potential savior to Gould, just as he had to the Northern Pacific. He let Greeley believe he was a substantial holder of Erie stock and also the holder of proxies from a number of European friends, enough to provide Gould with the margin of victory. But Gordon-Gordon had a price for his aid. He wanted the management of the railroad reformed and an active voice for himself, but, he generously added, he was prepared to leave Gould in charge. Gould was ecstatic—and grateful. He handed over to Gordon-Gordon $1 million in negotiable securities and cash in "a pooling of interests" that could only be considered a bribe.

Soon after this transaction, large chunks of stock began appearing for sale. Gordon-Gordon was quickly cashing in on his profits from the gullible Gould. Convinced he had been swindled, Gould sued Gordon-Gordon, who immediately threw in with Gould's business rivals. But time was running out for Gordon-Gordon. On the witness stand he cheerfully reeled off the names of important European personages he knew and represented in the Erie deal. Before his references could be checked, he decamped to Canada with a large portion of Gould's money.

When located in Canada, Gordon-Gordon had little trouble convincing the authorities there that he was a man of high breeding and that charges by various Americans, Gould in New York and railroaders in Minnesota, were ill founded and malicious. He told people in Fort Garry, Manitoba that he intended to invest huge sums in the area and that the Americans were being vindictive because he would not utilize the funds in their country.

Convinced they would never get the scoundrel back to face charges by any legal means, a group of Minnesotan railroaders, perhaps financed by Gould, attempted to kidnap Gordon-Gordon. They actually snatched him in July 1873 and were only apprehended at the border by a group of the swindler's friends and a contingent of Northwest Mounted Police. The kidnappers, including two future governors of Minnesota and three future congressmen, were clapped into prison and allowed no bail.

The Gordon-Gordon affair blew up into an international incident. Gov. Austin of Minnesota ordered the state militia to be ready to march and demanded the return of the kidnap party. Thousands of Minnesotans volunteered for an invading expeditionary force. Finally, negotiations between President Ulysses S. Grant and his secretary of state, Hamilton Fish, and Canadian prime minister Sir John MacDonald produced an agreement in the interests of international amity that allowed the raiding party to go free on bail. Gordon-Gordon was safe in Canada, since the treaties between the United States and that country did not provide for extradition for such minor offenses as larceny and embezzlement.

All might have gone well for Gordon-Gordon had not news of the incident reached Edinburgh. The owners of Marshall and Son, Jewelers became convinced that the description of Lord Gordon-Gordon matched that of the long-gone Lord Glencairn. They dispatched a clerk who had dealt with His Lordship to check up on Gordon-Gordon in person. He made a firm identification and the master swindler was ordered returned to England to clear up the matter. Gordon-Gordon undertook a legal battle, but when it was obvious he had lost, he shot himself to death.

Grand Central fruit stand swindle

One of the most bald-faced swindles in history occurred in 1929 when two well-to-do Italian fruit dealers bought the rights to convert the information booth at New York's Grand Central Station into a fruit stand. It all began when a well-dressed stranger dropped into their bustling fruit store in midtown and presented them with his card:

T. Remington Grenfell
Vice President
GRAND CENTRAL
HOLDING CORPORATION

Mr. Grenfell told the fruit dealers, Tony and Nick Fortunato, that they had been selected, after an intensive investigation, to be offered the rights to the information booth. He explained that the railroad was upset because too many travelers were jamming the big circular booth in the center of the station to ask unnecessary questions. So, it had decided to let the ticket sellers answer all questions and this opened up the information booth for commercial use, ideally as a fruit stand. The rental would be $2,000 a week with the first year's rent paid in advance. The $100,000 payment did not faze the Fortunato brothers—in 25 years in the country they had amassed a goodly fortune through hard work, without ever really catching on to the sharp American ways—but they did ask for time to think it over.

Mr. Grenfell was somewhat curt. He said that wouldn't be possible. He mentioned the name of a nearby competitor of the Fortunato brothers and said he was to get second option if they refused. Quickly, the brothers agreed. It seemed like a good opportunity. While $2,000 a week was certainly high rental, the traffic at Grand Central was enormous. Besides the ordinary fruit sales, travelers would undoubtedly be buying expensive baskets to give as gifts.

The brothers followed Mr. Grenfell into a building connected with Grand Central to the door of a suite of offices that bore the legend:

Wilson A. Blodgett
President
GRAND CENTRAL
HOLDING CORPORATION

They were ushered past a blond secretary into Mr. Blodgett's office. Blodgett was a very busy man and could not spend much time on such a trifling matter. When the brothers again hesitated, Mr. Blodgett seemed to take it that they would have trouble raising the $100,000. Imperiously, he started to dismiss them, but thanks to Mr. Grenfell's intercession and the brothers' hasty assurances, he relented. It was agreed that the brothers would close the deal the following morning by presenting a certified check for the full amount.

The next morning the transaction went like clockwork. The check changed hands and the papers were signed. The brothers were to take possession at 9 A.M. on April 1, coincidentally April Fool's Day.

Shortly before the appointed hour, Tony and Nick Fortunato arrived at the station accompanied by a small gang of carpenters. Some remodeling was, of course, necessary to transform the information booth into a plush fruit stand. Eager to get started, the brothers ordered the carpenters to start doing the lumber work outside the booth. The puzzled information booth clerks wondered what was going on. At exactly 9 o'clock, Tony Fortunato approached the booth and ordered the clerks out. The clerks then began asking the questions, with the indignant Fortunatos shouting answers. Railroad guards appeared, trying to clear away the carpenters, who were blocking travelers from getting to the information booth.

Finally, one hour and one melee later, the Fortunatos were escorted into the administrative offices of the New York Central Railroad. They flaunted their written contract but were told that there was no such thing as the Grand Central Holding Corp.

Undaunted, the Fortunato brothers promptly led the officials to the offices of that firm—or at least where the offices had been. The officials of the railroad tried to explain to them that they had been the victims of a confidence scheme. The brothers were convinced that a rich American corporation was trying to cheat two foreigners out of $100,000 and then lease the booth to another fruit dealer. In the end, they were forcibly ejected from the terminal. The brothers took their complaint to leaders of New York's Italian community, who complained to the police. But while the police had extensive files on confidence game operators, they could not identify Grenfell or Blodgett. It had been a perfect crime, one that many in the Italian community continued to believe had been cooked up by a rich corporation to take advantage of naive Italians. For many years thereafter, Tony and Nick Fortunato would come into Grand Central Station and glare at the poor information clerks, hurling insults of shaking their fists at them, thus becoming, after a fashion, another strange sight for tourists arriving in Gotham.

Grannan, Riley (1868–1908) gambler and gunfighter

Although he was reputed to be fast on the draw, Riley Grannan is best remembered as a truly successful Western gambler, a brilliant student of horse racing and the inventor of modern form-betting. He once bet $275,000 on a horse and won.

Born in Paris, Ky. in 1868, Grannan arrived on the Western scene fairly late and soon grasped that with the closing of the frontier, the old style of the cheating gambler was outdated. He came up with the idea of establishing a gambling palace that could offer customers satisfaction for all their desires and, an idea still relatively unique for the West, honest gambling. For the locale of this great dream, Grannan picked out a plot of land at Rawhide, Nev. in 1907 and plunked down $40,000 for its purchase. There were those who considered it a foolish idea to try to build a great gambling center in the desert, and they appeared to be right. When Grannan died suddenly in April 1908, he was flat broke, his dream having drained away virtually all his funds.

Four decades later, a leading hoodlum named Bugsy Siegel would come up with the same dream and lose millions of the crime syndicate's money building the Flamingo. Eventually, the gambling paradise of Las Vegas was to prove that Siegel, and Riley Grannan before him, were right.

great diamond hoax

In 1872 two seedy prospectors named John Slack and Philip Arnold pulled off a monumental fraud, fooling some of the best business brains of this country and the diamond experts of Tiffany's.

Slack and Arnold visited the Bank of California in San Francisco and asked to have a leather pouch deposited in the vault. After first refusing to say what it contained, they finally shrugged and spilled out the pouch's glittering contents, a hoard of uncut diamonds. By the time they left the bank, the head teller was already in the office of the bank's president, William C. Ralston. A for-

mer miner himself, and probably selected by Slack and Arnold for that very reason, Ralston soon went looking for the two prospectors. His offer: to form a mining syndicate for harvesting the diamonds. Slack and Arnold conceded they could use some help, but they were not about to reveal the source of the diamonds until they had cash in hand. The diamonds were sent over to a jeweler's office in San Francisco to determine their genuineness and the answer came back that they were indeed the real thing. Still, caution prompted Ralston and his associates to double-check with Tiffany's in New York. Tiffany's proved even more enthusiastic, suggesting the diamonds sent them meant that those in hand were worth at least $1.5 million.

Now convinced there was a pot of diamonds at the end of the rainbow, Ralston & Co.'s next step was to find a way to separate the diamond find from the grizzled prospectors. Slack and Arnold were first brought into the mining syndicate and then offered $300,000 apiece for their shares—provided they would reveal the source of the diamonds. The two prospectors rubbed their whiskers and said that was a good enough offer since they weren't the greedy kind. The fact that the mining company had in its possession an estimated $1.5 million in gems made it a very good deal for Ralston and the others, some might even say a swindle. That, of course, is the secret behind many a great swindle—the cheated must believe they are cheating the cheaters.

Before the money was turned over to the pair, they would have to prove the diamond field existed. This they agreed to provided the man sent with them to check its authenticity, mining expert John Janin, went and returned blindfolded. Slack and Arnold stated they would not reveal the field's location until they were paid. They traveled a day and a half by train and then two days by pack mule with Janin blindfolded all the way. What the mining expert found at the end of the trip made him ecstatic. There were diamonds all over the place, just below the ground, between rocks, in ant hills! When the three returned to San Francisco, Janin refused to make his report until he was permitted to buy into the mining corporation. That ignited the whole thing. A diamond craze hit the West. Ralston's company paid off the prospectors, who headed east, and then prepared to mine the diamond field before other fortune hunters found it. The company sent out phony search groups to mislead other prospectors. At least 25 expeditions were launched to find diamonds. However, before the Ralston combine could really get its operation off the ground (the company first wanted to set up its own, and the country's first, diamond-cutting industry in San Francisco), the bubble burst. A prominent geologist, Clarence King and two others set out to find the field. When they did, King quickly determined it had been "salted." Some of the diamonds found by King showed lapidary marks.

The news was electrifying. The *San Francisco Evening Bulletin* headlined the story:

THE DIAMOND CHIMERA
It Dissolved Like the Baseless
Fabric of a Dream
The Most Dazzling Fraud of the Age

Investigation in Europe revealed that Slack and Arnold had come to Amsterdam with $25,000 they'd won gambling and bought up a huge amount of flawed uncut diamonds. This was what they salted the desert with. Very

few reputations came through the scandal unmarred. Charles Lewis Tiffany had to admit that his experts, who were the best in America, hadn't ever worked with uncut diamonds and thus simply were not aware how much of a raw stone was lost when fashioned into a jewel. Many of California's tycoons dropped huge amounts of money and Ralston's bank collapsed. Ralston committed suicide.

Slack and Arnold fared better. Private detectives found Arnold living quite happily in his original home in Elizabethtown, Ky. on his $300,000 take. The courts there did not look kindly on efforts to have him extradited to California. He and Slack were admired, even lionized, by much of the country. After all, even if they had taken some supposedly sharp tycoons for $600,000, hadn't those greedy men swindled them out of a "billion dollar" mine? Finally, in return for giving back $150,000 of his haul, Arnold had all charges against him dropped. Nothing more was heard of Slack for many years. Just before leaving California, he had told his friends that he intended to drink up his $300,000 or die in the effort. Then years later, he turned up as a well-to-do coffin maker in White Oaks, N.M.

Great Michigan "free land" swindle

There have been any number of swindles involving the sale of vacation or retirement plots, but never has there been anything to rival the fantastic ripoff worked early in the 20th century by two colorful rogues, Col. Jim Porter, a former Mississippi steamboat gambler, and his young assistant, who over the years would become famous as Yellow Kid Weil.

Col. Porter had a cousin who was a county recorder up in Michigan and the owner of several thousand acres of undesirable or submarginal land. Porter and his assistant bought a large chunk of this land at $1 an acre and then set up a Chicago sales office, showing the usual artist's concept of a clubhouse, marina and other features that would be built. However, they said nothing was ready for sale yet. Meanwhile, Porter, posing as an eccentric millionaire, and Weil started ingratiating themselves with hundreds of people by giving away free lots. No one was immune to the offer. Porter on certain evenings would give away 30 to 40 lots to prostitutes, madams, waiters and bartenders. Weil even gave some to Chicago police detectives. But they admonished each recipient not to mention the gift because then everyone else would want one. Naturally, they would also inform the happy recipients that they should immediately write and have the transaction recorded at the county seat. The fee for this, it developed, was $30; it had been just $2 before the swindle, but Porter's cousin had raised the fee to $30 with the understanding that $15 of it would go to Porter and Weil, netting the pair $16,000, and the rest he would keep for himself. The operation was entirely legal since all they had done was give away some valueless land, and not taken a penny from any recipient.

green goods swindle   confidence game

The green goods game is an old swindle by which a victim is sold what he thinks is an extraordinarily well-executed set of counterfeit money, only to find out later he has bought a bundle of worthless paper.

The racket made its first appearance in 1869. The mark would be shown a batch of genuine bills, told they were perfect counterfeits and given the chance to buy them at an extremely reasonable rate. Invariably, the victim would jump at the opportunity, but just before the sale was completed, the money package would be switched for one containing cut-up green paper.

By the 1880s several green goods gangs flourished in this country. They set about picking their victims in a scientific manner. First, a list of people who regularly bought lottery tickets was compiled and scouts were sent out to determine whether they were likely to go for a dishonest scheme and whether they had the funds to make fleecing them worthwhile. In this fashion quite a number of small-town bankers and businessmen were targeted and then caught in the swindlers' net. Rather brazenly, the approach would even be made by mail. One circular issued in 1882 read:

> *Dear Sir:*
> *I will confide to you through this circular a secret by which you can make a speedy fortune. I have on hand a large amount of counterfeit notes of the following denominations: $1, $2, $5, $10 and $20. I guarantee every note to be perfect, as it is examined carefully by me as soon as finished, and if not strictly perfect is immediately destroyed. Of course it would be perfectly foolish to send out poor work, and it would not only get my customers into trouble, but would break up my business and ruin me. So for personal safety, I am compelled to issue nothing that will not compare with the genuine. I furnish you with my goods at the following low price, which will be found as reasonable as the nature of my business will allow:*
> *For $ 1,200 in my goods (assorted)*
>   *I charge 100*
> *For $ 2,500 in my goods (assorted)*
>   *I charge 200*
> *For $ 5,000 in my goods (assorted)*
>   *I charge 350*

For $10,000 in my goods (assorted)
I charge 600

Faced with the glowing prospect of making a considerable sum of money, very few carefully screened recipients of such letters notified the authorities. In a few rare cases the sellers of the "counterfeit" money were seized when they appeared to close the deal, but they were released when an examination showed their money was genuine. In one case a fast-talking swindler convinced a New England police chief that he represented a bank executive who was planning to offer an important position to a local banker but wanted to test his honesty first.

Among the swindlers who worked the green goods game over the years were Reed Waddell, Tom O'Brien, George Post, Pete Conlish, Yellow Kid Weil and Fred Buckminster. For a time the New Orleans Mafia pulled green goods swindles, and even Mafia godfather Carlo Gambino supposedly worked it several times. Although most victims never reveal that they have been swindled, police bunco squads get a few such reports each year.

See also: REED WADDELL.

Gypsy Curse swindle   enduring con game

The Gypsy Curse is a concept that goes back many centuries in Europe and endures to the present in this country. Witch doctors have gouged the gullible since colonial times, placing on or removing curses from believing victims.

The greatest practitioners of the art in the 20th century were two audacious swindlers, Mrs. William McBride and Edgar Zug, who produced terror in hundreds of people and then bilked them of fortunes. Dressed in weird ceremonial costumes, the pair told wealthy victims they, their property and money were under evil spells. Then they explained that Zug, as the sole living white witch doctor in the United States, could be the instrument of their salvation. "The only way to relieve this deadly spell," Zug would intone, "is to buy your way out of it. These evil spirits respect cash."

In 1902 Zug and Mrs. McBride put the curse on an elderly rich couple, Mrs. Susan Stambaugh and her palsy-ridden husband. "I see your profiles on the side of a distant mountain . . . and through the brains of these profiles, evil spirits have thrust long needles. This was done many years ago and the needles are now rusty. When these needles break, a day not long off, you both will die."

Upon hearing this prediction Mrs. Stambaugh fainted and her husband had a spasmodic fit. When they came to, Mrs. McBride had some good news; Edgar Zug could save them from their awful fate. There was a way Zug could convince the spirits to withdraw the fatal needles. Zug nodded but warned, "It will take money, a lot of money." Within seven days the scheming pair had stripped the Stambaughs of all their savings and the deeds to their many properties. Then Zug had some bad news for them. The spirits were not satisfied. "You are going to die," he intoned with an air of resignation, "unless you can come up with at least another five thousand." But there was then some good news; the Stambaughs would end up getting more back than they paid in through a hidden treasure that the spirits would reveal to them.

The now desperate but hopeful couple hysterically hunted for more money, trying to secure loans from friends. Finally, one of them revealed the reason for the cash and the Gypsy Curse swindlers were arrested and convicted of fraud. As they were being led from the courtroom, Zug cried, "That's what I get for being kind!"

Police report that variations of the Gypsy Curse swindle are still worked today on the elderly rich in almost every ethnic community in big cities.

handkerchief switch   Gypsy bunco operation

A famous confidence game dating back as far as Gypsy fortune-tellers, palmists and card readers, the handkerchief switch has been used to bilk thousands of gullible Americans out of millions of dollars annually.

At first, the victim is told his fortune for a small fee, during which the fortune-teller gauges his or her gullibility and means. The victim is then told that the fortune-teller's power of prayer will solve his or her problems. The prayer must be accompanied by the burning of a candle, and the size and price of the candle determine how long these potent prayers will continue. Once a likely prospect has been found, the fortune-teller informs the victim that evil spirits are within him or her, and must be routed. The victim may be asked to bring a raw egg on the next visit, at which time the fortune-teller, by sleight of hand, breaks the egg, displaying a black mass inside. This, the victim is informed, constitutes the evil spirits that transfer their potent bad luck on everything the victim comes in contact with.

By further prayers, the fortune-teller discovers the reasons these evil spirits remain in the victim's body. It is because of the money the victim has. If he or she gets rid of the money, the evil spirits will depart. The victim is then instructed to bring a large sum of money, preferably in big bills. The fortune-teller places the money in a very large handkerchief, which is then folded up and sewn together at the ends. In the process, another stuffed handkerchief is substituted while the victim is not looking, and the substituted handkerchief is buried in a cemetery, flushed down a toilet or thrown in a river or the ocean. Sometimes the victim himself is permitted to throw the handkerchief in the ocean or to flush it down the toilet. Occasionally when the money is to be flushed down a toilet, the use of the handkerchief is discarded, and the victim is permitted to watch the roll of money flush away. In such cases, the toilet's plumb-ing has been altered so that the-money is trapped in the pipes, to be extracted later.

Hargraves, Dick (1824–1882) gambler and killer
Probably the epitome of the Mississippi gambler, Dick Hargraves cut a dapper and deadly figure on the river in the 1840s and 1850s.

A fashion plate who ordered boots from Paris and clothing from his native England, Hargraves came to New Orleans at the age of 16 and went to work as a bartender. He turned to professional gambling after winning $30,000 in a legendary poker game. Thereafter, he was a fixture on the river, where he became famous as an honest but pitiless gambler. Since at least 90 percent of all Mississippi gamblers were dishonest operators, Hargraves prided himself on being "square" and always felt that characteristic made it totally unnecessary for him to feel any sympathy for those he won money from. He supposedly shot at least eight or 10 men who sought vengeance after losing their money and often all their possessions to him. At the peak of his prosperity, Hargraves was worth an estimated $2 million.

As the best-known gambler in New Orleans, it was inevitable that women would be attracted to Hargraves. One of his numerous affairs resulted in scandal and death rivaling a Greek tragedy. Hargraves became involved with a banker's wife and was challenged to a duel by the enraged husband. He killed the banker with dispatch, and when the dead man's brother warned he would shoot the gambler on sight, Hargraves met him at a Natchez-under-the-Hill gambling den and killed him in a desperate battle. When Hargraves returned to New Orleans, the banker's widow stabbed him and then committed suicide. He recovered from his wounds and married a girl whose life he had saved in a fire. Tired of river gambling, he joined a filibustering campaign to Cuba and during the Civil War served as an officer in the Union Army. After the war Hargraves, a wealthy but ill man, moved to Denver, where he died of tuberculosis in 1882.

See also: RIVERBOAT GAMBLERS.

Hoffman, Harold Giles (1896–1954) governor and embezzler
One of the most flamboyant politicians in recent American history, Harold G. Hoffman lived a double life, that of an elected public official and an embezzler, whose total depredations remain undetermined. At the high point of his career, in 1936, he was boomed by New Jersey Republicans for president of the United States. At the low point in his life, in 1954, investigators closed in on him and he became an almost certain candidate for prison.

Hoffman was an army captain in World War I, a small-town banker, mayor of South Amboy, assemblyman, congressman, state commissioner of motor vehicles and, lastly, governor of New Jersey. At the age of 33, he began looting money. By the time he left the governorship in 1937, he had stolen at least $300,000, a considerable sum in Depression dollars. He spent the last 18 years of his life juggling monies in order to cover his embezzlements.

As near as could be determined, Hoffman started stealing from his South Amboy bank, dipping into dormant accounts to keep up his free-spending ways. Whenever an inactive account became active, Hoffman was able to shift money from another quiet account to cover his looting. Some of Hoffman's stolen funds went to promote his political career. Eventually, he reached Congress. Happily, Washington was not too far away from South Amboy, so he could keep a lid on things at the bank. When Hoffman suddenly left Congress to take the post of state commissioner of motor vehicles, which to many seemed a political step-down, some observers theorized that the move was part of Hoffman's plan to eventually run for governor, but the real reason was that he needed access to public funds. Sooner or later, an examiner might discover the shortages at the bank, so it was extremely advantageous for Hoffman to be able to juggle the funds of the motor vehicle department. When money had to be at the bank, it was there; when it had to be in the state coffers, it was there. In the process, more and more stuck to Hoffman's fingers.

When Hoffman won the governorship at the age of 39, he enjoyed wide popularity in his state and grew to be a national political power. However, he became a center of controversy in the sensational Lindbergh kidnapping case. His interference and attempts to reopen the investigation after Bruno Richard Hauptmann was convicted brought him widespread criticism. When he granted Hauptmann a few months' reprieve, he provoked a storm of criticism. He would never again be elected to any public office. Upon completing his term, Hoffman was named director of the unemployment compensation commission, an agency with a budget of $600 million, and he was able to continue his money-juggling operations.

While still governor, Hoffman had become president of the Circus Saints and Sinners, a group devoted to the twin duties of providing help to old circus folk and providing themselves with a good time. Hoffman became known as a boisterous buffoon, but inside he must have been a frightened, lonely man trying to keep his crimes hidden.

In 1954 newly elected Gov. Robert B. Meyner suspended Hoffman pending investigation of alleged financial irregularities in his department. Exorbitant rentals were apparently being paid for some department offices, and the state's attorney general subsequently found that favored groups stood to make nearly $2 million from a modest investment of $86,854. Other irregularities appeared in the purchase of supplies.

Hoffman put up a joyous front. The day following his suspension he appeared before the Circus Saints and Sinners. Harry Hershfield, the famous wit, cracked, "I knew you'd get into trouble in Jersey, fooling with a Meyner." Hoffman answered, "I can't even laugh." And he broke into raucous laughter.

The next two months, however, were lonely ones for Hoffman as he waited for the ax to fall. One morning in June he got up in the two-room Manhattan hotel suite provided by the Saints and keeled over with a fatal heart attack.

Later, more and more facts came out. The state became concerned when they discovered Hoffman had deposited $300,000 of public money in his own bank in a non-interest-bearing account. Officials then learned that not only was the interest missing but so was the principal.

Hoffman had written a confession to one of his daughters to be opened only upon his death. It said, ". . . until rather recently I have always lived in hope that I would somehow be able to make good, to get everything straight."

Howe and Hummel shyster lawyers

Howe and Hummel were easily the grandest shysters ever to seek out a loophole, suborn a witness or free a guilty man. Practicing in New York from 1869 to 1906, they made a mockery of the law. Rotund, walrus-mustached William F. Howe was a great courtroom pleader who could bring sobs to any jury. Young Abe Hummel was a little man who was marvelously adept at ferreting out loopholes in the law, to the extent that once he almost succeeded in making murder legal.

At the age of 32, Howe came to America from England, where his career as a medical practitioner had terminated in a prison term for performing an illegal operation on a woman patient. He studied law and within three years he opened up shop on New York's Centre (later called Center) Street. Howe was an instant success because of his resonant voice and a face that could turn on and off any emotion he wished to display for a jury. Years later, David Belasco, the theatrical producer, watched Howe's tearful performance winning an acquittal for a woman who had shot her lover full of holes. "That man," he said, "would make a Broadway star."

In the late 1860s Howe hired young Abe Hummel as his law clerk and in almost no time promoted him to partner. Anyone so adept at finding holes in the law was too good to lose. One case that illustrated Hummel's ability involved a professional arsonist named Owen Reilly. Hummel suggested they save the prosecution the trouble of a trial by pleading Reilly guilty to attempted arson. Only after the plea was accepted did anyone notice that there was no penalty for the crime of attempted arson. However, the statutes did say that the sentence for any crime attempted but not actually committed was to be one-half of the maximum allowable for the actual commission of the crime. Since the penalty for arson at the time was life imprisonment, obviously the defendant's sentence had to be half a life. Howe made nonsense of that standard.

"Scripture tells us that we knoweth not the day nor the hour of our departure," he told the judge. "Can this court sentence the prisoner at the bar to half of his natural life? Will it, then, sentence him to half a minute or to half the days of Methuselah?" The judge gave up and set Reilly free; the state legislature rushed to revise the arson statutes shortly thereafter.

On another occasion the pair almost managed to make murder legal in New York State. It happened in November 1888, when a client named Handsome Harry Carlton was convicted of having killed a cop. Since the jury failed to recommend mercy, the death penalty was mandatory. Little Abe studied the statutes very carefully and pointed out to Howe that in the month of November there was no death penalty for murder on the books, the state having abolished hanging the previous June, with the provision that it be replaced by the electric chair. The new death-dealing apparatus was to start functioning on the following January 1, and as Hummel noted, the law specifically said that electrocution should apply to all convictions punishable by death on and after January 1.

When Carlton came up for sentencing, early in December, Howe objected as the judge prepared to pronounce the death penalty. In fact, he objected to any sentence being passed on Carlton. If the jury had recommended mercy, Carlton could be sentenced to life imprisonment, the lawyer noted. "However, my client has been convicted of first-degree murder with no recommendation of mercy and there is no law on the books covering such a crime.

He then read the precise language in the new law and concluded that all the judge could do was turn his client free. Nonplussed, the judge delayed sentencing while the case moved to the state supreme court. Quite naturally, Howe and Hummel's contention made headlines across the country. In New York the public reaction was one of utter shock. According to the lawyers' contention, anyone committing murder between June and the new year could not be executed. Other murderers confined in death cells clamored to be released on the ground that they were being wrongfully held and could not be executed.

The district attorney's office vowed to fight the matter, and Inspector Thomas Byrnes of the New York Police Department's Detective Bureau pledged to the public that his men would continue to clap murderers behind bars, law or no law.

In the end, Howe and Hummel lost out on their interpretation; the high court ruled that no slip in syntax could be used as an excuse to legalize murder. Harry Carlton swung from the gallows two days after Christmas, a nick-of-time execution. However, if Carlton had lost out, Howe and Hummel did not; their crafty efforts brought many felons and murderers to their office door.

Buoyed by the publicity, the two shysters coauthored a book entitled *In Danger, or Life in New York: A True History of the Great City's Wiles and Temptations*. They explained in the preface that it was published in the interest of justice and to protect the innocent from the guilty, but what they actually turned out was a primer on every type of crime—blackmail, house burglary, card sharping, safecracking, shoplifting, jewel thievery and, of course, murder.

It became an immediate best-seller, with bookstore owners noticing a lot of traffic in their shops by persons who did not appear to be frequent book buyers. The book became required reading for every professional or would-be lawbreaker, from streetwalkers to killers. More and more when Howe and Hummel asked a new client, "Who sent you?" the stock reply was, "I read about you in the book."

No one ever computed exactly what percentage of murderers Howe and Hummel got off scot-free, but a prosecutor once estimated it was at least 70 percent, and "90 percent of them were guilty."

Whenever they had a client who was obviously as guilty as could be, the pair went into their bandage routine, having the defendant appear swathed in yards of white bandage, as though to suggest so frail a mind that his brains might fall out at any moment. One contemporary account tells of a Howe and Hummel client who simulated a village idiot's tic by "twitching the right corner of the mouth and simultaneously blinking the left eye." As soon as he was cleared, the defendant's face "resumed its normal composure, except for the large grin that covered it as he lightly removed the cloths from about his forehead." Another client, whose supposedly blithering insanity was accompanied by muteness and an ability to communicate only by sign language, seized Howe's hand gratefully when the verdict was announced in his favor and boomed, "Silence is golden."

The pair did not always resort to such trickery. When it was more convenient, they simply bribed witnesses and appropriate officials to get records changed, yet somehow they never ran into deep trouble until after Howe died in 1906. The following year Hummel was caught paying $1,000 to facilitate a divorce action. He was sentenced to two years in prison. Released at the age of 60, Hummel retired to Europe and died in London in January 1926, a regular to the end in the visitors' section during trials at the Old Bailey.

See also: IN DANGER.

In Danger primer for criminals

Probably no book ever published in America was more blatantly an instruction guide to criminality than *In Danger, or Life in New York: A True History of a Great City's Wiles and Temptations,* which appeared in 1888. The book was signed, "Howe and Hummel, the Celebrated Criminal Lawyers." Howe and Hummel indeed were celebrated attorneys and probably the most corrupt New York has ever seen. As they declared in a moral-toned preface, the two wrote the book after being moved by a clergyman's sermon in which he had declared, "It had been well for many an honest lad and unsuspecting country girl that they had never turned their steps cityward nor turned them from the simplicity of their country home toward the snares and pitfalls of crime and vice that await the unwary in New York." That was the last piece of high-minded drivel to appear in the book, the rest of which was given over to a detailed guide on what to steal and how.

By way of invitation, Howe and Hummell wrote of "elegant storehouses, crowded with the choicest and most costly goods, great banks whose vaults and safes contain more bullion than could be transported by the largest ships, colossal establishments teeming with diamonds, jewelry, and precious stones gathered from all the known and uncivilized portions of the globe—all this countless wealth, in some cases so insecurely guarded."

Having thus whetted the appetites of novice and would-be criminals, they hastened to add that "all the latest developments in science and skill are being successfully pressed into the service of the modern criminal." The ever-helpful authors went into detailed technical descriptions of various devices used by jewel thieves and shoplifters, such as "the traveling bag with false, quick-opening sides . . . the shoplifter's muff . . . the lady thieves' corsets." There were instructions for making one's own burglar tools and descriptions of the methods used in various skin games and the mathematical formulas used for rigging cards. And did crime pay? Howe and Hummel never said so in so many words, but, e.g., of shoplifting they stated, "In no particular can the female shiplifter be distinguished from other members of her sex except perhaps that in most cases she is rather more richly and attractively dressed."

The great shysters also touted certain legal services available at "what we may be pardoned for designating the best-known criminal law offices in America."

In Danger was severely criticized by the police and denounced from the pulpits, but each fresh denunciation merely produced more sales of the book.

See also: HOWE AND HUMMEL.

Insull, Samuel (1860–1938) stock manipulator

Among the most grandiose swindlers of the 20th century, Samuel Insull built up a multi-billion-dollar Midwest utility empire, one of the great financial marvels of the 1920s, by merging troubled small electric companies into an apparently smooth-running combine. He was hailed by the nation's press as the financial genius of the age, and lucky was the banker from whom Mr. Insull deigned to borrow money.

Clearly outdoing even Horatio Alger, Insull began his career as a 14-year-old dropout in his native London and rose to the pinnacle of high finance. He first worked as an office boy for $1.25 a week and later became a clerk for Thomas A. Edison's London agent. He was so impressive that he was recommended to Edison as a youth worth bringing to America, and the great inventor made him his secretary in 1881; Insull was 21 at the time.

Soon, Insull was handling the organization of several Edison companies, and by 1902 he was president of Chicago Edison. In 1907 he merged all the electric companies there into Commonwealth Edison. He then struck out on his own, joining small, often poorly run utilities into one operation. By the 1920s he was among the nation's richest men, worth $100 million, and people felt they were making the smartest investment in America when they purchased his stock.

The secret of Insull's success was to have one of his electric companies sell properties to another of his companies at a handsome profit over the original cost. The second company would not be hurt because it would later sell other properties to yet another Insull company. Thus, even in 1931, at the depths of the Depression, Insull's Middle West Utilities group reported the second most profitable year in its history. Of course, by this time Insull had to do more than sell properties to himself. He started cutting depreciation allowances in his various utilities or eliminating them entirely.

Then Insull had to spend huge sums—which he took in from gullible investors—to fight off takeover bids from other Wall Street operators eager to latch onto a strong financial organization. The problem was that if a takeover occurred the buyers would soon discover that Insull had done it all with mirrors. The swindler spent $60 million in the battle and won, but his financial empire was now so weak the bubble had to burst. The collapse came in June 1932, with investor losses estimated at $750 million.

Broke at the age of 72, Insull fled to Paris, where he lived on a yearly pension of $21,000 from a few companies of his that hadn't gone under. Facing extradition back to the United States on embezzlement and mail fraud charges, the old man left France and went to Greece. The Greek government let him stay a year but then bowed to U.S. pressure and ordered him out. For a time Insull drifted about the Mediterranean in a leased tramp steamer, but he finally had to put in at Instanbul for supplies. The Turks arrested him and shipped him back home for trial.

Because Insull's financial capers were so involved and often fell into areas where the law was not really clear, the government failed to prove its charges and he was able to go back to Paris. He dropped dead on a street there at the age of 78. At the time, he had assets of $1,000 cash and debts of $14 million.

insurance frauds—faked deaths

Cases of "dead men" turning up alive are common in insurance company fraud files, although the industry has never seen the virtue of publishing any statistics on the subject. There is, of course, even less information on those who have gotten away with such fraud. One of the most publicized disappearance frauds of all was perpetrated in the 1930s by John H. Smith, who had once run for governor of Iowa. Smith made it look as if he had been burned to death in an auto accident, substituting an embalmed body in his fire-gutted car. Mrs. Smith later confessed her husband had faked his own death to fleece an insurance firm out of $60,000 stating, "Under our plan, I was to collect the insurance or accept it when the insurance company paid it to me, and then meet John when he got in communication with me, which might be from one to two years."

Smith might have gotten away with his plot had he not developed a roving eye. He committed bigamy during his disappearance by marrying an 18-year-old Kansas farm girl. That was something Mrs. Smith hadn't agreed to, and since her wounded pride meant more to her than $60,000, she screamed for the law as soon as she learned what her husband had done.

Probably the longest successful insurance disappearance was pulled off by socially prominent Thomas C. Buntin of Nashville, Tenn. who vanished in 1931. Shortly thereafter, Buntin's 22-year-old secretary also disappeared. Buntin had $50,000 in insurance, and after waiting the customary seven years, the insurance company paid off the claim. However, the firm, New York Life, did not close the case. It kept up a search for Buntin, and in 1953—some 22 years after he vanished—the company found him living in Orange, Tex. with his ex-secretary under the name Thomas D. Palmer. For 22 years the couple had posed as Mr. and Mrs. Palmer and had even raised a family.

A trust fund had been established with the money from Buntin's insurance policy, and there was still $31,000 left when he turned up alive. The insurance company immediately launched legal action to get the money. As for Buntin, he obviously had not benefitted personally from the fraud. What was the reason? Very often a husband wishing to leave his wife and knowing he cannot expect a divorce will use a disappearing act to get out from under. Along with acquiring his freedom, the man can feel he has discharged all his duties as a husband and father by defrauding an insurance company into providing for his family. In the end, Buntin and his former secretary suffered no penalties from the law. In fact, after they were exposed, their neighbors sent them flowers.

Of course, producing a dead body will make a faked death even more convincing, but this often entails murder. In the 1930s Philadelphia's notorious Bolber-Petrillo murder ring specialized in killing off husbands so their wives could claim the insurance. Occasionally, they worked with a loving couple who wanted to enjoy the fruits of the husband's life insurance policy while he was still alive. In such cases the ring would kill an itinerant stranger and use him as a stand-in corpse for the husband.

Another famous insurance fraud murderer was Charles Henry Schwartz, a sort of mad scientist. When Schwartz ran his business into the ground in the 1920s, he looked for someone to use as a substitute corpse so that he could collect $200,000 in insurance. He settled on a traveling evangelist, Warren Gilbert Barbe, and murdered him in his Berkeley, Calif. laboratory. Since Barbe didn't look much like him, Schwartz worked hard on his substitute. Because Schwartz had a scar on his own chest, he burned away a section of Barbe's chest. He pulled out two teeth from the murdered man's upper jaw to match his own missing teeth. To take care of the difference in eye color between the two, Schwartz punctured his victim's eyeballs, and then for added protection, he blew up the laboratory. Despite all this, the corpse was soon identified as someone other than Schwartz and the latter was exposed. To avoid imprisonment he committed suicide.

Beyond doubt the prize victim of all insurance swindles was a beautiful but gullible model named Marie Defenbach. She was persuaded by a Dr. August M. Unger to join him and two accomplices in a fraud in which she was to take out $70,000 worth of life insurance and then fake her own death. The men were to be her beneficiaries and were to give her half the money. Dr. Unger assured Marie he would personally handle her "demise." He would give her a special medicine of his own that would induce a deathlike sleep. Later, the doctor convinced her, she would be revived in the back room of an undertaking establishment and spirited away, with an unclaimed body left in her place for cremation. If Marie had had

any sense, she would have realized that it would save the man a lot of bother and money if they just fed her some old-fashioned poison. But Marie was already mentally counting her loot.

On the evening of August 25, 1900, Marie blithely informed her Chicago landlady she was feeling ill, and she sent a messenger to get her some medicine. Fifteen minutes after taking it, she died in terrible agony. In due course, the true nature of Marie's death was uncovered by a suspicious uncle, whose investigation finally led to the arrest and conviction of the culprits.

In a curious sidelight to insurance frauds, the man responsible for the fact that few insurance company investigators carry weapons while on the job was a New Jersey man named J. R. Barlow, who had a wife and a $200,000 life insurance policy. One day he swam out from a beach and never swam back. His wife reported him as missing and applied for the insurance. The insurance company was suspicious, however, and after an intensive investigation traced Barlow to Mexico. When he was confronted by an insurance agent, Barlow turned violent, and in the ensuing struggle the investigator was forced to shoot him. Ironically, the insurance company was then compelled to pay off on his death. Soon after, the company issued a rule forbidding investigators to carry weapons.

See also: WARREN GILBERT BARBE, BOLBER-PETRILLO MURDER RING.

Internet crime   keyboards beat guns

A 28-year-old Los Gatos, Calif. woman suddenly discovered she was much "richer" than she thought. She possessed a new $22,000 Jeep, five credit cards, an apartment and a

$3,000 loan listed in her name. The trouble was she never asked for any of it. It turned out the woman had been a victim of "identity theft" via the Internet.

Another woman was impersonating her. All the second woman needed was to get hold of the woman's employee-benefits form and it was shopping time. The victim spent months and months straightening out the mess. There were scores of angry phone calls, court appearances and lots of legal expenses. And she constantly had to demonstrate she was the real her, rather than her impersonator!

Internet identity theft is getting to be a very common crime, committed by very sophisticated swindlers. One expert calls it "the next growth industry in crime." All a crook has to do is have a keyboard—no guns necessary. All he or she needs is your full name or Social Security number to access Internet databases that spew out your address, phone number, name of employer or driver's license. Then they use your good name to get great credit, and leave you to explain later if you can.

Everyone notes how amazingly the Internet is growing. Well, so is Internet fraud. The Internet Fraud Watch, operated by the National Consumers League, reports that complaints from 1997 to early 1999 shot up by an astonishing 600 percent. The number one complaint involves auctions. In 1997 auctions made up 26 percent of the total frauds reported, and the following year increased to 68 percent. The top auction companies work with authorities to try to cut auction scams, but the fact is as a Internet Fraud Watch spokesperson notes, "More people are online, and more people are being scammed. Consumers need to remember that con artists are everywhere—even in cyberspace."

While most frauds on the Internet are in auctions, many consumers do well in auctions, but with the traffic soaring the need for consumer protection and increased education is a must.

The top 10 scams on the Internet in order are auctions, general merchandise sales, computer equipment and software, Internet services, work-at-home, business opportunities and franchises, multilevel marketing and pyramids, credit card offers, advance fee loans and employment offers.

Anyone can be a target for Internet frauds, even those who don't have a computer. Hacker programs have turned up on the Web allowing people to generate credit card numbers using the same algorithms as the ones used by banks. Crooks open accounts with created numbers and then order products on-line—without even having the plastic.

In some cases consumers using auto-buying services have paid money on the assumption the service will search auctions looking for the car they want. Result: no car and no money back.

Irving, Clifford (1930–) Howard Hughes book forger

In 1971 writer Clifford Irving pulled off what was undoubtedly the most celebrated literary hoax of the 20th century when he swindled the McGraw-Hill Book Co. out of $765,000 for a fake autobiography of billionaire recluse Howard R. Hughes. Irving also conned *Life* magazine, which planned to print excerpts of the book with 20 pages of handwritten letters by Hughes. After examining the letters, a number of handwriting experts had declared all of them to be genuine.

Together with a friend who was a children's book author, Richard Suskind, Irving wrote an engrossing 1,200 page book, which veteran newsmen who had long covered the enigmatic Hughes found to be most "authentic." The scheme was so daring and so outrageous it was widely accepted even after Hughes said in a telephone call from his hideaway in the Bahamas that he had never met with Irving and that the work was "totally fantastic fiction." Irving's hoax was finally wrecked when a Swiss bank broke its vow of secrecy to reveal that a $650,000 check from the book publisher to Hughes had been cashed in one Swiss bank by "H. R. Hughes" and deposited in another under the name "Helga R. Hughes"—actually Irving's wife.

On March 13, 1972 Irving pleaded guilty to federal conspiracy charges. He was forced to return what was left of the publisher's money and was sentenced to two and a half years in prison. He served 17 months.

In 1977 Irving was asked by the editors of the *Book of Lists* to compile a list of the 10 best forgers of all time. He listed Clifford Irving as number nine.

Clifford Irving's phony biography of Howard Hughes earned him a dubious distinction from *Time* magazine.

jailhouse shopping network
convict's credit card con

Credit card fraud is a billion-dollar business, but there are some frauds, in a manner of speaking, more fraudulent than others. That is perhaps the only way to describe the scam that became known as the "nationwide jailhouse shopping network" in the early 1990s. It was conceived in Miami's Dade County jail, where there was a legal requirement that inmates be provided with access to telephones. The scam was thought up by Danny Ferris, a shrewd con man convicted of murder who, for more than four years, made local calls and 1-800 calls free of charge.

What Ferris did was simply order all sorts of merchandise over the telephone and steal an estimated $2 million in that fashion. It turned out that Ferris' accomplices on the outside provided him with hundreds of credit card numbers (retrieved from hotel dumpsters and the like), and the convict in turn used the numbers to order from catalogs by telephone. He arranged to have the goods delivered overnight to his accomplices who then sold the goods and split the profits with Ferris.

Ferris ordered incredible numbers of video camcorders, Rolex watches, champagne, gourmet gift baskets and gold and silver coins and raked in a fortune.

Later he admitted to interviewers, "I split right half with everybody. I mean, I never took more than half. I got robbed a lot, but, again, you kind of take it on the chin. You know what I mean? It was like you said, 'Heck, it was all free.'"

When at last Ferris was exposed, jail officials found they could not legally deprive him of his phone rights. They did, however, raid his cell and confiscate hundreds of credit card numbers.

That failed to knock Ferris out of business, as he managed to salvage a single number and used it to order a newspaper ad and a telephone answering service. He ran the ad in *USA Today* offering, "Cosmetics package, $89.95 value for only $19.95. All major credit cards accepted. Please call Regina Donovan Cosmetics." Danny supplied a 1-800 number but never sold any cosmetics. But he got what he really was after—a brand new batch of credit card numbers.

Eventually Danny Ferris was sentenced to five years for credit card fraud. Since that was in addition to the life sentence he was already serving, that hardly upset him. However, he was transferred to a tougher Florida state prison, where more stringent controls were placed on telephone calls. Meanwhile, back at Dade County jail it was discovered that other inmates were pulling Danny's surefire scam, one con even operated in the departed Danny's personal cell. Finally after the CBS television program *60 Minutes* featured the case, Dade County jail officials removed the in-cell telephones, requiring prisoners to make their calls in open corridors and the like, figuring that would put a serious crimp in their operations.

Without the old master's tutelage, the restrictions appeared to work.

Johnny Behind the Deuce (1862–1882)
gambler and killer

One of the West's most colorful and deadly gamblers, Johnny Behind the Deuce won a fortune at cards, killed several men, was saved from a lynch mob by Wyatt Earp and went to his own reward in a blazing gunfight—all before he reached his 21st birthday.

Nothing is known of his early life, but Johnny turned up in Tucson, Arizona Territory in early 1878 at the age of 16, giving his surname, at various times, as O'Rourke and his Christian name as either Michael or John. He worked as a hotel porter and seemed to spend all his free moments learning to manipulate a gun and a deck of cards. By 1880 he was famous throughout the territory as Johnny Behind the Deuce, a hard man to beat at any game of cards. In time, a suspicion developed that as he sat in the saloon gambling, Johnny would watch for a man passing out from drink and then leave the table for a short period. When the drunk sobered up the next day, he would find his belongings had been burglarized. Hardly anyone accused Johnny Behind the Deuce of such crimes, since he had already demonstrated a deadly knack for dealing with critics.

In January 1881 in Charleston a miner named Henry Schneider dared to call Johnny a thief when he found his poke had disappeared from his shack. He died with a bullet between the eyes after, Johnny Behind the Deuce alleged, drawing a knife. Marshal George McKelvey hustled the gambler off to Tombstone before the miners could start thinking of a lynching. Upon his arrival in Tombstone a crowd quickly gathered but a shotgun-armed Wyatt Earp held them off long enough for the prisoner to be moved to Tucson, where he was able to break out of jail. Since Johnny Behind the Deuce often dealt in the Oriental Saloon, of which Earp owned a piece, it is very likely that the latter felt he owed the young gambler something.

What happened next is guesswork, but a popular theory that summer was that the fugitive gambler came across the notorious Johnny Ringo, Wyatt Earp's mortal enemy, sleeping off a powerful drunk under a gnarled oak in Turkey Creek Canyon. Johnny Behind the Deuce supposedly figured he owed Earp one, so he shot the outlaw through the head. Whether true or not, the story was generally believed by Ringo's gunfighter friends. One of these, Pony Deal, got into a card game with Johnny Behind the Deuce in Sulphur Springs Valley. After a few hands Deal called Johnny a four-flusher, cheater and murderer. Angered, the gambler went for his gun, but Deal outdrew him and shot him dead.

Johnson, Mushmouth (?–1907) gambler

Perhaps the most successful black gambler in America, John V. "Mushmouth" Johnson dominated black gambling enterprises in Chicago from the mid-1880s until his death in 1907. Johnson, a flamboyant man with the obligatory cigar in mouth, controlled the city's policy racket, as well as scores of faro, poker and crap games in the black sections. His influence also extended over the Chinese quarter, where he charged all gambling enterprises a fee for protection. Mushmouth had considerable clout with the law as a result of his ability to deliver large blocks of black votes in elections.

Generally believed to have been a native of St. Louis, Mushmouth Johnson first appeared on the Chicago scene as a waiter at the Palmer House in the 1870s. In the early 1880s Andy Scott hired him as a floor man in his gambling emporium on South Clark Street and soon became so impressed with Mushmouth's abilities that he gave him a small interest in the operation. Mushmouth decided that what Chicago needed was a good nickel gambling house. A few years later, he opened his own place at 311 South Clark and did a thriving business with tables that catered to all races, offering bets as low as 5¢ in any of the games. Mushmouth sold off his interest in the place in 1890 and opened a saloon and gambling hall at 464 State Street, which operated without interruption for the next 17 years despite reform waves that shut down other gambling resorts at various times.

Together with two other big-time gamblers, Bill Lewis and Tom McGinnis, Mushmouth opened the Frontenac Club on 22nd Street. The club catered strictly to whites, and to be admitted, one was required to display a certain amount of cash. The fact that the Frontenac excluded blacks did not hurt Mushmouth's standing with his fellows; on the contrary, his success in the white world was a matter of black pride.

A total nongambler himself, Mushmouth is generally believed to have accumulated a quarter of a million dollars, a sizable sum for any man in that day and a colossal sum for a black man. Yet, shortly before his death in 1907, Johnson told a friend he had only $15,000, all the proceeds of his saloon business, and that he had lost money on his gambling ventures through the years. He said that he had spent $100,000 on fines and that police protection had always drained him, claiming, "I have had to pay out four dollars for every one I took in at the game." Johnson also implied he had been forced to pay more than his white counterparts because of the color of his skin.

When the claim gained currency following Mushmouth's death, an unnamed police official was outraged, denouncing Mushmouth Johnson as a "whiner" and a "damnable liar." It was unclear whether the official objected to Johnson's statement that he had paid for protection or, simply, that he had been discriminated against in the rates charged.

Jones, William "Canada Bill" (?–1877) gambler

Probably the greatest three-card monte cheater this country has ever produced and a fine all-round gambler, Canada Bill Jones cut a mangy figure along the Mississippi in the middle of the 19th century. In his autobiography *Forty Years a Gambler on the Mississippi*, George Devol, another legendary gambler, described Canada Bill as *a character one might travel the length and breadth of the land and never find his match, or run across his equal. Imagine a medium-sized, chicken-headed, tow-haired sort of a man with mild blue eyes, and a mouth nearly from ear to ear, who walked with a shuffling, half-apologetic sort of a gait, and who, when his countenance was in repose, resembled an idiot. His clothes were always several sizes too large, and his face was as smooth as a woman's and never had a particle of hair on it.*

Canada was a slick one. He had a squeaking, boyish voice, and awkward gawky manners, and a way of asking fool questions and putting on a good natured sort of a grin, that led everybody to believe that he was the rankest kind of sucker—the greenest sort of country jake. Woe to the man who picked him up, though. Canada was, under all his hypocritical appearance, a regular card shark, and could turn monte with the best of them. He was my partner for a number of years, and many are the suckers we roped in, and many the huge roll of bills we corralled.

Normally, three-card monte favored the dealer two-to-one, but Canada Bill seldom gave a sucker such a decent break. He was probably the century's greatest manipulator of cards and could show a victim two aces and a queen and then, virtually in the act of throwing the cards, palm the queen and introduce a third ace so that the sucker could never find the queen. About 1850 Canada Bill formed a partnership with Devol and two other talented gamblers, Tom Brown and Hally Chappell. The larcenous quartet operated on the Mississippi and Ohio and other navigable streams for close to a decade. When the partnership dissolved, each man's share of the profits was more than $200,000.

As quickly as both he and Devol made their money, however, they squandered it,

both being suckers for faro. Canada Bill, who truly loved gambling for its own sake, was the originator of what was to become a classic gamblers' comment. He and a partner were killing time between boats in a small Mississippi River town when Bill found a faro game and started to lose consistently. His partner, tugging at his sleeve, said, "Bill, don't you know the game's crooked!"

"I know it," Bill replied, "but it's the only game in town!"

When river traffic dwindled and then virtually disappeared by the start of the Civil War, Canada Bill shifted his operations to the rails. The railroads, however, did not always exhibit the same tolerance for gamblers that the riverboats had, and three-card monte players were ejected when spotted. In 1867 Canada Bill wrote to one of the Southern lines offering $25,000 a year in exchange for the right to operate without being molested. He promised to give the railroad an additional percentage of the profits and said he would limit his victims to very rich men and preachers. Alas, his offer was refused.

Alternately flush and broke Canada Bill continued his itinerant gambling style until 1874, when he settled in Chicago and, with Jimmy Porter and Charlie Starr, established some very lucrative and dishonest gambling dens. Within six months he was able to pull out with $150,000, but in a short time, he lost his entire poke at faro. Canada Bill worked Cleveland a bit, winning and then losing, and in 1877 he wound up in Reading, Pa., an area noted as a refuge for gamblers. While down on funds he was committed to Charity Hospital and died there in 1877. He was buried by the mayor of the city, who was later reimbursed by Chicago gamblers for the cost. As two old gambling buddies watched Canada Bill's coffin being lowered into the grave, one offered to bet $1,000 to $500 that the notorious cheat was not in the box.

"Not with me," the other gambler said. "I've known Bill to squeeze out of tighter holes than that."

See also: GEORGE DEVOL.

Keating, Charles H., Jr. (1923–)
savings and loan scandal figure

Throughout the entire savings and loan (S&L) scandal, which rocked American finance in the late 1980s, Charles H. Keating Jr. remained the most blatant participant. Keating's case—estimated to have cost U.S. taxpayers some $2.6 billion—even jeopardized the reputation of the U.S. Senate because of the actions of the so-called Keating Five. It was a prime example of unfettered S&L officials living high on the hog and playing fast and loose with depositors' and investors' money.

The Keating story can be told in the form of a chronology:

February 1984—American Continental Corp., formed by Keating, buys the Lincoln Savings and Loan of California for $51 million.

March 1986—The Federal Home Loan Bank in San Francisco starts an examination of Lincoln's rapid growth and hectic investment activities.

Mid-1986—San Francisco bank examiners urge Washington officials to come down hard on Lincoln for questionable accounting and loan procedures.

November 1986—Five U.S. Senators—Alan Cranston of California, John Glenn of Ohio, Donald W. Riegle of Michigan and Dennis DeConcini (all Democrats) and Republican John McCain of Arizona—meet with examiners on behalf of Keating, who has made large political contributions to them.

May 1987—Examiners recommend that Lincoln be seized for operating in an unsound manner and dissipating its assets. Nothing happens.

April 12, 1989—American Continental files for bankruptcy protection, making its junk bonds worthless.

April 14, 1989—The government now takes control of Lincoln and puts the bailout at an eventual cost of $2.6 million, the most expensive in history.

September 1990—A California grand jury charges Keating and three others with securities fraud, saying they had deceived investors into buying junk bonds without telling them the risk. Many Lincoln investors thought they were buying government-insured bonds.

February 1991—After a three-and-a-half month investigation, the Senate Ethics Committee renders a verdict in the case of the Keating Five. It declares there was "substantial credible evidence" of misconduct by Senator Cranston (leading to a severe rebuke from the Senate in November). Riegle and DeConcini are described as giving the appearance of impropriety, but no further action is taken against them. Glenn and McCain are criticized less severely.

December 4, 1991—After a four-month court case, Keating is convicted of securities fraud and sentenced to a 10-year state jail term in California. He still faces federal charges.

July 3, 1993—Keating, convicted of federal charges of fraud, is sentenced to 12 years and seven months, the sentence to run concurrently with the state sentence.

The S&L scandal provoked a tightening of regulations against such institutions, which took their investments far afield. The impact on politics was immense so that by 1999 only John McCain of the Keating Five still was in the Senate.

Keely, John E. W. (1827–1898) swindler

Few swindlers have ever deceived their victims and the public longer than ex-carnival pitchman John Keely of Philadelphia. In 1874, he convinced four top financiers, Charles B. Franklyn, an official of the Cunard steamship line, Henry S. Sergeant, president of the Ingersoll Rock Drill Co., John J. Cisco, a leading banker, and Charles

B. Collier, a lawyer, that he could convert a quart of water into enough fuel to power a 30-car train a mile a minute for 75 minutes. Over the next 24 years he held frequent demonstrations in his workshop that seemed to confirm he was about to revolutionize the entire field of energy. The previously mentioned foursome organized the Keely Motor Co. and over the years advanced him large sums of money for his research. Company stock was traded on exchanges in this country and Europe and Keely proved adept at getting money out of people besides his primary backers. Clara Jessup Moore, a wealthy widow, not only invested an estimated half-million dollars in Keely's so-called invention but also authored a book entitled *Keely and His Discoveries*. At one stage, John Jacob Astor "wanted in" to the tune of $2 million.

The Scientific American attacked Keely's claims as ridiculous, but this did nothing to cool the ardor of thousands of investors. Finally, after Keely's death in 1898, investigators dismantled his house and found Keely's mysterious force was nothing more than compressed air. Buried under the kitchen floor of the house was what *The Scientific American* in its February 4, 1899 issue described as "a steel sphere forty inches in diameter, weighing 6,625 pounds." This sphere was "an ideal storage reservoir for air . . . at great pressure." The compressed air traveled upward to a second-floor workshop, where Keely gave his demonstrations, through steel and brass tubes nine inches in diameter with a three-inch bore, strong enough to withstand the tremendous pressure. Between the ceiling of the room on the first floor and the floor of the workshop was a 16-inch space "well calculated to hide the necessary tubes for conveying the compressed air to the different motors with which Keely produced his results." It was a setting in which "for a quarter of a century the prince of humbugs played his part." Concealed in the walls and floor of the workshop were spring valves that could be operated by foot or elbow to "run" a motor whenever desired. Clearly, the whole setup was similar to the fun and mystery houses Keely had seen during his carnival days.

Kelly, Joseph "Bunco" (1838–1934)
shanghaier and murderer

Oddly, the two greatest shanghaiers in America were named Kelly—Shanghai Kelly and Joseph "Bunco" Kelly. At age 26, Joseph Kelly of Liverpool, England set up in Portland, Ore. in 1859 and for the next 35 years made thousands of men into unwilling seamen, filling orders from crew-short sea captains. Totally without conscience, he hesitated at sending no one to sea, recruiting his victims from anywhere along the waterfront. He often used two doxies, Liverpool Liz and Esmeralda, as sex lures to coax drunks from Erickson's Saloon, where it took 15 men to tend the block-long bar, or from the Paris House, the city's biggest brothel, or from Mark Cook's Saloon. If such tactics failed, he simply bludgeoned hapless passersby and carted them off to a ship ready to sail.

Kelly sometimes had trouble acquiring accomplices, and for good reason. After once receiving an order for 10 men, he and two assistants deposited eight drunks into a ship's hold. "Here," said the skipper, "I need ten men, I told you."

Kelly nodded, battered his two aides senseless and collected for a full consignment. The profitability of the procedure was unassailable: in addition to collecting a fee

for his assistants—as well as the other shanghai victims—he also saved the money he would otherwise have had to pay them.

Kelly picked up his nickname Bunco for another of his double-dealing deeds. He would bring an apparent victim wrapped in a blanket aboardship and deposit him directly in a bunk, telling the captain, "drunkenest sailor I ever seen." Kelly would collect his $50 stipend as the ship set sail. Not until the next morning would the angered captain discover Kelly had slipped him a cigar store Indian instead of a drunken sailor.

Bunco's biggest coup occurred when he came across 24 waterfront bums either dead or dying in the basement of an undertaking establishment, where they had partaken of barrels filled with embalming fluid under the illusion they were inside the next building, which was a saloon. At the time Bunco found them, he had an order outstanding for 22 shanghai victims at $30 a head. The master of the craft was extremely pleased when Kelly oversupplied the order by two, and gratefully handed him $720 for the bunch. The next day the redfaced captain had to dock in order to unload 14 corpses and another 10 men whose lives could be saved only by energetic stomach pumping. The captain vowed never again to do business with Bunco Kelly, but he probably broke his resolutions, since in Portland a ship's master almost had to deal with Kelly, even if wisdom required a close inspection of any goods purchased from him.

Despite actions by the police, which varied from largely indifferent to modestly determined, Kelly continued his nefarious trade until 1894, when he was apprehended for murdering a retired saloon keeper, 73-year-old George Washington Sayres. Kelly denied the charge, claiming it was a frame-up by competitors who wanted to take over his business. "I am being tried not as the person who killed poor old George Sayres," Bunco said in a statement. "I am being tried for all the crimes ever committed in the North End. I am on trial because I am operating a successful sailor's boardinghouse—the finest on this coast. I am being tried because I have no influence with the city's politicians. I had nothing against George Sayres."

That last statement, at least, was accurate. The jury concluded Kelly had committed the murder for $2,000 given him by Sayres' enemies.

Kelly did 13 years in the Oregon State Penitentiary and was released in 1907. He got a newspaperman named John Kelly, no relation, to help him write a book, *Thirteen Years in the Oregon Pen,* in which he continued to proclaim his innocence. Kelly left Portland in 1909 and eventually was said to have ended up in South America, where, as proof of the adage that only the good die young, he lived until the ripe old age of 96.

See also: SHANGHAIING; SHANGHAI KELLY.

Kelly, Shanghai (1835–?) shanghaier

Without doubt the most-feared name wherever Pacific sailors gathered in the 19th century was that of Shanghai Kelly, a stubby, red-bearded Irishman who became the most prodigious shanghaier on San Francisco's Barbary Coast.

Kelly maintained a saloon and boardinghouse at 33 Pacific Street. There is no way to precisely estimate how many men passed through his notorious shanghai pipelines but it was at least 10,000. He got the best deal from shipmasters because he generally provided bona fide sailors rather than unsuspecting landlubbers who happened to stumble along. Not that Kelly didn't turn a dishonest dollar in his shanghai operations whenever he could. Occasionally, among a boatload of drugged victims, Kelly would toss in a corpse or two. Since the usual transaction only allowed time for a head count of men in various degrees of stupor, it is easy to see how a captain might not discover he had been "stiffed with a stiff," as the saying went, until he was well out into the Pacific. Police could only wonder how many murder victims were turned over to Kelly to be disposed of for a price, thus providing him with a double fee. The master shanghaier knew that such a corpse would receive a quick and unrecorded burial far out at sea.

Feared as he was, Kelly still had no trouble keeping his boardinghouse stocked with sailors, many of whom knew the fate that lay in store for them. The popularity of Kelly's place rested on his reputation of providing free women to go along with his free liquor. To many a sailor the price of their next voyage was little enough to pay. Once, in the 1870s, though Kelly received an order for 90 sailors at a time when he was understocked. Chartering a paddle-wheel steamer, he announced he would celebrate his birthday with a picnic at which there would be all the liquor a celebrant could drink. Naturally, there was an admission charge, since Kelly firmly believed in getting all he could out of any deal. He kept a close count of the willing celebrants clamoring aboard and as soon as the number reached 90 the gangplank was pulled up and the steamer paddled off. Barrels of beer and whiskey were opened and the happy picnickers toasted Kelly's health. Of course, all the drink was heavily drugged and within a couple of hours everyone aboard except Kelly and his men was sound asleep. The paddle steamer pulled up to the two ships that had ordered crews, and Kelly handed over the agreed-on number to each and collected his pay. On his way back, he rescued survivors from the *Yankee Blade* which had sunk off Santa Barbara. Luckily for Kelly, the landing of the rescued men caused great stir and nobody noticed that his picnic guests were missing. Of course, he would have felt even luckier if he had been able to sell the rescued seamen as well.

Kelly was active in his trade till near the end of the 19th century, when he faded from sight.

See also: JOSEPH "BUNCO" KELLY, SHANG-HAIING.

key racket   B-girl swindle

The so-called key racket, where a bar-girl gives a customer the supposed key to her apartment in exchange for cash, is still practiced.

Shortly after its birth in San Francisco, it reached the proportions of a minor industry in that city. The practice began in the Seattle Saloon and Dance Hall, perhaps the lowest dive on San Francisco's Barbary Coast after the earthquake of 1906. The second floor of the Seattle was an assignation floor, where the 20-odd "waiter girls" could adjourn with customers. The ladies developed a lucrative sideline making dates to meet drunken customers after the Seattle closed at 3 A.M. In this scam a woman would promise to spend the night with a customer but only if the meeting were kept secret from her boyfriend, who met her each night after the saloon closed and escorted her home. It would therefore be impossible for the customer and the woman to leave the resort together. Instead, she would offer to sell the

man a key to her flat for a price ranging from $1 to $5, depending on what she thought the traffic would bear, so that he could join her an hour after closing. If the customer objected that he was paying for a pig in a poke, the woman would counter that since she did not know him, she would be stuck with the expense of changing the lock on her door if he didn't show up. To a man with a liquor-logged brain, the argument often made sense. After handing over the cash, the customer would write down the woman's address, which would be some nearby building but, of course, not the one where she really lived.

Some popular waiter-girls at the Seattle often sold a dozen keys a night. The custom was soon picked up in most of the other Barbary Coast resorts, so that on a typical night, long after the dance halls closed, scores of furtive figures would be seen staggering through the streets, key in hand, trying to find a door that would open. For a time, watching the "key men" became a slumming sport for those San Franciscans who were rather proud of their city's reputation as the vilest this side of decadent Paris. The lucrative practice continued for about a year until the police cracked down on it as a result of newspaper exposés that published hundreds of complaints from reputable householders plagued by drunks trying to unlock their doors.

Koretz, Leo (1881–1925) swindler

A contemporary of Charles Ponzi, Leo Koretz is not as well remembered today as a notorious swindler, certainly not as well as he should be. True, Ponzi is believed to have netted something like $7 million while Koretz appears to have stolen a mere $5 million. But Koretz carried off his scheme for much longer and, unlike Ponzi, who preyed to a great extent on unsuspecting immigrants, Koretz robbed the elite of the Chicago business world. In fact, Koretz' depredations may well have been greater than Ponzi's since a number of businessmen were known to have taken their losses in silence, fearing that any revelation that they had been swindled would damage their reputations as shrewd businessmen.

Koretz' scam was based on stock in the Bayano Timber Syndicate of Panama, which had supposedly garnered a fortune in mahogany from its vast land holdings and then discovered oil on its property. Koretz started selling stock in Bayano in 1917. Within no time at all the company was rewarding its stockholders with a quarterly dividend of 5 percent on their original investment. In reality, there was no Bayano Timber Syndicate. The swamp land it allegedly held was owned by the Panamanian government, since no one had any interest in mining or having anything to do with its only known commodity, mosquitoes.

Koretz' ignorant stockholders were happy with their dividends. Of course, in theory, he had to pay the investors their dividends out of their original investments, creating the same kind of impossible pyramid structure that eventually brought Ponzi to grief. The more cunning Koretz solved that troublesome matter by encouraging his investors to take their dividends in additional stock, each certificate as worthless as the originals.

The stockholders adored Koretz, even as the news of Ponzi's fraud was breaking; in fact, they started calling him "Lovable Lou . . . Our Ponzi." They regarded him as the first true financial genius to come down the pike since John D. Rockefeller. Once, Koretz was feted at a sumptuous dinner at Chicago's Congress Hotel. Sitting next to him was Arthur Brisbane, William Randolph Hearst's top editorialist and himself a big Koretz sucker. During the dessert, newsboys broke into the hall with an extra announcing, "Leo Koretz' oil swindle." For a moment everyone was stunned. Then Brisbane rose laughing. He had had phony newspapers printed up as part of the evening's entertainment. Then, embra-cing Koretz, he shouted, "Mr. Koretz is a great and honorable financier!" Everyone learned differently at the end of 1923, when his great hoax was exposed.

In 1922 a large group of happy stockholders thought it was about time that they visited the company's vast holdings. Koretz succeeded in stalling them for almost a year, but when they sailed from New York in November 1923, Koretz knew his time had run out. Taking $5 million with him, he fled to Canada and assumed an identity he had established there years ago as Lou Keyte. What brought Koretz down was his diabetes, for which he had to take insulin, then a rare and expensive commodity. He was traced thanks to his dependency on the drug and finally arrested in Halifax.

In the ensuing investigation, it was found that his elderly mother had invested $50,000 in his scheme and his brother $140,000. Even his secretary had parted with $3,000. Koretz said he had accepted the investments because he didn't know how to turn them down without arousing suspicion.

Koretz spent only about a month behind bars for his crimes. He induced a lady friend to bring him a five-pound box of chocolates. He ate the entire box on January 9, 1925 and promptly keeled over dead, certainly one of the most bizarre prison suicides in history.

land frauds

The Western land frauds of the late 19th and early 20th century remain one of the great raids on the public purse in the history of the United States. Almost 40 million acres of valuable public land were set aside as forest reserves and the General Land Office was put in charge of protecting this natural treasure. Almost immediately, land office agents began peddling the rich forest acreages to private parties, who then turned around and made a quick killing reselling the property to lumber companies.

By the time of Theodore Roosevelt's administration, these land looters had become so influential in Congress that they were able to strip the Department of Justice of an investigative force charged with collecting evidence against the wholesale frauds. Finally, however, an investigation launched by Secretary of the Interior Ethan A. Hitchcock uncovered the manipulations carried out by members of the General Land Office, including the agency's own detectives. Much of the evidence in the land frauds cases were gathered by William J. Burns, then the star agent of the Secret Service, and in a total of 34 cases that went to trial, 33 ended in conviction. Among those convicted were U.S. Sen. John H. Mitchell and Rep. John N. Williamson, both of Oregon. Sen. Mitchell appealed his conviction but he died in 1905 before his case was reviewed by a higher court. The Senate departed from custom and did not adjourn its session or send a delegation to Mitchell's funeral.

In later years some of the prosecutions were found to be politically tainted and corrupt. Many charges were brought against Burns, among them that witnesses had been intimidated into providing perjured testimony. In 1911 a report made to President William Howard Taft by Attorney General George W. Wickersham said there was no doubt that Burns had stage-managed the selection of jurors. Although the same accusation was made against the flamboyant Burns in numerous cases over the years, there is little doubt about the guilt of most of those charged in the land frauds.

Las Vegas

Las Vegas was built on mob money. During World War II it was a jerkwater town with a few greasy spoons, filling stations and some slot machine emporiums. Gangster Bugsy Siegel first conjured up the idea of Las Vegas as a glittering gambling mecca in the desert. Using $6 million in mob funds, he built the Flamingo Hotel, which was initially a bust, largely because it took time to build up public interest. The mob was upset with Siegel due to the lack of return on its investment, and when it learned that Bugsy had pocketed some of the construction money, he was killed.

Nonetheless, the Bug's idea still made sense. Slowly, the Flamingo began to flourish and once the public accepted the idea of trekking through the desert to dice and roulette tables, one casino after another sprang up. State authorities adopted strict oversight measures to ensure the new casinos would not fall under mob domination, but to little avail. Syndicate money was traced directly to many major gambling establishments. Meyer Lansky financed much of the Thunderbird. Although some others fronted as its proprietors, the Desert Inn was largely owned by Moe Dalitz, head of the syndicate's Cleveland branch. The Sands was controlled—from behind the scenes—by Lansky, Joe Adonis, Frank Costello and Joseph "Doc" Stacher. The Sahara was launched by the Chicago mob—the Fischetti brothers, Tony Accardo and Sam Giancana. The Dunes was a goldmine for New England mafioso Raymond Patriarca.

When Frank Costello was shot in 1957, police found tallies in his coat pockets that matched the revenues of the Tropicana for a 24-day period. Up until then, presumably only the Nevada Gaming Control Board was unaware that the Tropicana provided a great source of income for Costello and his New Orleans partner, Dandy Phil Kastel. The word on Caesar's Palace was that almost everyone in the mob had a piece of it. Comedian Alan King said of its decor: "I wouldn't say it was exactly Roman—more kind of early Sicilian."

The value of Las Vegas to organized crime is difficult to measure. Its casino-hotels made huge profits, and when some of the revenues were skimmed off the top so that taxes would not have to be paid on them, the take was much greater. It was later alleged that in an eight-year period Lansky and some of his associates skimmed $36 million from the Flamingo alone. In addition, the vast exchange of money across the gaming tables offered a perfect opportunity to launder funds from other, illegal enterprises. Jimmy Hoffa invested Teamsters' pension funds in the hotels in the form of interest-free "loans" that were never paid back, providing the mob with additional capital.

One thing Vegas proved was that given the opportunity to run a gambling setup honestly, the mob would still operate it dishonestly. Despite the huge profits, by the mid-1950s the mob had started selling off some of its properties to individuals and corporations. In the 1960s billionaire Howard Hughes started buying one casino after another.

In the early 1970s the mob's interest in Vegas was reportedly at a low point, but by the close of the decade, many observers concluded, mobsters were returning to the scene.

See also: FLAMINGO HOTEL; BENJAMIN "BUGSY" SIEGEL.

Levine, Dennis (1953–) Wall Street inside trader

It was the "singing" of Dennis Levine that broke open the 1986 Ivan Boesky scandal that exposed the boundless avarice existing on Wall Street. The Securities and Exchange Commission discovered that Boesky, a millionaire hard-ball stock trader and arbitrager, had agreed to pay Levine a total of $2.4 million for his illegal tips. But Levine was also an illegal stock trader in his own right.

Over a period of five years Levine illegally traded in at least 54 stocks and stashed away $12.6 million in profits. At the time he was unmasked, Levine was a hotshot managing director of the investment banking firm of Drexel Burnham Lambert. He conducted his personal trading through a secret bank account in the Bahamas.

Using his Wall Street position, Levine profited from information about various companies' dealings before that information reached the public. The extent of Levine's ease in making illegal profits was typified by his 1985 activities in Nabisco stock. With inside information he had obtained, Levine made two phone calls on the stock and walked away with almost $3 million in illicit profits. Later Levine would tell the CBS news show *60 Minutes*: "It was this incredible feeling of invulnerability. . . . That was the insanity of it all. It wasn't that hard. . . . You get bolder and bolder and bolder, and it gets easier, and you make more money and more money, and it feeds upon itself. And looking back, looking back I realize that I was sick, that it became an addiction, that I lived for the high of making those trades, of doing the next deal, making the bigger deal."

After he was caught, Levine pleaded guilty to securities fraud, perjury and tax evasion, and cut a deal for himself by exposing Boesky and his own circle of wheeler-dealers. Levine gave up $11.6 million in illegal profits and served 15 months in the federal penitentiary in Lewisburg, Pennsylvania. He was

Illustrative of his insider trading skills, Levine made just two phone calls concerning Nabisco stock and waltzed off with almost $3 million in booty.

released in 1988 and thereafter claimed to have turned his life around, lecturing college students around the country about what he'd learned from his past mistakes and operating his own financial consulting firm.

Some questioned how much Levine had changed. Since that time Levine was involved in a number of dubious "up-front" deals, bringing together struggling businesspeople needing financing and supposed financial institutions willing to make money available in exchange for an up-front commission. For his part Levine also received thousands of dollars in fees. The only trouble was no monies were ever advanced and some Levine clients said they were out almost $200,000. One Levine client said he had been told by Levine that a person named Jim Massaro could help out on the deal. The client said Levine described Massaro as a friend he'd done business with during his days at Drexel.

Levine actually met him at Lewisburg where they had been jailmates.

Levine insisted he had exercised the required "due diligence" in all cases and that it was not accurate for him to be described as the consummate con man. He insisted, "I have never conned anybody in my life. . . . People are entitled to their own opinions, but it's not true. I have to live with myself. I don't think I've done anything wrong."

Lustig, "Count" Victor (1890–1947) con man Probably the only confidence operator who could be classed as the equal of the legendary Yellow Kid Weil was "Count" Victor Lustig, a remarkable rogue who not only pulled the most outrageous swindles of the 1920s and 1930s but also constantly courted danger by victimizing the top gangsters in America, including Al Capone and Legs Diamond.

Born in 1890 in what is now the Czech Republic, Victor Lustig soon established himself as the black sheep of the family (although when he became a successful international confidence swindler, his brother Emil followed in his footsteps).

Lustig pulled a number of swindles in Europe as a young man and was hunted by police in several countries. Consequently, he came to the United States just after World War I and immediately emerged as the leading practitioner of the "money-making machine" swindle. A sucker would be informed that the Count had discovered a secret process for making real currency out of plain paper that he fed into a machine. He demonstrated the process several times, although what came out were other genuine bills that he had secreted in the machine earlier. As outrageous as the dodge was, Lustig had such a gift for grift that he sold the machine—often for sums up to and even exceeding $10,000—to bankers, businessmen, madams, gangsters and small-town lawmen.

An incorrigible rascal, Lustig believed in flimflamming as a matter of principle, and no one was exempt. He originated one of the con man's favorite petty swindles, that of "tishing a lady." Lustig was a habitue of brothels and paid extremely well, at least in a manner of speaking. Upon taking leave of a lady, he would produce a $50 bill, fold it up, lift up her skirt and pretend to tuck it in her stocking. Actually, he would palm the bill and stuff in a wad of tissue paper. Then the Count would explain to the woman that it was trick money and that if she removed it before morning, it would turn to tissue paper. The lady would promise to leave it there but after Lustig's departure she would eagerly retrieve her pay—and indeed, it had turned to tissue paper!

In the mid-1920s Lustig returned to Europe and twice succeeded in selling the Eiffel Tower. He had read in the newspapers that the great tourist attraction was in need of repairs and would be very costly. The Count had a brainstorm. When he arrived in Paris, he sent out letters to six leading scrap metal dealers inviting them to a secret government meeting in a luxury hotel. Lustig introduced himself as "deputy director-general of the ministry of mail and telegraphs," and explained to the dealers that since it was too costly to repair the Eiffel Tower, it would have to be torn down and sold for scrap. However, the government was fearful of public reaction, so the plans had to be kept secret. Then when the government announced how much money would be saved, the public would accept the idea.

The dealers were invited to bid for the scrap metal from the tower. All turned in secret bids. Then Lustig informed one of the dealers that for a fee his bid would be accepted. The dealer paid eagerly, and Lustig immediately fled to Vienna. When the story of the swindle failed to make the newspapers, he realized the dealer had been too frightened or too ashamed to go to the police. So he returned to Paris and swindled another dealer. This one, however informed the law when he realized he had been taken and Lustig realized he couldn't sell the Eiffel Tower again and returned to America.

For a time Lustig operated in the worthless security field, selling bogus paper that he often presented as "stolen." He found a number of underworld buyers who agreed to take the hot stuff off his hands for as little as 10¢ on the dollar, with the idea of holding it several years before disposing of it. Among those so taken were Big Bill Dwyer, Nicky Arnstein and Legs Diamond, who actually thought he was buying some retirement security. Oddly, when the gangsters found out they had been taken, they could do nothing because Lustig said he would spread the word on how they'd been suckered, making fools of them. Even the maniacal Diamond saw the humor of the situation and left Lustig alone.

The Count once swindled Al Capone out of $5,000 and the famous gangster never realized he had been taken. Lustig asked Capone for $50,000, promising to double it in 60 days in a scam he was working. Capone gave him the money, warning what he did to welchers and swindlers. Lustig simply put the money in a safe-deposit box for the allotted time and then dolefully informed him his plan had failed and he had not made any money. Capone was about to explode, thinking he had been taken, when Lustig returned his $50,000, keeping up a spiel of apologies. Capone was not prepared for this situation. Initially figuring Lustig had swindled his money, he now was faced with the obvious fact that the Count was playing square with him.

"If the deal fell through," Capone said, "you must be down on your luck." He peeled off five $1,000 bills and handed them to Lustig. "I take care of guys who play square with me." The Count gratefully left with the $5,000, which was what he was after from the beginning.

One of the Count's prize patsies was a renowned madam of the period, Billie Scheible, operator of a string of very plush houses in Pittsburgh and New York. He once sold the madam a moneymaking machine for $10,000 after telling her he was too impatient with it since it could only turn out one $100 bill every 12 hours. When Billie determined she had been hoaxed, she had some of her strong-arm boys run the Count down in Philadelphia.

Lustig refunded Billie's $10,000 and then turned on the charm full voltage to sell her $15,000 in worthless securities. "The Count had a way with him," Billie once explained.

Since many of Lustig's swindles involved money schemes, it was only natural he would also venture into counterfeiting. But counterfeiting was another matter and the Count, who had never done time for any of his cons, was caught in 1935.

On September 1, the day before he was supposed to go on trial in New York City, Lustig, using a rope fashioned from nine bed sheets tied together, climbed out a lavatory window of the Federal House of Detention and started his escape descent. Part way down, Lustig noticed lunch-hour pedestrians watching him. Immediately, he began to go through the motions of cleaning the window. Down he went, floor by floor, scrubbing every pane he passed. When he hit the sidewalk, he ran. It was several minutes before one puzzled onlooker approached the small wicket in the formidable jail doors and asked, "Do you know your window cleaner has run away?"

The Count's fantastic escape made headlines throughout the country, as did the ensuing manhunt for him. Billie Scheible was questioned but knew nothing. Perhaps Arthur "Dapper Don" Collins did. Collins, reputed to be one of the country's greatest con men, had been pals with Lustig before his arrest. But he was not too helpful either. It turned out Lustig had swindled him out of several thousand dollars and, quite naturally, failed to keep in touch.

Finally, Lustig was run to earth in Pittsburgh. He was convicted and sentenced to 15 years for the counterfeiting charge and five more for his escape. He died in prison in 1947.

See also: MONEY-MAKING MACHINE.

McDonald, Michael Cassius "Mike"
(1832–1907) gambler and fixer

Chicago gambling, confidence swindling, vice and the political fixing during the 30 years after the fire of 1871 starred Michael Cassius McDonald.

A professional gambler while still in his early teens, Mike became the King of the Bounty Jumpers during the Civil War, heading an organized gang of crooks who reaped a fortune collecting bounties for enlisting in the Union Army and promptly deserting to repeat the process elsewhere. McDonald masterminded the movements of his men, keeping track of their "enlistments" on a large war map. He came out of the war with a stake large enough to open a gambling house at 89 Dearborn Street.

In 1869 McDonald swindled $30,000 out of an assistant cashier who, in turn, was embezzling money from the large company he worked for. McDonald was arrested for the swindle but beat the rap by hiring scores of witnesses to testify that his gambling place ran honest games and that his victim had begged him, with tears in his eyes, to be allowed to play. However, the trial drained McDonald's finances, and he was unable to keep up protection payments to the police, which resulted in raids on his establishment several times a week. The experience left him with a hatred for policemen, which continued into his later life when he was the greatest fixer in the city and even named police chiefs. Years after, a patrolman came to him and said: "We'd like to put you down for two dollars, Mike. We're burying a policeman."

"Fine!" Mike replied. "Here's ten dollars. Bury five of 'em!"

Like all other gambling and vice operators, McDonald was wiped out by the Chicago Fire, but because he was one of the quickest to get back in business, he was able to "build a poke" before the police became organized enough to collect protection payments again. By 1873 he and two partners had opened a four-story resort in a building that would later become the home of the Hamilton Club. The first floor was a top-notch saloon; the second floor housed McDonald's office and a large set of gambling rooms. The third and fourth floors were run by his wife Mary, who rented furnished flats to select gamblers and bunco men, such as Kid Miller, Snapper Johnny Malloy, Dutchy Lehman, Jew Myers, Charley Gondorf, Boss Ruse and Black-Eyed Johnny. Another of his cronies, Hungry Joe Lewis, took Oscar Wilde for several thousand dollars during the English writer's tour of the United States in 1882. The same year two others, Johnny Norton and Red Jimmy Fitzgerald, swindled diplomat Charles Francis Adams out of $7,000.

In this famous resort, called The Store, McDonald uttered a number of phrases that were to become part of the American vernacular. When a partner objected that his plans were too lavish and that they would never attract enough customers, McDonald replied, "There's a sucker born every minute." While later writers would attribute the remark to P.T. Barnum, it was McDonald who coined it as well as another equally famous saying: "Never give a sucker an even break."

By 1880 McDonald's stature had grown to the extent that he controlled all vice operations except for prostitution, a business activity he found repulsive. "A crook has to be decent to work with Mike," a friend of his once explained. And working with Mike meant making good money. McDonald moved into politics, refining the political fix to a fine art. A criminal wishing to operate freely had to pay Mike as much as 60 percent of his take, which was then divided among the police, various city officials and judges and McDonald's own syndicate. McDonald became close friends with such Chicago mayors as Harvey Colvin and Carter Harrison. During the terms of these two mayors, Mike's minions were allowed to run wild. In 1882, during one of the mayoral reigns of

Carter Harrison, McDonald flexed enough muscle to have Superintendent of Police Simon O'Donnell, who was both honest and efficient, reduced in rank to captain and replaced by his own man, William J. McGarigle. McGarigle later had to skip town following the disclosure of a cleaning and painting swindle of a governmental building that netted McDonald's company $67,000. While some of the governmental grafters went to prison, McDonald remained untouched.

McDonald continued to control the Chicago rackets until the turn of the century, pulling in his horns whenever a reform administration came in and then swinging back into action when the heat was off. After accumulating several million dollars, he started to lose interest in his business because of marital problems. In the mid-1880s his wife ran off with a minstrel singer. McDonald finally tracked her down in San Francisco and brought her home, but in 1889 she took off again, this time with a Catholic priest who used to say mass at a private altar in the McDonald mansion. The lovers went to Paris, where they lived for six years until the priest entered a monastery and McDonald's wife returned to Chicago to operate a boardinghouse. Mike meanwhile had obtained a divorce and married Dora Feldman, four decades his junior. In the ninth year of this second marriage, Dora shot and killed a young artist named Webster Guerin, who, it developed, had been her secret lover during almost all of the marriage. The now-retired political fixer never recovered from the shock of the disclosure and his wife's comments to the press that she had always disliked him; he died on August 9, 1907. Nevertheless, McDonald had left his second wife a large portion of his estate and had set up a special defense fund of $40,000 for her murder trial. Chicago being Chicago, Dora McDonald was acquitted in 1908.

See also: BOUNTY JUMPING.

McPherson, Aimee Semple (1890–1944)
evangelist and alleged kidnap victim

For a decade before 1926, Sister Aimee Semple McPherson was America's most successful, if controversial, female evangelist, billing herself the World's Most Pulchritudinous Evangelist, until a bizarre "kidnapping" started her career in decline.

Born near Ingersoll, Ontario, Sister Aimee married a Pentecostal evangelist, Robert Semple, with whom she served as a missionary in China. When he died, she returned to the United States and remarried. She left her second husband, Harold McPherson, in favor of a life of preaching that took her all over the United States, Canada, England and Australia. When she finally settled in Los Angeles, she was without funds but had a large, devoted following, which she organized into a religious movement called the International Church of the Four-Square Gospel. The church appealed especially to transplanted midwesterners and southerners who had difficulties coping with California life.

Raising $1.5 million from her devout followers, Sister Aimee built the huge Angelus Temple, where 5,000 of the fervent could attend her meetings, which featured faith healing, adult baptism by immersion, an aura of hope and Cecil B. DeMille–style spectacle. Sister Aimee would appear in a white silk gown, her hair adorned with flowers and colored lights dancing on her figure. A 50-piece band played patriotic songs and rousing religious music. Sister Aimee's lectures were broadcast live from the group's own radio station in the church. The sheer size of the operation required a weekly payroll of $7,000.

As well known as Sister Aimee was, she became even more famous in the spring of 1926, when she went to a lonely section of beach near Venice, Calif. and disappeared after being seen entering the water. Her mother, active in the temple, summoned the faithful and bade them to pray for her. "We know," she said, "she is with Jesus." Besides praying, the faithful kicked in $25,000 as a reward for anyone helping Sister Aimee to return. About 100 of her devoted followers hurled themselves into the waters where Sister Aimee had disappeared. One drowned and another died of exposure. A young girl became so distraught at the loss of her spiritual mentor that she committed suicide. A plane scattered lilies over Sister Aimee's watery departure spot.

Then, 32 days after her disappearance, Sister Aimee limped out of the desert near Douglas, Ariz., the victim of an alleged kidnapping. She said that while she was on the beach, her secretary having returned to a nearby hotel, she was kidnapped by a couple and a second man who said they wanted her to say prayers over a dying baby. Instead, they drugged her and imprisoned her in a hut in Mexico. They told her that if she didn't raise a half-million dollars in ransom, they would sell her to a Mexican white slaver. One of the men burned her with cigars when she would not answer all his questions. On June 22 the trio had gotten careless in their vigil and Sister Aimee was able to slip away, hiking for 13 hours across the desert to Douglas, Ariz.

While several of the faithful gathered outside the hospital, Sister Aimee showed burns on her fingers and assorted bruises and blisters she said she had gotten while tied up and during her long trek to freedom. The story did not sit too well with many, however. Her shoes and clothing didn't seem scuffed enough for such a hike across sun-baked sands, and some thought it odd that after such an ordeal Sister Aimee hadn't even asked for a drink of water.

Los Angeles District Attorney Asa Keyes investigated and was dubious, so dubious that in due course he indicted Sister Aimee and her mother for obstruction of justice because of their story of the "disappearance" and "kidnapping." Keyes produced evidence that while the evangelist's flock was praying for her return, the good Sister was trysting with the married radio operator of her temple, Kenneth G. Ormiston, at various hotels. At her trial Sister Aimee announced, "I am like a lamb led to slaughter," and she blamed her troubles on "the overlords of the underworld." Keyes ignored such comments and called to the stand a parade of hotel maids, house detectives and others who identified Sister Aimee as the woman who accompanied Ormiston on various stopovers while the nation puzzled over her disappearance.

Keyes also had flushed Ormiston out of hiding in Harrisburg, Pa. Previously, he had supposedly mailed an affidavit to Keyes admitting to the hotel trysts but insisting his companion was really "Miss X" whom he would not embarrass by identifying. The district attorney had been unimpressed by the paper since it bore a signature that closely resembled the hand of Sister Aimee. However, Keyes failed to call the radio operator to testify, and midway through the trial he suddenly moved for an acquittal. Keyes never explained why, but it is worth noting that in later years the district attorney himself went to prison for taking bribes in a number of strong cases that had been dropped or plea-bargained.

Officially cleared, Sister Aimee returned to her spiritual work, but the ardor had gone out of many of the faithful. She took to touring Europe and the Orient but never fully recaptured a style one historian described as fusing "economies and ecstasy, showmanship and salvation, carnival and contrition." Sister Aimee later had a short marriage with a radio man named Dave Hutton and then dropped from public view. In September 1944 she died in Oakland, Calif., apparently from an overdose of sleeping pills.

Maxwell, Robert (1923–1991) intercontinental superswindler

While the 1980s have been called the decade of the superswindler—producing such financial felons as Michael Milken, Ivan Boesky, Charles Keating, and the like—Robert Maxwell was in a class of his own.

Maxwell, a flamboyant Czech-born British publisher, was regarded by many as a brilliant ringmaster who fought his way up from poverty and personal tragedy to build a financial empire that made him one of the business world's most feared operators. In the 1980s Maxwell eagerly sought the mantle of savior of downtrodden newspapers, such as Britain's Mirror Group newspapers and New York's *Daily News*.

Then began what may be called Maxwell's "Operation Siphon." It will take years into the 21st century to unravel the full extent of Maxwell's depredations, but it became clear that he and perhaps a few others siphoned off at least $1.63 billion from pension funds and the two flagship companies of his publishing empire, Mirror Group and Maxwell Communications Corp. The total losses to the pension funds and other creditors will at some point escalate by many billions of dollars more.

Maxwell died at sea, having either fallen, been pushed or jumped from his luxury yacht, *Lady Ghislaine.* Was he murdered to be silenced? Had he died accidentally? Or had he finally decided the jig was up and taken his own life? Of the alternatives, the last seems the more likely since, according to investigators, he faced certain exposure in a matter of days.

Actually the most amazing aspect of his crimes was that Maxwell had gotten away with them for so many years, considering that 20 years earlier Great Britain's Board of Trade found that he was not "in our opinion a person who could be relied on to exercise proper stewardship of a publicly quoted company." Nevertheless, Maxwell continued to thrive, proving that nothing succeeds in fraud like excessive success. Even while picking up the nickname "The Bouncing Czech," Maxwell blithely went from one megadeal to the next, using looted assets to keep afloat the heavily indebted private companies at the heart of his empire.

In the firestorm after Maxwell's death, even the most austere elements of the British press descended to colorful and livid terms to denounce him as a "fraudster on a grand scale." Whittam Smith, editor of *The Independent,* declared, "He was a crook. Shareholders other than his family were lambs to be fleeced; pensions were fair game." Peter Jenkins wrote in the same publication: "Ask anyone with knowledge of financial matters the secret of his success, and they would explain how he could make money move from bank to bank, company to company, faster than the eye could see. Some called this wizardry business, but most

Super swindler Robert Maxwell was for a time hailed as the savior of the ailing *New York Daily News* when he took it over. Then he began what was later called "Operation Siphon," looting pension funds at the News and his other holdings and cheating creditors out of many billions.

knew in their hearts that Maxwell was simply not kosher, no friend of widows and orphans."

Within a month of Maxwell's death, his financial empire had crumbled in bankruptcies. Perhaps Maxwell knew the house of cards was rushing headlong to collapse. In a television interview shortly before his death, Maxwell said in response to a question that in the hereafter he couldn't say if he would meet his "maker . . . or the banker."

Maxwell left a few somewhat laughing—but far many more stone-cold broke.

Means, Gaston Bullock (1880–1938) swindler and rogue

In the pecking order of J. Edgar Hoover's pet hates, Gaston Bullock Means stood close to the top of the list and deservedly so, since Means was perhaps the most outrageous figure to appear on the Washington scene in the 20th century.

At one point this rogue of unsurpassed effrontery stood almost at the top of the list of future candidates to become head of what was then called the Bureau of Investigation, later renamed the Federal Bureau of Investigation. He was, in William J. Burns' words, "the greatest natural detective ever known." The word "detective" easily could have been replaced by such terms as con man, swindler, hoaxer, spy, influence peddler, blackmailer and, quite possibly, murderer. His depredations were astonishing. Only Gaston Means, for instance, could do more to besmirch the administration of Warren G. Harding than the Ohio Gang and Teapot Dome. Always the opportunist, he made more money out of the Lindbergh kidnapping than did Bruno Hauptmann.

Means, born in North Carolina in 1880, had a most undistinguished record as, among other things, a towel salesman and sometimes lawyer. When he joined the Burns Detective Agency in 1910, it was in this period that Means so impressed Burns, using such standard private detective cons as "secret informants" and other phony methods indicative of investigative prowess to impress his superior.

In 1915 Means left the agency for bigger and better things, becoming bodyguard and financial overseer for madcap heiress Maude R. King. There is strong reason to suspect that Means gained Mrs. King's confidence by arranging to have a thug fake a robbery attempt on her and some friends on a Chicago street, a crime frustrated by the gallant appearance of Means. In no time at all, the con artist was managing the woman's financial affairs and by 1917, he had bilked her out of some $150,000. Even as flighty a

person as Maude King eventually got a bit upset about her losses, but Means solved this problem by taking her on a hunting trip to North Carolina. Mrs. King, unaccustomed to such sport, was shot to death on the trip. Means was tried for murder but acquitted; the conclusion was that the woman had committed suicide.

Means' activities were not confined to swindling heiresses. During World War I he hired out as both a secret agent for the Germans (with duties to disrupt British shipping) and at the same time, as a counterspy for the British against the Germans. Eventually—before the United States entered the war—Means severed his German connections, probably less because of patriotism than because of the difficulty he encountered in collecting his pay. Quite naturally, he shifted his activities to U.S. Army Intelligence.

When the Harding Administration came to power in 1921, Burns brought his old friend Means into the Bureau of Investigation, which enraged Hoover, who was made assistant director of the agency. Although the bureau was rife with bribe takers during this period, Means upgraded the graft system to a fine art. He was also busy, as he subsequently revealed, in the employ of Mrs. Harding, secretly investigating her husband's love affairs and paternity situation. For a time Means came under such a cloud that he was dropped from his job, but he was quickly reinstated as an "informant" through Burns' good offices. A short time later, Means was indicted for a scheme in which he had swindled a number of bootleggers by telling them he was collecting graft for Secretary of the Treasury Andrew Mellon. During a Senate committee investigation, Means told how he had acted as a go-between in the payment of $50,000 to an associate of Attorney General Harry Daugherty to have a $6 million government suit against an aircraft concern killed.

In this same period Means was also busy attempting to blackmail the Hardings for $50,000 with the accusation that the president had fathered a child by Nan Britton, an undistinguished young poetess from Ohio. After Harding died in office, Means tried to make his money by coauthoring a book with Nan Britton entitled *The President's Daughter*. Eventually, Means went to prison for his bribery scams. When he emerged in 1930, he further pursued his literary career with a scandalous best-seller, *The Strange Death of President Harding*, in which he implied Mrs. Harding had poisoned her husband.

Means capped his career of unbridled roguery by concocting a swindle to capitalize on the Lindbergh baby kidnapping. He convinced another flighty heiress, Mrs. Evalyn Walsh McLean, that through his underworld contacts he could recover the child. Mrs. McLean gave him $100,000 for the ransom and $4,000 for his own expenses. The child was not recovered, and Means did not give back the money, instead telling the woman one preposterous story after another. He finally insisted he had returned the money to an associate of Mrs. McLean, but his story was proved false and he went to prison for 15 years.

When Means suffered a heart attack in 1938, Hoover dispatched FBI agents to his prison hospital bed to learn the whereabouts of Mrs. McLean's money. Means gave them a puckish smile and died.

medical quackery

In a century that has seen monumental strides in pharmaceuticals, general medicine and surgery, medical quackery has become among the most lucrative criminal activities in the United States. The public wastes hundreds of millions and probably billions of dollars each year on "miracle" and "sure-cure" medicines, cosmetics, drugs and therapeutic devices. Particularly victimized are persons who have incurable diseases and those with great fear of going to doctors.

Typical cures are those that will grow hair on a bald head and renew sexual vigor in older men. In fact, there are nostrums for every human ailment from hemorrhoids to cancer. Devices offered include a magnetized copper bracelet with magical powers against rheumatism and arthritis, an electric rolling pin that melts fat and a plug-in vibrating cushion that cures arthritis and varicose veins. Concentrated seawater, according to those who sell it, will do away with such varied ailments as diabetes, baldness and cancer, among other things, while offering our bodily glands "a chemical smorgasbord."

One of the more unique instruments sold some years ago was a set of two small rubber hammers for people tired of wearing glasses all the time. They were instructed to tap their eyes with the hammers 200 times a day as a method of "strengthening" them. Then they were to put a mask over their eyes for total relaxation and rest. When the mask was removed, quite a few of the victims sported two perfect black eyes. But the promoter even turned this development into a plus by insisting that the discoloration indicated the victim was eminently susceptible to the treatment and that if the hammers were used on the male genital organs, such tapping would increase virility.

Probably the biggest con man in the cancer field was Norman Baker, who battled postal inspectors with every available legal delaying tactic for almost a decade before he was put out of business. Baker's empire mushroomed to include a number of hospitals and radio stations, and he even published a newspaper in Iowa. It was charged that he fed his patients large amounts of flavored waters and acids as a cancer cure. Since he gave the patients in his hospitals no substantial foods, his operating expenses were greatly reduced. In the process, a great many of his patients, understandably, died, but Baker was nonetheless able to accumulate millions of dollars. His achievement was even more monumental consi-dering the punishment he later received: four years imprisonment and a $4,000 fine.

According to postal inspectors, the two main obstacles to successful prosecution of medical quacks are the fact that potential chief witnesses against them often die before the case reaches court and the mistaken belief of many of their victims that they are getting treatment the "medical interests" and the American Medical Association in particular conspire to keep from the public.

Milken, Michael R. (1946–) king of junk bonds

As a result of the scandals and prosecutions of the 1980s and early 1990s a debate left unsettled was who among the perpetrators did the most damage and walked away with the most loot. For a time Ivan Boesky was labeled by the press as the most "successful." However, Boesky could make the point that he was nowhere near being the biggest crook in American finance. He could point to Michael R. Milken, the junk bond king of Drexel Burnham Lambert, Inc., who was nailed after Boesky's cooperation.

Milken had risen to fame as the main force creating the huge market for junk bonds, the high-yield, high-risk debt securities that marked the corporate takeover boom of the 1980s. Milken did not go down easily, spending an estimated $1 million a month for several years fighting the federal government's case against him. He finally reversed his tactics and pleaded guilty in 1990 to six felony counts involving securities fraud and agreed to pay the lion's share of a cash settlement by himself and his cohorts, which was eventually fixed at $1.3 billion in fines and restitution costs to victims.

Still, there were those who objected to the deal, insisting that Milken had forced the government to drop the more serious charges of racketeering and insider trading. They also complained about his being able to keep about $125 million of his personal fortune. In addition, his immediate family maintained more than $300 million in assets, meaning that the settlement could leave the convicted junk bond dealer with close to a half billion dollars. Milken drew a 10-year prison term, with sentencing judge Kimba M. Wood declaring, "When a man of your power in the financial world, at the head of one of the most important banking houses in this country, repeatedly conspires to violate, and violates, securities and tax laws in order to achieve more power and wealth for himself and his wealthy clients, and commits financial crimes that are particularly hard to detect, a significant prison term is required in order to deter others."

The 10-year sentence was not permanent. Milken negotiated with the government and provided evidence against others (although critics said his offerings were less than adequate). For his cooperation Judge Wood reduced Milken's sentence to 33 months and 26 days so that he could be released on parole after 24 months. The judge said she also took into account Milken's good behavior in prison, where he had been tutoring other prisoners and had set up a prison library. Milken was also sentenced to 1,800 hours of community service. Barred from doing any more stock deals, Milken hardly maintained a low profile in business matters.

Miller, William F. (1874–?) swindler

A 24-year-old Brooklyn, New York City bookkeeper, William F. (520%) Miller was one of the greatest swindlers this country has ever produced. Charles Ponzi did nothing but lift Willy Miller's modus operandi; and while the latter could not be credited with having originated the idea of robbing Peter to pay Paul, he certainly carried it to dizzying heights during 11 incredible months in 1899, while he trimmed an array of suckers out of well over $1 million.

For years Miller was an insignificant bookkeeper who tried in vain to make a killing in the stock market. He made small investments, in the hundreds of dollars, with money borrowed from friends in his community. Miller was good for it, though, and always repaid his debts promptly—by the simple expedient of borrowing a slightly larger sum elsewhere. It took Miller some time to figure out this robbing-Peter-to-pay-Paul tactic was one of the great secrets of high finance.

One day he posted a sign in his window:

WM. F. MILLER
Investments
The way to wealth is as plain as the road to market.—B. Franklin

Miller was a great admirer of Benjamin Franklin.

By the following Sunday everyone in the neighborhood had seen the sign and Miller was asked about it in the adult Bible class he ran at the local church. With a very earnest expression he said, "It's not fair that the Morgans and the Goulds and the Vanderbilts are making so many millions when us little people are making so little—and I've decided to do something about it."

Then he confided a great secret. Everyone knew he was always hanging around Wall Street. Well, he had learned the investment secrets used by the big boys. Naturally, he couldn't tell what they were, but he was now in a position to pay 10 percent interest on money invested with him. A few persons expressed interest, since that rate was substantially more than what the banks were paying.

"You don't understand," Miller said matter-of-factly. "I don't mean ten percent a year. I mean ten percent a week."

"Holy smoke!" one parishioner exclaimed. "That's 520 percent a year!"

"I suppose it is," Miller said modestly.

Now, many of his students were impressed and wanted to invest right on the spot. Righteously, Miller said he wouldn't take any investments on the Sabbath. The next night when he got home from work, there was a line of investors waiting at his door. True, many had only tiny sums, undoubtedly cautious about so remarkable an investment opportunity. Miller took many amounts of less than $10, but he told each investor to return in one week for their first interest payment.

Sure enough, after seven days an investor who had given $10 got $1 back as interest. By the time 10 weeks passed, all the original investors had made back initial investments and were still drawing more. All of these people were investing larger sums now, as were others who had joined the eager procession as soon as Miller started making payments.

Miller's fame spread far beyond his Brooklyn community. He was known as 520% Miller and money flowed in much more rapidly than he was paying it out. Some investors thought they were being rather shrewd by promptly reinvesting their interest as soon as Miller handed it to them. In 11 glorious months Miller trimmed his suckers for well in excess of a million dollars. According to some later accounts, while he lived high on the hog, he managed to salt away $480,000 and possibly more, considering that in one month in 1899 he made an estimated $430,000 profit.

But Miller never did get to enjoy his money. The great con man was himself conned out of half of the $480,000. A fixer named T. Edward Schlesinger told Miller that for a cut of the take, he would show him how to keep the law off his neck. Gullible Miller, the genius swindler, dutifully handed over the money. Schlesinger, however, didn't offer Miller any foolproof method to avoid legal harassment. He simply took his $240,000 and caught a fast boat for Europe, finishing out his days in Baden-Baden.

Miller's turn at playing the sucker would come again. His second bit of gullibility resulted from his meeting with a slick lawyer named Robert Ammon. He hired Ammon to give him legal advice on how to stay out of jail once it became known that when new investments stopped coming in, Miller would be unable to pay any more juicy 10 percent dividends.

Ammon's advice was that Miller leave the country. As for the $240,000, Miller said he had left, Ammon suggested he leave it with him "because if you are caught and have the money in your possession, it would be proof of your guilt."

Miller went to Canada after getting Ammon's firm promise that he could have his money sent to him whenever he wanted it. He never did get a penny of the loot he left with Ammon and was eventually caught and sent to prison, but only for 10 years, a surprising ending to one of the most fabulous crime careers in American history. Well, maybe not quite the ending. Miller was sent to Sing Sing, where he finally was able to make a deal with the law to get out of prison in 1907, having served only five years. The authorities were very much interested in lawyer Ammon and Miller told everything he knew about him. Ammon screamed that Miller had given him nowhere near $240,000. In any event, Ammon went to Sing Sing and Miller got out. He returned to Brooklyn and, for a time, worked again as a bookkeeper. But after a few years Miller just sort of faded away, perhaps going off to enjoy the underestimated fruits of his crime.

Mina, Lino Amalia Espos y (1809–1832)
impostor and murderer

An impostor for whose favor much of early 19th century Philadelphia society vied, Lino Amalia Mina was a young man who passed himself off in that city as the son of the Spanish governor of California. He claimed to be stranded without funds until the arrival of a clipper rounding the Cape. Of the several important families that offered to house him, Dr. and Mrs. William Chapman won out. Dr. Chapman's wife, Lucretia, was overjoyed; she was very socially conscious and she thought having Mina as a houseguest would be a triumph. Within a week Mina's presence developed into a triumph in more ways than one. The servants saw Mina kissing Mrs. Chapman on a number of occasions, and the 41-year-old matron offered no resistance at all. If Dr. Chapman noticed anything, he said nothing, and within another month he was not able to say anything.

Mina went to a Philadelphia pharmacy and bought a huge amount of arsenic—for "stuffing of birds." Four days later, Dr. Chapman suddenly became ill and died. Two weeks after the funeral, Mina and the widow Chapman traveled to New York and were married. When they returned home, valuables in the mansion started disappearing. So did much of Lucretia's jewelry, and Mina set about cleaning out certain bank assets. He also posed as Dr. Chapman to complete certain financial dealings. This brought him to the attention of the authorities. Now suspicious, they ordered an autopsy performed on Chapman's body. Massive amounts of poison were found, and both Mina and Lucretia were charged with murder. Mrs. Chapman wept at the trial, insisting she had been totally taken in by Mina. A male jury was swayed and freed her but condemned Mina to death.

It was reported that a number of important personages attended Mina's hanging, perhaps more incensed over how the cad had bamboozled the city's high society than over the murder he had committed.

Minkow, Barry (1966–) teenage wolf of Wall Street

One cunning teenager who left Wall Streeters with very red faces—to say nothing of flattened portfolios—was Barry Minkow, who at the tender age of 16, launched his own rug-cleaning business from his parents' garage in Reseda, California. In less than four years, the still barely postadolescent punk engineered a stock scam that conned top Wall Street firms with a bald-faced ploy no different than the classic one used by legendary swindler Charles Ponzi—that of robbing Peter to pay Paul.

Ponzi was known to his gullible victims as the "man who invented money." Barry was hailed in the financial press as the kid wonder who "invented profits." Barry did not earn profits the old-fashioned way—by working for them; he hardly worked at all. His most laborious exertions seemed to have been naming his company, which was ZZZZ Best. After that the youthful entrepreneur simply went about convincing Wall Street that his tiny company had grown into a financial cash cow. In retrospect, Barry's company might have been a little more impressive if his business had actually earned a dime.

Daniel Askt, his biographer, said, "There was always a quality about Barry that suggested he held an MBA from the Dada School of Business."

Business methods to get capital had no restraints. He staged burglaries to collect insurance. He borrowed $2,000 from his grandmother and then stole her pearls for good measure. In 1984 he forged $13,000 worth of money orders from a liquor store.

ZZZZ Best prospered by such methods. By 1985 Barry hit on a lush source of income, opening up a merchant's account at a local bank, thus allowing him to take credit card payments. Whenever he needed money, he added bogus charges to customers' credit card accounts and got cash from the bank. If a customer noticed and complained, Barry ranted about forgeries by crooked employees, made refunds and then simply took from other accounts.

Since Barry wanted to eventually float stock in his company, he set up another firm called Interstate Appraisal Services. This company was headed up by a weirdo friend who collected guns and had a special fondness for Hitler and SS jewelry. Interstate's only activities were confirming ZZZZ Best's job contracts, which allegedly included large orders from insurance companies to repair fire-and-water damage in large buildings.

The phony revenues convinced banks and investors to put money into ZZZZ Best. Those who got in early reaped wonderful returns, which were of course provided by the investments of those who hopped on the bandwagon a bit later.

As late as 1986 nobody had actually seen a site where any of ZZZZ Best's work had taken place. Barry blandly explained that such information was confidential. Finally, an auditor for Ernst & Whitney insisted he'd have to see a site. Barry and his aides thus leased office space and put up signs indicating that ZZZZ Best was doing work on the premises. The actual work was handled by an outside contractor who was paid a big bonus to do the work. The ploy worked.

Barry enjoyed a massive success. He was featured in fawning newspaper stories, indulged on the Oprah Winfrey show and just about ready to make a smash entrance on Wall Street. He lived in high style with all the trappings of a successful millionaire and then some. Fostering an apparent smoldering hatred for his parents, he put them on the ZZZZ Best payroll just so he could have the pleasure of threatening to dismiss them. Always a believer in the fix, he

coached a girls' softball team with which his girlfriend was involved and passed out up to $100 a piece to spectators to cheer for his team.

Barry negotiated with the securities firm of Rooney, Pace (a company that would soon be defunct) to take his company public, so that he could start shearing thousands of small investors who saw him as epitomizing the American Dream. In December 1986 ZZZZ Best stock made its debut on Wall Street, and Barry got a hero's welcome. By the following March the shares were worth $64 million and a month later $100 million. At its peak ZZZZ Best commanded a stock market valuation of $200 million without having any actual value. Eventually its assets would be auctioned off for $64,000.

Oddly, it was Barry's credit card frauds, not the nonexistent fire-and-water jobs revenues, that were exposed. Biographer Askt, a former reporter for the *Los Angeles Times* and the *Wall Street Journal,* had originally been conned by Minkow and wrote a flattering article in 1985, which helped establish the myth of Barry's acumen. On May 22, 1987, he revealed the credit card skulduggery in a story headlined: "Behind 'Whiz Kid' Is a Trail of False Credit-Card Billings." The next day ZZZZ Best stock fell 28 percent and continued plummeting straight to nowhere. In December 1988 Barry Minkow was convicted of 57 counts of fraud and sentenced to 25 years in prison. *Barron's,* the financial weekly, stated: "ZZZZ Best had earned a chapter in the long history of financial scams written by the 'Eighties."

When Barry was released with good behavior time off, he followed a hallowed trail of many con artists and hit the lecture circuit, warning folks not to be taken by the likes of him.

Mississippi bubble 18th-century fraud

Although the fraudulent Mississippi Bubble was developed in France and felt most there, the scourge of criminality it introduced into the New World left its mark for decades to come.

The Bubble was a swindle conceived by a resourceful and unscrupulous Scot named John Law, who founded the Mississippi Company in 1718 to extract the supposedly vast riches of French Louisiana and convinced the French government to back his scheme. With the aid of the French regent, Law soon had all of France caught up in a frenzy of speculation. Frenchmen invested their entire savings in the glorious company that was to yield enormous riches, and the national currency was inflated to further the bogus operation. In fact, a few who sold at the right time made 36 times their investment. Unfortunately, most held out for more. Not only was there no more, there was just plain nothing, except Law's lavish promises. Millions of Frenchmen were wiped out, and France itself tottered on the brink of ruin. Law, disguised as a beggar, barely escaped the country before being lynched.

But what of Louisiana itself? In its zeal to reap the wealth of this new land, the government had peopled it with a type of colonial not found anywhere else in the New World, at least not in comparable numbers. Historian Albert Phelps noted

John Law concocted the Mississippi Company, which left investors flat broke when the bubble burst.

The government went boldly to the task of ransacking the jails and hospitals. Disorderly soldiers, black sheep of distinguished families, paupers, prostitutes, political suspects, friendless strangers, unsophisticated peasants straying into Paris, all were kidnapped, herded, and shipped under guard to fill the emptiness of Louisiana. To those who would emigrate voluntarily the Company offered free land, free provisions, free transportation to the colony and from the colony to the situation of their grants, wealth, and eternal prosperity to them and their heirs forever; for the soil of Louisiana was said to bear two crops a year without cultivation, and the amiable savages were said so to adore the white man that they would not allow these superior beings to

After Law's wild caper of an "investment" in the New World, British promoters did the same with the South Sea Company, which also went bust. In the aftermath of the scams, "bubble cards" became collectibles for the outrageous schemes.

labor, and would themselves, voluntarily and for mere love, assume all the burden of that sordid necessity. . . . And now the full tide of the boom began to reach Louisiana. The emigrants, hurried out to fill seignorial rights, began to arrive in swarms and were dumped helplessly upon Dauphin Island. . . . Crowded, unsheltered and unfed, upon that barren sand heap, the wretched emigrants sickened, grew discontented, starved and died. . . .

The seed of the Mississippi Bubble planted in Louisiana, particularly in New Orleans, bloomed into a level of criminality that for the next 100 years was unmatched in any locale on the North American continent.

Mona Lisa swindle

Probably the most audacious—and still unsolved—art swindle ever perpetrated in this country was the sale of six copies of the famed *Mona Lisa* to American art collectors in 1911–12.

In 1908 an international art crook, using a variety of aliases, came to America and befriended a number of millionaire art collectors. He made separate secret agreements with six of them to sell each one the *Mona Lisa* if he could steal it from the Louvre Museum in Paris. Meanwhile, he had an expert art forger make six copies of the Da Vinci masterpiece and had the fakes stored in New York. Then in 1911 the genuine *Mona Lisa* was stolen by a Louvre employee named Vincent Peruggia, who kept the painting in his apartment for two years. To this day it is unclear whether the art crook had arranged this theft or whether it happened coincidentally while his own plans were afoot. In any event, Peruggia was arrested in Italy in 1913, when he attempted to sell the original for $95,000. In the meantime, the cunning art crook had sold each of the six millionaires a copy of the masterpiece, collecting a total of $2 million. At his trial in Florence, Peruggia based his defense on patriotism, claiming he merely wanted to return the painting to the land of its creator, and got off with a mild sentence of a year and 15 days in prison. The art crook who had swindled the six American collectors was never caught.

money-making machine   swindle

A racket that dates back to the 19th century is the "money-making machine," which is sold to a victim with a bizarre tale that it can duplicate a bill of currency so exactly that no expert can tell the real from the fake. The only thing that is different is the serial number, which the machine changes with a special "scrambling" device. However, this particular part of the process is very slow, and it takes the machine six hours to complete the entire procedure for duplicating a single bill. The swindler demonstrates the machine by placing a plain piece of white paper on a tray inside the machine and closing it up. He then places a genuine bill in another compartment of the machine and inserts it into the machine. Then he and the victim remain by the machine until the entire procedure is finished. After the six hours have elapsed and the victim is convinced that no trickery has taken place in the meantime, the genuine bill is removed and the tray in which the plain paper was inserted is opened. Inside is a new, apparently perfect bill. The victim is advised to take the bill to a bank and change it. He does and it is readily accepted. Naturally, the victim is now most eager to buy the machine. The swindler is at first loathe to sell it, but he does allow that he is impatient with the machine because it takes so long to produce a new bill. At the rate of only four in a 24-hour period, the machine will produce just $400 a day at most. Perhaps if he got a good offer. . . .

There are cases of the machine being sold or leased for as much as $50,000. The deal is closed as soon as the gullible buyer brings the money. The swindler leaves and the eager victim waits for his first new bill. It comes out right on schedule. Merrily, he puts in another plain sheet of paper. Six hours pass . . . out comes the same blank piece of paper. The victim tries it again but gets the same results. Finally, it dawns on him that he has been conned. By that time, of course, the crook has had a minimum of 12 hours to get away. The secret of the money machine is the tray in which the plain paper is loaded. As the swindler closes the tray, he presses a pin that drops a false top which holds a real bill previously concealed there. When the tray is opened six hours later, this is the bill that appears.

In the 19th century, money-making machines were quite the vogue both in America and England. As late as the 1930s, one American operator, "Count" Victor Lustig, is reputed to have made well over a million dollars with the scheme. Even today, police bunco squad experts estimate that the swindle is worked hundreds of times annually in this country. Bankers, stockbrokers and other professional men are the usual victims. Because of the advances made in photocopying techniques, authorities say, supposedly sophisticated individuals are now more likely to become victims.

See also: "COUNT" VICTOR LUSTIG.

Monk, Maria (1817–1849)   anti-Catholic hoaxer

One of the most infamous impostors of her time, a young girl named Maria Monk became a rallying point in the 1830s for American Protestants against what was regarded as the evils of popery, fanning emotions that were later exploited fully by the Know-Nothings. Maria arrived in New York in January 1836 in the company of a Canadian clergyman, the Rev. W. K. Hoyt, who told all who cared to listen that he had saved her from a life of sin in the famous Hotel

Dieu nunnery in Montreal. More likely, Rev. Hoyt had, as Maria was to admit in moments of candor, met her following a street corner solicitation.

The pair had with them the first draft of what they claimed was Maria's memoirs of her years as a novice and nun at the Hotel Dieu. When published under the title of *The Awful Disclosures of Maria Monk*, it was to say the least most shocking in its charges. According to Maria, the remote cellars of the nunnery were strewn with the bones of nuns who had resisted the advances of amorous priests. She said the sisters were called upon nightly by priests from a nearby monastery, who ventured through subterranean passages to conduct their amorous and abusive exercises. Maria had a tiny tot with her whose origin she traced to these nocturnal visits from the neighboring clergyman. A later investigation by Canadian authorities turned up rather convincing evidence that the gentleman who had fathered the child—though not in the nunnery—was a Montreal policeman.

Maria and Hoyt found as sponsors for the book the Society for the Diffusion of Christian Knowledge, especially its president, Dr. W. C. Brownlee, pastor of the Collegiate Dutch Reformed Church and himself the author of a militant anti-Catholic best-seller, *Popery*. Dr. Brownlee thought so highly of this supposed refugee from a nunnery that he took her into his own house under the care of his wife, leading in time to complaints by the Rev. Mr. Hoyt that Maria was a "damned jilting jade."

By that time Maria was worth fighting over; her book sold an astonishing 20,000 copies almost immediately. Anti-Papists could delight in a variety of chilling charges; for example, one nun's punishment for some minor infraction was to be stretched out on a mattress

> with her face upwards, and then bound with cords so that she could not move. In an instant, another bed [mattress] was thrown upon her. One of the priests, named Bonin, sprang like a fury first upon it with all his force. He was speedily followed by the nuns until there were as many on the bed as could find room, and all did what they could do, not only to smother, but to bruise her. Some stood and jumped upon the poor girl with their feet: and others, in different ways, seemed to seek how they might beat the breath out of her body. After the lapse of fifteen or twenty minutes, Father Bonin and the nuns ceased to trample on her and stepped from the bed. They then began to laugh. . . .

Maria assured her readers "speedy death can be no great clamity to those who lead the lives of nuns," and she offered to visit the Hotel Dieu "with some impartial ladies and gentlemen, that they may compare my account with the interior parts of the building, and if they do not find my description true, then discard me as an impostor."

Her challenge was not taken up, but in time even firm believers in Maria developed doubts. Maria's mother in Montreal denied that her wastrel daughter had ever entered a nunnery. Moreover, she insisted that she had been visited in 1835 by the Rev. Mr. Hoyt, who offered her $500 to say such were the facts. Eventually, Dr. Brownlee concluded he had been hoodwinked; not only did the girl's story appear contradictory but she had also run off in the meantime with his young clergyman protege, John J. L. Slocum. In 1836 Slocum brought suit against the publishers of the book for Maria' share of the royalties, all of which had been appropriated by the Society for the Diffusion of Christian Knowledge. The resulting trial clearly demonstrated Maria's story to be a hoax.

This, however, did not stop Maria. In August 1837 she turned up at the house of a Dr. Sleigh, a Philadelphia clergyman, and told a tale of being kidnapped by a group of priests and held captive in a nearby convent. She had escaped, she said, by promising one of the priests that she would marry him. The result of all this was, of course, a sequel to her first book, *Further Disclosures of Maria Monk*.

The second publication also did rather well, but Maria evidently saw little of the financial rewards. Slocum persuaded her to sign over to him a number of rights to both publications and he then decamped for London to arrange for their foreign publication.

Maria's life plunged downward. She became a habitue of the dives of the Bowery, a drunken hag before she was 30. She was confined in jail for picking a man's pocket in 1849 and died that year at the age of 32, although her true identity went unnoticed for some time. But *The Awful Disclosures of Maria Monk* has outlived her. To date, well over 300,000 copies have been sold.

Morse, Charles W. (c. 1860–1942) swindler

One of the most proficient American swindlers and confidence operators was Charles W. Morse, a Midwesterner who pulled off hundreds of crooked deals and bilked victims out of millions of dollars with every conceivable financial scam.

His greatest coup occurred two years after he was arrested, for the first and only time, in 1910 and sentenced to 15 years for tampering with the books of the Bank of North America. In 1912 President William Howard Taft granted him a full presidential pardon after government physicians reported he was dying of Bright's disease. To the amazement of the medical men, the cunning swindler thrived and lived for 30 years after his release. It was finally discovered he had faked the symptoms of the disease with a special concoction composed mainly of different soaps.

Murphy game   confidence swindle

Originally conceived during the 19th century as a sex swindle, the Murphy game has changed with the times. It was apparently named after an engaging rogue named Murphy who had the face of a pimp a man could trust. In the swindle the con artist would describe the delightful and talented young lady he had in store for the lascivious pigeon. Then the "pimp" would convince the pigeon to leave the money for the whore with him so that the woman would not be liable to a bust for accepting money in exchange for services rendered. The pigeon would be sent up the stairs of a building to a nonexistent apartment, and by the time he returned to the street, either puzzled or enraged, the Murphy man had disappeared.

Today, the original Murphy game is fast dying out but a substitute sex object has been found in the form of what is often called the "$75 Sony Trinitron." A pair of hustlers will start patronizing a bar, actually several in different parts of town, and one will make a big show of delivering to the other an expensive radio or other electronic item for something like a dime on the dollar. Then the boys will let slip that the seller has a contact at a wholesaler's warehouse and can get almost anything. But right now he has a big deal cooking. The inside man at the warehouse has found a way to cover up the disappearance of 10 Sony Trinitrons in perfect condition. The only thing is that he has to move them all at once. Naturally, all the barflies are interested when they hear the price for the $600 sets is only $75 apiece, or $750 for all 10.

Naturally, the deal falls in place and the suckers are taken to the warehouse in a rented van. The con artist collects all the money and disappears into the warehouse to make the payoff and have the sets brought out on the loading platform. The suckers in the van wait and wait and wait. What else can they do? Go into the warehouse and ask, "Where's that crooked employee of yours who's going to heist ten Trinitrons for us?" Meanwhile, the con artist has long since disappeared via another exit.

Musica, Philip (1877–1938) swindler

As a 20th century swindler, Philip Musica in many ways surpassed the great Charles Ponzi. He stole more money, and while Ponzi lasted only a matter of months, Musica lasted years. In his prime he was a pillar of society, a patron of the arts, a bosom friend of the great tenor Enrico Caruso and a charming, cultured gentleman. On Wall Street he was known as a financial genius, in the midst of the Morgans, Astors and Rockefellers. Not at all bad for a man who had previously been, among other things, an ex-convict, stool pigeon, swindler, forger, rumrunner, smuggler, bootlegger, gunrunner, hijacker and briber. With a record like that, it might seem odd that Musica was able to make *Who's Who in America*, but then again, that illustrious publication is better known for judging people for what they appear to be rather than what they are.

Musica had qualified for *Who's Who* under one of his other identities (he used several during a long criminal career).

It was his final and greatest identity, that of F. Donald Coster, about whom the book of the nation's notables declared:

> COSTER, Frank Donald, corpn. official; b. Washington, D.C., May 12, 1884; s. Frank Donald and Marie (Girard) C.; PhD., U. of Heidelberg, 1909, M.D., 1911; m. Carol Jenkins Schiefflin, of Jamaica, L.I., N.Y., May 1, 1921. Practicing physician, N.Y. City, 1912–14; pres. Girard & Co., Inc. (succession to Girard Chem. Co.), 1914–26; pres. McKesson & Robbins, drug mfrs., since 1926; also pres. McKesson & Robbins, Ltd.; dir. Bridgeport City Trust Co., Fairfield (Conn.) Trust Co. Methodist. Clubs: New York Yacht, Bankers, Lotos, Advertising (New York); University, Black Rock Yacht (Bridgeport); Brooklawn Country. Home: Fairfield, Conn. Office: McKesson & Robbins, Inc., Bridgeport, Conn.

In 1883 six-year-old Philip Musica came to America from Italy with his parents, and by the time he was in his early twenties, he had become the most Americanized of all the children as well as the active head of the family. He kept telling Papa Antonio that things were different here than in the old country and that there were different standards of ethics. Quickly, he involved his father and a number of brothers and sisters in dishonest schemes, starting off with an imported cheese business made all the more lucrative by bribing customhouse weighers. Soon, the Musicas could afford a mansion in the fashionable Bay Ridge section of Brooklyn, complete with landscaped grounds, horses, stables and a carriage house. In 1909, however, the roof fell in on Musica's financial empire. Several customhouse weighers confessed to taking bribes and young Musica was sentenced to a year in prison. He served only a few months, however, before winning a presidential pardon, apparently because he came across as somewhat gallant, shielding his father from a jail term by accepting all the blame himself.

Once freed, Musica moved immediately into a new line of business, that of importing human hair from Italy to supply the needs of American females. By 1913 he had established a thriving business and was once more a leader in Italian-American social and financial circles. Then the William J. Burns Detective Agency dug up evidence that Musica had swindled 22 banks out of $1 million by taking loans on hair shipments based on phony invoices. When the cases of supposedly long hair were opened, they were found to contain tissue paper and short hair, worth no more than $1 a box and known as trash in the field.

The entire Musica family was captured in New Orleans shortly after boarding a liner for Honduras. One of Musica's sisters tried to throw overboard $18,000 she had stashed in her girdle. Musica had $80,000 in cash and $250,000 in other money instruments on him. Again, he accepted full blame for the swindle. He was lodged in the Tombs Prisons in New York City because he promised to make full restitution and said that from there he could better help authorities round up his assets. While in prison, Musica endeared himself to a succession of prosecutors by becoming a professional stool pigeon who spied on other prisoners. It paid off. In 1918 these grateful officials got him a suspended sentence for the hair fraud.

That was the last seen of Philip Musica until he emerged from his final cover, F. Donald Coster, in 1938. Musica became "William Johnson," an "investigator" for the district attorney's office, a career that was cut short when he was indicted for perjury in a murder trial in which he had testified against two men. William Johnson promptly disappeared.

He was replaced by "Frank Costa," a copartner in a firm called the Adelphi Pharmaceutical Manufacturing Co., which was entitled to 5,000 gallons of alcohol a month during Prohibition for production of its hair tonics and the like. The innovative Mr. Costa so scented and colored Adelphi's products that running them through a simple still would return them to high-proof straight alcohol. Cut with water and spiked with the proper coloring and flavoring and presto— "great stuff right off the boat." Eventually, Adelphi's real business was discovered by revenue agents and one of the owners was caught, but not Costa, who disappeared.

Musica reemerged as F. Donald Coster, president of Girard and Co., and obtained a new alcohol license. By this time Papa Musica was dead and Philip was the acknowledged leader of the family. Because he was still being hunted on the perjury charge, Philip severed all ties with his Musica past. Girard was the new family name he gave to Mama Musica and her daughters— save for one, who, in Philip's words, "disgraced our whole family by running off and marrying a gardener." Girard and Co. also gained three new officials, "George Vernard," "George Dietrich" and "Robert Dietrich"—really Musica's three brothers, Arthur, George and Robert.

By 1925 F. Donald Coster had become a man of high society, more than 13 years after Philip Musica had cavorted about so flashily. Of course, "Doctor Coster" was nothing like Philip Musica. He was starting to gray on top and in his trim mustache, and he was American-born and a Methodist now, not Italian and a Catholic.

In 1926 he moved to the pinnacle of the Wall Street heap by buying the 93-year-old drug firm of McKesson and Robbins. He did so after obtaining a loan against Girard and Co., an easy matter since its books, thanks to bootlegging activities, were in excellent shape. Once in control of McKesson and Robbins, Coster swung a stock flotation and money flowed in. A large portion of this new money was used to establish a Canadian "crude drug" department. It was Coster's master swindle. George Vernard became fiscal agent and representative in charge of the department, which proved to be the world's easiest job. The Canadian crude drug department consisted of large inventories of drugs in half-a-dozen warehouses. But there were no drugs and no warehouses in Canada. There was just George Vernard—and he wasn't even Vernard. Unwittingly, through its new owner the reputable McKesson and Robbins "bought" drugs from phantom companies and shelled out hard cash, which wound up in the pockets of F. Donald Coster. Receipts, inventories, invoices, bills of lading and the like from the crude drug department carried the names of Coster, Vernard and Dietrich, and no questions were asked.

The Depression of 1929 hit McKesson and Robbins as hard as most companies but the firm continued to look robust because of its inventories of crude drugs, which rose in value by several million dollars. Coster became known as the wizard of the drug field. "No one can match Coster when it comes to crude drugs," honest directors of McKesson told one another.

Up in Fairfield, Conn., Coster relaxed in the splendor of his 16-room mansion and aboard his 135-foot oceangoing yacht. He contributed lavishly to charity and even established a free heart clinic in Bridgeport, Conn. out of his own money. Why not, there was plenty more where that had come from. But beneath the facade of luxurious tranquility, Coster was troubled. Business was crashing downward and more and more he had to cover up his lootings with forgeries. By 1935 he was paying $25,000 a year in blackmail money to those who knew him as Philip Musica and Frank Costa. Then there were reports that he used McKesson facilities to smuggle guns and munitions to Franco Spain. Franco received rifles packed in cases labeled, "Milk of Magnesia." However, there were indications that Coster was rather impartial. He appeared to be selling to the Loyalists as well, although there were also reports that the Franco forces were informed—for a price—where the Loyalists' shipments were going so that they could seize them, allowing Coster to collect twice.

Coster's undoing came from two quarters. First, he took to adulterating his own drug products, and in September 1938, agents of the Pure Food and Drug Administration seized some of the firm's adulterated quinine in New Jersey and New York. Meanwhile, the business recession of 1937 had battered the firm and Julian F. Thompson, a Wall Street figure whom Coster had hired as the window-dressing treasurer (George Dietrich was assistant treasurer and handled all illegal matters), demanded that Coster reduce the crude drug inventories to give the company more cash assets. Coster stalled. He couldn't produce something out of nothing. After a year of stalling, Thompson launched a quiet investigation of his own and found that an alleged $21 million worth of inventories carried no insurance. Checking further, he discovered they weren't insured because they didn't exist.

Thompson took his findings to the New York Stock Exchange and early in December 1938 all trading in the firm's stock was halted. Each of McKesson's 82 vice presidents shuddered, but none more than George Vernard and George and Robert Dietrich. The master swindler remained calm as story after story about him hit the newspapers. Inevitably, tips about Coster came in and authorities took a deep interest in his past. On December 14 Coster was fingerprinted in his home. "This is a pesty business," he grumbled.

Within 24 hours newspapers revealed the life story of Philip Musica, a long-vanished swindler and perjurer. On December 16 government agents arrived at his house to place him under arrest, but he had shot himself to death in the bathroom.

Musica left two notes, one to his wife pleading for her forgiveness and the other, eight pages long, trying to rationalize his underhanded dealings.

McKesson, he insisted, would have gone into receivership in 1930 and 1932 had he not bolstered its paper profits. He asserted all the alleged "lost" millions were merely fictional "profits to save the company . . . what is missing is the alleged profits plus expenses and blackmail money paid to maintain it. . . ."

"As God is my judge," he concluded, "I am the victim of Wall Street plunder and blackmail in a struggle for honest existence. Merciful God bring the truth to light! F. D. Coster."

For their part in the swindle, Musica's three brothers got off with mere three-year sentences, possibly because not all of Coster's claims were hogwash. True, he had indeed siphoned off $8 million or $10 million for his own use, but the rest of the "loot" probably never existed, being mere figure juggling to keep up the firm's profit margins. The conventional wisdom on Wall Street was that without Coster's shady dealings McKesson and Robbins would have been forced into bankruptcy years earlier and the stockholders wiped out. Instead, the firm weathered the storm and the stockholders had been both robbed and saved.

New York Lottery swindle

One of the earliest lottery swindles in America was unearthed in New York in 1818, when it was found that lottery operators had arranged for certain numbers to win in return for kickbacks from the prearranged winners.

The lottery, much of whose proceeds were allegedly slated for the unfortunate, was exposed by Charles Baldwin, the editor of the *New York Republican Chro-nicle,* who wrote:

> *It is a fact that in this city there is SWIN-DLING in the management. A certain gentle-man in town received intimation that a number named would be drawn on Friday last and it was drawn that day! This number was insured high in several different places. A sim-ilar thing had happened once before in this same lottery; and on examination of the man-agers' files the number appeared soiled as if it had been in the pocket several days. . . .*

Baldwin was sued for libel by several of the operators and a select committee was appointed to look into the matter. What they found was that one of the complainants, John H. Sickles, was a secret supplier of the lottery forms and had provided certain politi-cians with the winning numbers in advance. By using political figures in the scheme, Sick-les and others assured that the lottery would enjoy general governmental approval and support. Based on these findings, Baldwin was acquitted and became famous as the first of New York's journalistic muckrakers.

Norfleet manhunt

In 1919, while stopping at a Dallas hotel, a Texas rancher named Frank Norfleet was taken by a group of confidence men. Using a variation of the "big store" racket, they roped Norfleet in by letting him "find" the lost wallet of an obviously rich man. When Norfleet returned the wallet, he was offered a $100 reward, which he refused. The wealthy man, a supposed speculator on the Dallas Cotton Exchange, then said that he would invest the money for him and let him have the winnings. Soon, Norfleet's "win-nings" totaled $73,000. However, it developed he had to post some $45,000 as security before he could get his money. Norfleet was "put on the send," i.e., sent back home to empty his savings account and put a mortgage on his ranch. He returned with the money and gave it to the five crooks, who soon decamped with it.

Norfleet so far had behaved like the ideal sucker, but he didn't continue to. Vowing vengeance, he went after the gang. After raising another $30,000, he spent the next four years on a private manhunt, running down the confidence men one by one. His prize catch was the gang's leader, Joe Furey, a legendary swindler. In Denver, while on the trail of another of the crooks, W. B. Spencer, Norfleet infiltrated a phony stock exchange operation and gathered evidence that led to the arrest and conviction of three dozen con

men. But his quarry was not among them. He later caught up with Spencer in Salt Lake City. When caught, Spencer complained bitterly, "None of us had a minute's peace since you got on our trail."

Also caught in the Norfleet net were two lawmen who provided protection for confidence operators. In all, Norfleet covered 40,000 miles and spent $30,000 in his four-year vengeance hunt. The Texas legislature took note of the plucky rancher's tenacity and daring and appropriated a small amount of expense money for him, but the action was ruled illegal. The matter was taken under advisement in 1923 by the governor and the legislature, seeking to find some way to reimburse Norfleet. In 1960, at the age of 95, Frank Norfleet said whimsically, "Far as I know, the thing is still 'under advisement.'"

Ohio Gang   Harding Administration grafters

Without doubt, the so-called Ohio Gang, a group of political cronies from Ohio who put Warren G. Harding in politics and eventually in the White House, took more from the public coffers in their two-year and five-month stay in Washington than any other corrupt group in American history. Including Teapot Dome, their total depredations have been estimated to total as much as $300 million, or five to 10 times what the Tweed Ring made off with.

The unofficial head of the Ohio Gang was President Harding's attorney general Harry M. Daugherty, who had guided Harding's political career from 1900 until his triumphant arrival in Washington in 1921. The Ohio Gang, as the group was soon labeled, let it be known that they had come to Washington for only one reason, to make money. A price tag was placed on everything they controlled. Judgeships, lucrative Prohibition-agent jobs, public lands and oil reserves were all up for sale. Bribes and payoffs were made at the House on 16th Street. The Little Green House on H Street featured poker games, bathtub gin and women to convince the dubious to join the graft game.

Daugherty and his Ohio henchman, Jess Smith, are believed to have a hand in every payment of graft, and there is little doubt that Harding knew much and suspected more. "My God," he told William Allen White, "this is a hell of a job. I have no trouble with my enemies. I can take care of them all right. But my damn friends, White, they're the ones that keep me walking the floor nights."

Harding didn't really spend much time walking the floors; he sat in on the poker games. Actually, the president didn't know how to control Daugherty and was a little afraid of him. Daugherty knew of Harding's illegitimate child and he had also advanced him $100,000, which he dropped in the stock market. As the stocks dipped, Daugherty's hold on Harding tightened.

The Ohio Gang's plundering was so massive that scandals started to break even before Harding died in 1923. There were rumors of frauds in the Veterans Bureau running as high as $200 million. Eventually,

Colonel Charles R. Forbes was sent to prison for taking kickbacks from contractors building veterans hospitals. Jess Smith, the Ohio Gang's bagman, killed himself and the newspapers speculated whether it was because of pangs of conscience or whether he had been murdered to ensure his silence. Albert B. Fall, Harding's secretary of the interior, served his time for his part in the Teapot Dome Scandal along with oil man Harry Sinclair. Harry Daugherty narrowly escaped conviction in a bribery complicated case involving the alien property custodian. In the final analysis, the Ohio Gang could not have functioned if Harding had been a strong president, but Daugherty probably would not have promoted him if he had possessed that potential. As Sen. Frank Brandegee of Connecticut said at the time of his nomination, Harding was "no world-beater but he is the best of the second-raters."

panel house   brothel specializing in robbing customers

The panel house, a bordello designed more for robbery than for prostitution, may not have been an American invention, but its operation was certainly raised to a fine art in this country. In these dens, sliding panels were installed in doors and walls so that a prostitute's customer could be robbed while he was otherwise occupied. A chair for the customer's clothing would be placed right near a panel. If the man deposited his clothes elsewhere, a hooked pole was used to retrieve them. One advantage of the operation was that the prostitute normally could not be charged with robbery, since she clearly had not done the robbing.

A New York and Philadelphia madam named Moll Hodges, who operated during the 1850s and 1860s, is generally credited with becoming the first panel house operator. In 1865 Lizzie Clifford, a former employee of Moll Hodges in New York, opened a panel house in Chicago, and by 1890 there were an estimated 200 such establishments in that city. A police report

A 19th-century print warns readers to beware of panel houses.

in 1896 calculated the amount of money stolen in Chicago panel houses at $1.5 million a year. For several years complaints of such robberies came in at the rate of 50 to 100 every 24 hours. The establishments were finally eliminated around 1900 thanks to the efforts of a single Chicago police detective, Clifton Wooldridge, a colorful and resourceful character who came up with the idea of arresting the property owners who rented buildings to the panel houses operators. No property owner appears to have been imprisoned, but as police bore down on them, the practice came to a quick end.

See also: CREEP JOINT.

pedigreed dog swindle

A short con, or quick hustle, the pedigreed dog swindle is less important for its own sake than it is for the more lucrative swindles it fathered.

The 19th century victim of such a caper was often a bartender, who was approached by a strange customer with a dog, most often a mongrel terrier. The customer would explain that the dog was a prize winner and produce some impressive-looking papers to prove the point. "Look," he might say, "this dog is really valuable and I have an important meeting with some bankers and I can't take him with me. I'll give you ten dollars to watch him for a couple of hours."

Naturally, the bartender would agree. After the dog owner left with a final word about how valuable the dog was, another customer would walk in. He would pretend to be very impressed by the dog, declaring he really liked the animal and that his kids would be wild about it. After this buildup he would offer the bartender $50 for the animal. The bartender would explain the dog was not his, but the man would only grow more insistent, raising the offer to $100. Patiently, the bartender would refuse and keep refusing as the ante was raised. Finally, the customer would say, "Listen, I'll stop conning you. I know my dog flesh. That's a valuable dog. If you'll sell it, I'll go to five hundred dollars."

By now the bartender would be in agony, turning down such an offer. The customer would then say, "Look, I'm from out of town. If you can swing a deal for me for the dog, I'll give you the five hundred, but I have to catch a train in an hour and I'll stop back just before I have to leave."

A half an hour later the dog's owner would reappear, looking downcast, and order a drink. The bartender would serve him, asking if anything was wrong. Sorrowfully nodding, the dog owner would explain that his business deal had fallen through. "I was really counting on that deal, now I don't know what I'll do."

The bartender, trying to curb his enthusiasm, might then offer to help the poor dog owner. He had taken a liking, he would explain, and was willing to pay $100 for it. The dog owner wouldn't consider it, again pointing out how valuable the animal was. The bartender would have to raise the bid to $300 before the owner would agree to part with the valuable animal, but only with the proviso that he could buy the dog back the following month for $400 if he solved his financial problems. That detail wouldn't worry the bartender. He could always say the dog had been trampled by a horse.

The bartender would take the money from the register and exchange it for the mutt. Now, with the original owner gone, he only had to wait for the return of the prospective buyer to realize a $200 profit. Of course, this proved to be a wait considerably longer than the dog's life span.

The pedigreed dog swindle was a favorite with the short con operators for decades, and eventually, it evolved into a bigger con, with the profits increasing 10- to 100-fold. The victim changed from a bartender to a greedy banker or businessman, and instead of selling a pedigreed dog, the con man would offer a gold mine or some oil stock, invariably worthless, which, for some reason, he could no longer keep.

Peters, Frederick Emerson (1885–1959)
check passer

Probably the most prolific passer of bad checks in American history, Frederick Emerson Peters, starting at age 17, cashed thousands of bad checks all over the United States, using hundreds of different names. One of his favorite ploys was to pose as the son or some other relative of a well-known figure, especially Theodore Roosevelt, whose appearance he could somewhat emulate. He would engage a shopkeeper in conversation, casually let drop his identity and then make a purchase with a check for a somewhat larger amount. Few small shopkeepers, impressed by having a celebrity as a customer, would turn him down; in fact, any number of them would eventually frame the bad check and proudly recall the time they "got took by Teddy Roosevelt's kid."

Asked once why he continued to write bad checks after a number of convictions, Peters shrugged and said it was so easy that it would take the "rock-like willpower of the Sphinx to resist such temptation." He stated his record achievement was to pass 30 worthless checks in one day in a small Indiana town whose name he could no longer remember. Much of his life was spent behind bars; during those tours he often helped establish prison libraries. One day while he was making his check-passing rounds in New Haven, Conn., he suffered a fatal stroke; Peters was 74 years old at the time. He was given a pauper's funeral, although it was observed that with some advanced warning he could have given the undertaker a handsome check.

See also: CHECK PASSING.

pigeon drop   con game

Probably the most-practiced confidence game of all time, the so-called pigeon drop comes in many varieties but all follow a basic pattern. Con man number one finds a wallet, purse, attache case or even a paper bag apparently filled with money. An unsuspecting victim standing nearby witnesses the discovery. Just then con man number two appears and claims he is also entitled to a share of the booty as much as the other two. If it hasn't occurred to the victim as yet, he now realizes he ought to share in the proceeds. An argument ensues about whether they should divide the money immediately or first check to find out if it is stolen. Con man number one says his "boss" has police connections and can check. This is done by phone and the report comes back that the money was probably dropped by some big gambler or tax evader and that the three should share it. The "boss" offers to hold the money until all three can produce a substantial amount of their own money to demonstrate that they are acting in good faith and are responsible enough to keep the secret. Con man number two, apparently determined not to be cut out of the deal, produces a large sum of money on the spot to prove his reliability. Con man number one and the victim then hurry off to get their money. When the victim returns and hands over his share, it is the last he sees of the two con men or the "boss."

While the plot appears almost incredible, it must be remembered that the acting is high powered; in particular, the bickering bet-

143

ween the two con men makes the victim fearful he will be "left out" unless he abides by all the conditions of the agreement. The reliability of the employer—in some scams he is alleged to be a police detective—is the convincer. The money involved is always so great that the victim wants to believe. In a 1979 incident in the Bronx, New York City, two sisters in their sixties leaped to their deaths in a joint suicide after realizing they had been swindled out of their life savings of $17,000 by a version of the pigeon drop.

Ponzi, Charles (1877–1949) swindler

Among the greatest swindlers ever to prey on the American public was Charles Ponzi—ex-dishwasher, ex-forger, ex-alien smuggler—who came to America from his native Italy in 1899. And for a time, he was also the most-beloved, especially among those who got in early on his fantastic scheme and actually made money. Once when Ponzi was being hauled before an official hearing to explain his money-trading operations, he was cheered by crowds in front of the State House in Boston. A voice from the crowd called out, "You're the greatest Italian of them all!"

"No, no," Ponzi responded, "Columbus and Marconi. Columbus discovered America. Marconi discovered the wireless."

"Yes, but you discovered money!"

That last claim was to prove debatable indeed. Not that Charles Ponzi didn't have money-making acumen. He discovered he could buy up international postal-union reply coupons at depressed prices in some foreign countries and sell them in the United States at a profit of up to 50 percent. It was, in fact, a classic get-rich-slowly operation, and as such, it bored Ponzi. So he figured out a better gimmick. He simply told everyone how he was making the money and said he needed a lot of capital to make a lot of money. For the use of their funds, he offered investors a 50 percent profit in three months. It was an offer they couldn't refuse, and the funds just came rolling into Ponzi's Boston office. In a short time, he had to open offices in neighboring states.

When Ponzi actually started paying out interest, a deluge followed. On one monumental day in 1920, Ponzi's offices took in an incredible $2 million from America's newest gamblers, the little people who squeezed money out of bank accounts, mattresses, piggy banks and cookie jars. There were days when a Ponzi office looked like a hurricane had hit it. Incoming cash had to be stuffed in closets, desk drawers and even in wastebaskets. Of course, the more that came in, the more Ponzi paid out. In that sense, Ponzi was merely following the example of the legendary Billy "520 percent" Miller who had pulled the same caper in Brooklyn, New York some two decades earlier.

As long as investors kept pouring in new funds, Ponzi could continue to pay the interest on the old funds. After about six months the newspapers started to investigate his operation, but he was able to buy more time by hitting them with huge lawsuits. Meanwhile, Ponzi became a great dandy. His wardrobe consisted of 200 suits; he sported more than two dozen diamond stickpins; and he owned an elegant mansion. But Ponzi's bubble had to burst. The *Boston Post* dug up his past record, which showed he had spent time in prison in Montreal for forgery and in Atlanta for smuggling aliens. It was enough to make large numbers of eager investors hesitate to put in more money; the moment that happened, Ponzi's fragile scheme col-

In the 1920's Ponzi made, many said, far greater discoveries than Columbus or Marconi. He discovered money.

lapsed, since it required an unending flow of cash. His books, such as they were, showed a deficit of somewhere between $5 and $10 million, or perhaps even more. No one ever knew for sure.

Ponzi went to federal prison for four years for using the mails to defraud and was then sentenced to seven to nine years in Massachusetts for theft. When he emerged from prison in 1934, he was sent back to Italy. At this point the picture of Ponzi blurs. Some accounts, apparently not all fanciful, have him furnishing his "financial genius" to the Mussolini regime. If he did, the Fascists obviously did not profit from the experience, for within a few years Ponzi had to leave the country. He ended up in Rio de Janeiro, working for an Italian company until 1939, when the war put him out of work. Ponzi's last years were filled with extreme privation. He became partially blind and paralyzed and ended up in the charity ward of a Brazilian hospital, where he died in January 1949.

pyramid schemes   confidence racket
Among the oldest con games, pyramid rackets have been used to swindle millions of dollars annually, employing everything from dollar bills in chain letters to more sophisticated schemes that sell franchises to unsuspecting individuals who then must sell more franchises to other victims and so on. In theory, pyramid schemes can continue on indefinitely, but in reality, the bubble eventually collapses from the sheer weight of the numbers involved.

A typical operation was the pyramid financial scheme that swept California in the late 1970s, leaving a trail of broken families and wrecked friendships. In the scheme each player paid an entry fee of $1,000. Then that player was required to bring in two new players, who contributed $1,000 apiece. Half of this amount, or $500, went to the top of the pyramid while the remaining $500 from each of the two newer players went to the player who recruited them. Thus, the first player got his money back and then waited to move up another rung on the pyramid as each of the second two players recruited two more players so that they could recover their original $1,000 investment. As each such step on the pyramid was mounted, the initial player moved from the number 16 rung, to the number eight rung, to the number four rung, to the number two rung and finally, to number one rung. Upon reaching number one or top rung, the player received the money that accumulated at the top for him, $16,000.

While it might seem simple for each player in a pyramid scheme to induce two others to join, the mathematics soon become astronomical. In essence, each player on the number 16 rung is responsible for the creation of two new pyramids and this progression of twos keeps getting bigger and bigger, for there are 16 players on the bottom rung, and it takes 32 players to get them to advance to the next rung. Each of these 32 players must now recruit two players, or a total of 64. The 64 then must recruit a total of 128. The total jumps to 256, at which point the first set of 16 players have reached the top of their pyramids. However, for the next set of players who started on the 16 rung, the total of new recruits needed jumps to 512, and for the next group the number required is 1,024.

It is thus apparent why, by June 1980, the mass pyramid craze in California collapsed. Even that state ran dry of enough gullible people to keep the scheme going. A member of the state attorney general's office reported that a number of operators had been arrested attempting to start new pyramids in New York, Florida and Canada. Ironically, such pyramid rackets even attract sophisticated victims who fully understand that a scheme must eventually collapse. No matter what the actual stage of recruitment is, they are told they are "getting in at the start, so there's no way you can lose."

Ragen, James M. (1881–1946) gambling czar and murder victim

From 1940 to 1946 James M. Ragen was the most powerful man in gambling in America, having taken control of the horse-racing wire business following the imprisonment of Moe Annenberg. Ragen waged war with the Chicago syndicate and held his own for a time until he became the victim of a mob execution.

Like many other members of the Chicago underworld in the early years of the 20th century, Ragen got his start as a circulation slugger for the *Chicago Tribune* during the period of the great newspaper wars, when Max Annenberg, Moe's older brother, was circulation manager. Among Ragen's coworkers were such criminals as Dion O'Banion, Frankie and Vince McErlane, Walter Stevens, Mossy Enright and Tommy Maloy—part of the roster of killers who kept the city of Chicago bloody for decades thereafter. Ragen managed to outlive most of his fellow sluggers and future gang bosses while maintaining a certain independence from the Capone mob.

When Moe Annenberg went to prison in 1940, the federal government was sure that the dismantling of his Nation-Wide News Service would be a crippling blow to illegal race horse betting throughout the country. But Ragen quickly moved in to fill the void. His Continental Press Service became the dominant racing wire in the nation, providing the latest results from scores of tracks directly to thousands of bookie joints. The Chicago mob had never tried to move in on Annenberg, perhaps because he was considered too powerful or because of some secret accommodation, but it soon informed Ragen they were dealing themselves in.

Ragen had survived the Chicago scene too long to just give up his business, even when he was offered a fine price to sell out. He told acquaintances he knew the ways of the mob, that even if he sold, he would not be permitted to live to enjoy his profits. Under Bugsy Siegel the mob set up Trans-American Publishing and News Service and forcibly gained control of the California market, supplying bookies with the necessary racing information for $100 a day. Ragen, however, held on to the rest of the country, and it soon became apparent that the only way to take over his empire was to kill him. In June 1946 he was hit by a fusillade of bullets from a passing car, but he survived and was rushed to a hospital.

From his hospital bed Ragen accused the mob of trying to eliminate him in order to assume control of his racing wire. His accusations proved an embarrassment to the mob. In September he died, apparently of his wounds. An autopsy later revealed he had been poisoned by mercury. The mob obviously had found a way to penetrate Ragen's around-the-clock police protection, and his death was listed as a gangland slaying. Several leaders of the mob were questioned, especially Jake Guzik, but nothing much developed from the investigation.

Ragen's murder became just another digit added to the column of unsolved gangland killings, which, during a period of a little over three decades, totaled more than 970.

See also: MOSES L. ANNENBERG.

Reading Game famous illegal crap game

The biggest crap game in the history of gambling on the East Coast, and perhaps in the country, was the so-called Reading Game, operating out of Philadelphia from 1959 to 1962, when the Federal Bureau of Investigation finally smothered it.

Each night big gamblers from all over the East would gather at a restaurant in the heart of Philadelphia. There, they would be picked up by "luggers" and driven 50 miles to Reading, where a million dollar dice game was played on three high-rolling "California tables."

A reformed hood later commented: "Everybody made a buck on that game. They rented their limousines from a funeral director, because they only used them from ten at night until seven in the morning." He indicated how much freedom organized crime had in Philadelphia at the time, stating: "They even had a cop out in front of the restaurant—he'd blow a whistle like a hotel doorman to signal a limo when he had a full load coming in for the game. It looked like opening night on Broadway. The cops never touched them."

Reavis, James Addison (?–1908) swindler and baron of Arizona

A former St. Louis streetcar conductor, James Addison Reavis went on to become the most colossal swindler-forger in American history, laying claim in 1881, as baron de Arizonaca and caballero de los Colorados, to 10.8 million acres of the Arizona Territory, including all of its largest city, Phoenix. As such, his claims were recognized as legitimate for over a decade, and he would point out to railroad executives, mine owners and big ranchers that they were trespassing on his property. However, he was willing to discuss rents. The tab for the Southern Pacific's right-of-way was set at $50,000 annually.

The origin and intricacies of Reavis' amazing fraud were never fully learned because he steadfastly refused to make a confession. However, it was revealed that as a youth in the Confederate Army, he had developed a knack for forging his commanding officers' signatures. After the Civil War, while working as a streetcar conductor in St. Louis, he used his skillful writing ability to forge a fraudulent real estate document that earned him a large sum. He moved west before he could be caught.

In Santa Fe Reavis got a clerical job in the records division of a special governmental commission that handled claims on property annexed by this country following the Mexican War. A treaty settlement required the United States to honor all legitimate claims of Spaniards and Mexicans and return to them the title of their lands. It was in this office that Reavis laid the groundwork for his incredible claim. He learned the pure Spanish used on ancient documents and eventually produced one that indicated he was the undisputed owner of a grant given by the Spanish Crown in 1758 to a nobleman, Miguel Silva de Peralta de la Cordoba, for military services rendered in the New World. In addition, Reavis presented himself as the husband of the last of the mythical Peraltas, a young woman he found working as a serving girl on a California ranch. The girl became convinced she really was a long-lost Peralta.

Government experts and others studied Reavis' documents, which he had forged, and checked them against historical records, which he had doctored over a five-year period, in Madrid, Seville and Mexico City. They concluded his claims were valid. As a result, until he was exposed in 1894, Reavis collected some $10 million in rent from hundreds of companies and thousands of families.

Finally, two tiny errors he had made were discovered. Reavis had used old inks and had found paper that appeared to be old, but a printer who was suspicious of him discovered that the watermark on the paper had not been designed until 1878. In addition, part of Reavis' hoax rested on proof that a pair of Peralta twins had been born long ago near San Bernardino, Calif. Their births were listed in the birth register at the Mission of San Salvador. Somehow Reavis had removed an entire page from the register and forged a substitute that included the names of the twins in place of the names of two other babies. What Reavis did not know was that births were also recorded each day in a separate volume that was kept hidden. Instead of the names of the twins, the secret volume listed two different names.

Reavis fought the case against him with the great wealth he had accumulated, but in the end, he was convicted and went to prison for six years. When he came out, he was a broken man, with no money left from his years of lavish living. He returned to Phoenix, once the scene of his great criminal triumph, as a vagrant. Until his death in 1908, he spent most of his time in the library reading old newspaper accounts of himself during his period of grandeur.

Remus, George (1874–1952) murderer

Often cited as one of the most farcical murder trials in American history, the conviction of George Remus for the murder of his wife, Imogene, in Cincinnati on October 6, 1927 should have been a cut-and-dried affair.

When Remus finished a prison term in the federal penitentiary at Atlanta for bootlegging, he returned home convinced his wife had been unfaithful during his years behind bars. So he shot her. As a lawyer, albeit disbarred, Remus insisted on his right to handle his own defense and won the judge's agreement despite his plea of not guilty on the basis of his own insanity.

While the prosecution paraded alienists to the stand to testify to Remus' sanity, the defendant set about proving, by his own behavior and by the testimony of his witnesses, that he was insane. The jurors were treated to the spectacle of a defendant getting his witnesses to say he was deranged and dangerous. In the end, they were convinced by his performance, taking only 19 minutes to bring in an acquittal by reason of insanity. The prosecution was not caught off guard by the verdict, however, moving quickly to get the judge to commit Remus to a state asylum on the basis of his witnesses' testimony that he was dangerously insane.

The Remus case was to have one more astonishing twist. Just four months later, Remus stood before the Ohio Court of Appeals, proved he was totally sane and walked out a free man.

riverboat gamblers

During the heyday of the riverboat on American waterways in the mid-19th century, it was estimated there were between 2,000 and 2,500 riverboat gamblers plying their trade. The first of the breed had appeared along the Mississippi near the beginning of the century. Far from the courtly gentlemen of Hollywood legend, they were tough, slovenly dressed characters who serviced the rugged flatboat sailors of the day both ashore and afloat. These gamblers were murderous types who would often kill those they couldn't cheat.

When the first steam packets appeared on the river to cater to higher strata of society, professional gamblers were not wanted and were usually heaved over the side or stranded on some lonely shore or sandbar. Slowly, the boat operators began to realize that during a long card session, players tended to spend huge sums on liquid refreshments. During one poker game in 1858 the liquor tab for the players came to $791.50. Soon, the gamblers, now often done up in exquisite finery, were welcomed with great respect and many owner-captains would not cast off until they were sure there was one aboard.

There is little doubt that some gamblers paid off captains for the privilege of being allowed to practice their art. Naturally, such overhead required most card sharks to ensure that winning wasn't left to mere luck or skill. One contemporary expert on the subject estimated that of the 2,000-odd gamblers, he could think of only four who were honest all the time.

Tom Ellison, a gambler turned honest in his later years, said:

I've seen fellows pick every card in a pack, and call it without missing once. I've seen them shuffle them one for one all through from top to bottom, so that they were in the same position after a dozen shuffles that they were in at first. They'd just flutter them up like a flock of quail and get the aces, kings, queens, jacks and tens all together as easy as pie. A sucker had no more chance against those fellows than a snowball in a red-hot oven. They were good fellows, free with their money as water, after scheming to bust their heads to get it. A hundred didn't bother them any more than a chew of tobacco would you.

Ellison told of a planter who lost

his whole tobacco crop in one night and get up and never mind it particularly. Many a time I've seen a game player just skin off his watch and ring and studs and play them in. Men often lost their goods playing in their way bills. I've seen them betting a bale of cotton at a crack, and it wasn't at all uncommon to hear an old planter betting off his Negroes on a good hand. Every man who ever ran on the river knows that these old planters used to play in their lady servants, valuing them all the way from $300 to $1,500. I saw a little colored boy stand up at $300 to back his master's faith in a little flush that wasn't any good on earth.

Few riverboat gamblers exercised their dishonesty alone. They either paired up or operated in groups of up to half a dozen. Often, one member of a crooked combination would disembark at a stop to be replaced by another gambler coming aboard there, thus allaying any suspicions that might be building up among the victims. A common procedure would be for a confederate to stand among the interested spectators and signal his partners what cards the suckers held. This trickery, known as "iteming," might be achieved by puffing on a cigar or by scratching certain parts of the anatomy to indicate certain hands. One such confederate used a walking stick as a signal, indicating various hands by the angle of the stick. Perhaps the most ingenious was a gambler's partner who played coded snatches of music on a violin while masquerading as a half-wit.

Among the top riverboat gamblers were Canada Bill Jones, perhaps the greatest practitioner of three-card monte; George Devol; and Dick Hargraves, the richest of the square gamblers. Another honest gambler was John Powell, the beau ideal of his river colleagues. Tall, handsome and always strikingly, though not vulgarly, dressed, Powell was well educated and a close friend of Andrew Jackson and Stephen A. Douglas. Although he turned down a chance to run for Congress from his native state of Missouri, Powell took a keen interest in politics. His advice was sought frequently by Louisiana politicians when he was ashore in the lavish home he maintained in New Orleans.

Powell once took part in a three-day poker game aboard the steamer *Atlantic*, during which he won more than $50,000 from a rich Louisiana planter named Jules Devereaux. It was said that in his most successful years—from 1845 to 1858—he netted at least $100,000 a year. In the fall of 1858 Powell won $8,000 from a young Englishman, who turned up on deck the next morning, shook hands with fellow passengers and, putting a pistol to his temple, blew his brains out. The gambler was so unnerved by the event that he sent the $8,000 and the lad's luggage (he had won that as well) to his family in England and retired from gambling for an entire year. When he returned to the river, his luck and skill deserted him and he went through his entire fortune within a year. Powell died in extreme poverty a few years later, a symbol to other gamblers of the perils of a guilty conscience.

See also: JAMES ASHBY, GEORGE DEVOL, DICK HARGRAVES.

Ross, Mrs. Hannah (c. 1880s) medium

Fake spirit mediums have used many tricks to make "spirits" appear before gullible victims, but none have matched the feat of a noted Boston medium, Mrs. Hannah Ross, in 1887. She actually seemed to make a long-dead baby materialize literally in the flesh. Mrs. Ross would seat herself in a cabinet in a darkened room and call the baby back from the beyond, and sure enough the baby's image would appear at the front of the cabinet. The grieving and awestruck parents of a departed baby would be able not only to see their baby but touch and kiss it as well. The baby would actually appear to be alive. And for good reason, as reporters from a Boston newspaper and the police discovered when they uncovered Mrs. Ross' act. She had a baby's face painted on her breast and would poke her breast through a slit in the curtain on the cabinet. With this exposure of her racket, Mrs. Ross decamped from the Boston area, undoubtedly to ply her trade in another venue.

salting   mine swindle

Easily the most prevalent form of larceny in the Old West and later in Alaska was the "salting" of worthless mining i.e., making an area of land appear to be rich in gold ore or other minerals. As Mark Twain once put it, "There was nothing in the shape of a mining claim that was not salable."

There were many ingenious ways to salt an area, a quite common one being to shoot gold dust into the ground with a shotgun. This method worked well in mine shafts, where the gold specks would convince a potential buyer/victim that a particular vein was not as yet played out. Shotgun salting on the surface could only be successful if some way was found to induce a sucker to search in the right area; salting a huge area would have been an expensive proposition.

According to one California mining legend, some prospectors stuck with a poor-paying claim devised an ingenious scheme to unload it on a group of Chinese fortune hunters. Unable to guarantee that the would-be buyers would look in the right spots, the miners hid one of their number in a gulch with a dead snake. When the Chinese arrived, the miners suggested areas for them to search, and as was to be expected, the potential victims, wary of a salting plot, said no and pointed into a far corner of the claim. As they approached the spot, the miner with the snake heaved it out of his hiding place. Quickly, a miner with the Chinese leveled his shotgun and shot the reptile. The fortune hunters became convinced of the miners' trustworthiness, for not only had they been saved from the snake but, after digging the area, they also found strong traces of gold.

One of the greatest silver saltings ever was that of a worthless hole called the North Ophir in the Comstock field in Nevada. During the 1860s great nuggets of silver turned up there and stock belonging to the North Ophir claim went through the ceiling. The bogus claim's promoters had cut silver dollars into pieces, pounded them into lumps, blackened the lumps and then salted the claim. The bubble burst when a "nugget" turned up with "ted States of" printed on it.

Many miners, looking ahead to the day when their claims would be played out, used

153

a special technique to prepare a salting for a future sucker. Since in the last century gold salts were widely used in the patent medicines miners took religiously for kidney ailments brought on by heavy drinking, they would urinate over large stretches of their claim so that traces of gold would still show up when they were ready to move on.

No tale was too tall for gold salters. A Calistoga Springs, Calif. promoter advertised that the local water was so rich in tiny particles of gold that he was filtering $5 to $10 worth out of each barrelful. While so-called flour gold was sometimes so fine that it would float in water, the Calistoga Springs water had none—except what this promoter had put there. It remained for Mark Twain to demolish the scam as only a master storyteller could. In response to an account about the claim, Twain wrote:

I have just seen your dispatch from San Francisco in Saturday evening's Post. This will surprise many of your readers but it does not surprise me, for once I owned those springs myself. What does surprise me, however, is the falling off of the richness of the water. In my time the yield was a dollar a dipperful. I am not saying this to injure the property in case a sale is contemplated. I am saying it in the interest of history. It may be that the hotel proprietor's process is an inferior one. Yes, that may be the fault. Mine was to take my uncle (I had an extra one at that time on account of his parents dying and leaving him on my hands) and fill him up and let him stand fifteen minutes, to give the water a chance to settle. Well, then I inserted an exhaust receiver, which had the effect of sucking the gold out of his pores. I have taken more than $11,000 out of that old man in less than a day and a half.

I should have held on to those springs, but for the badness of the roads and the difficulty of getting the gold to market, I consider that the gold-yielding water is in many respects remarkable, and yet no more remarkable than the gold-bearing air of Catgut Canyon up there toward the head of the auriferous range. This air, or this wind—for it is a kind of trade-wind which blows steadily down through 600 miles of richest quartz croppings—is heavily charged with exquisitely fine, impalpable gold.

Nothing precipitates and solidifies this gold so readily as contact with human flesh heated by passion. The time that William Abrahams was disappointed in love he used to sit outdoors when the wind was blowing, and come in again and begin to sigh, and I would extract over a dollar and a half out of every sigh.

I do not suppose a person could buy the water privileges at Calistoga now at any price, but several good locations along the course of Catgut Canyon gold-bearing trade-winds are for sale. They are going to be stocked for the New York market. They will sell, too.

Twain was right; almost any kind of salting plot would work because of the irresistible lure of easy treasure that had affected Western prospectors ever since the gold rush of 1849.

See also: GREAT DIAMOND HOAX.

Shanghai Chicken (1839–1871)
shanghaier's runner

The most famous of the runners who supplied bodies for the shanghaiers of San Francisco was Johnny Devine, better known as the Shanghai Chicken.

Little is known of the Shanghai Chicken except that he was born in New York and was shanghaied at age 18, turning up two years later in San Francisco, where he became an ornament of the waterfront. He quickly emerged a jack of all crimes, working industriously as a pickpocket, sneak thief, burglar, footpad and, eventually, pimp. He also hired out as a maimer and hit man for anyone who would pay his price, which was around $50. Although he was arrested seven times during his first nine months in San Francisco, he served no more than 50 days in jail.

With a record like that it was inevitable that Devine would soon attract the attention of Shanghai Kelly, probably the greatest kidnapper of sailors the world has ever known. In a few short years the Shanghai Chicken rose to be Kelly's chief of staff. He was one of the few in the trade who violated the rule that forbade stealing another runner's captives. Once, he tried to hijack a drunken sailor from Tommy Chandler, a particularly rough runner for Shanghai Brown. Chandler, a brute of a man, flattened the Chicken with a mighty punch to the jaw. The Chicken climbed to his feet and felled the sailor with a slungshot and then pulled a pistol and put two bullets into Chandler, leaving him incapacitated for months. The Chicken then lugged his prize off to Shanghai Kelly's boardinghouse.

In 1869 the Shanghai Chicken met his match in the person of Big Billy Maitland, another one of Shanghai Kelly's rivals. In an altercation at Maitland's saloon, Big Billy came after the Chicken with a knife; when the latter raised his arm to protect himself, Maitland neatly slashed off his hand at the wrist. Big Billy then tossed him out of his saloon. The Chicken brushed himself off with his one good hand and then screamed out to Maitland: "Hey, Billy, you dirty bastard! Chuck out me fin!"

Maitland flipped the severed hand out to the sidewalk, and the wounded Chicken staggered to Dr. Simpson's drugstore at Pacific and Davis, where he flung the gory hand on the counter. "Say, Doc," he said, "stick that on again for me, will you?"

He fainted before he could be informed that surgery had not yet advanced to that level of sophistication. The Chicken recovered from his wound and medical men attached a large iron hook to the stump of his left arm. Thereafter, he became an even more dangerous battler on the waterfront. While he earlier had earned the name of the Shanghai Chicken for some unknown reason, the hook now allowed him to fight in the manner of a battling cock. Keeping his hook honed to needle sharpness, the Chicken could cut open a foe with one quick thrust. But after his injury he drank so heavily that Shanghai Kelly fired him. Ever looking for ways to make an extra dollar, Kelly promptly attempted to shanghai the Chicken. Kelly's men got the Chicken as far as the boat landing, where he broke his bonds and started slashing away with his iron hook. The kidnappers fled, many bleeding profusely. The Chicken then made off with Kelly's boat and sold it to another shanghaier.

As a loner, the Chicken now had to make a living by rolling drunks and committing small thefts. He made the mistake of thinking a German sailor wouldn't resist; when the sailor did, he shot and killed him. The Chicken stowed away on a steamer scheduled to leave San Francisco but was discovered before the ship sailed. He was still wearing the victim's cap, since he had left his own hat at the murder scene. The Shanghai Chicken was hanged in 1871.

See also: SHANGHAIING, SHANGHAI KELLY.

shanghaiing

The custom of kidnapping seamen to fill out a ship's crew was practiced worldwide, but nowhere was the art so perfected as along the San Francisco waterfront.

In early times there were no ships sailing directly from San Francisco to Shanghai and back to San Francisco; the round trip involved a long dangerous cruise, which became known as a Shanghai voyage. When a man in San Francisco was forcibly impressed into a ship's crew, he was thus described as being "sent to Shanghai." This in time was shortened to just plain shanghaied.

By 1852, 23 known gangs in San Francisco were engaged in the shanghai trade. Some, of course, would waylay men foolish enough to walk the shadowy waterfront alone, but few shanghai gangs would wait so patiently for a fly to enter their web. The gangs employed runners to board incoming ships and induce sailors to come to boardinghouses they operated. As the *San Francisco Times* of October 21, 1861 reported:

> They swarm over the rail like pirates and virtually take possession of the deck. The crew are shoved into the runners' boats, and the vessel is often left in a perilous situation, with none to manage her, the sails unfurled, and she liable to drift afoul of the shipping at anchor. In some cases not a man has been left aboard in half an hour after the anchor has been dropped.

The runners would all carry the standard gear of their trade: a pair of brass knuckles, a blackjack or slungshot, a knife, a revolver, obscene pictures, several bottles of rum and whiskey spiked with Spanish fly and a flask of liquid soap. If the runners swarmed aboard at meal time, the soap would be slipped into soup or stew simmering on the galley stove. When this awful mixture was served, the seamen would be disgusted and much more receptive to the runner's spiel. First, the runners would offer the sailors some doctored liquor. After that began to take effect, the seamen would be shown obscene pictures and given an enticing, graphic description of what awaited them at a certain boardinghouse as well as the brothels of the Barbary Coast.

Usually, this was enough to convince at least one sailor, and he would be ushered to a runner's boat, where the boatman would give him more to drink. If the sailor showed signs of wavering or attempted to fight, the runner and boatman would club him into silence. Sailors who insisted on staying with their ship were often brass-knuckled or threatened with knives or guns. Often competing runners would settle on the same sailor and each would seize an ear with his teeth and bite down until the frightened man shouted out the boardinghouse he wished to go to. It was considered a serious violation of the runner's code for one runner to steal another's victim.

Some captains would try to protect their crew, but they were helpless when as many as a score of armed men stormed aboard. In addition, shipmasters were often warned by "certain interested parties," as the *San Francisco Times* put it in 1861, meaning the politicians and city officials who received payoffs from the boardinghouse masters, to look the other way or they would not be allowed to raise a crew when they were ready to sail.

Once a sailor reached the boardinghouse, his bag of possessions would be locked up and he would virtually be held prisoner until he was resold to an outgoing vessel. Captive sailors were sold whiskey laced with opium to keep them docile and, on occasion, prostitutes would be brought in to service them;

the boardinghouse master would get a percentage of the prostitutes' fees and whatever they could steal from the sailors. A shipmaster would pay the boardinghouse master between $25 and $100 for each crewman he supplied plus a customary two-months' advance salary to cover the seaman's bill in the boardinghouse. There was seldom any money left over for the sailor when the boardinghouse master figured out the bill.

Shanghaiing could exist on such an organized basis only because most sailors were brutalized men, long subjected to harsh treatment aboard ship and thus conditioned to receiving the same when ashore. Finally, with the rise of unions and a federal law against shanghaiing, the vicious practice began to disappear after 1906.

See also: JOSEPH "BUNCO" KELLY, SHANGHAI KELLY, SHANGHAI CHICKEN, SHANGHAI SMOKE.

Shanghai Kelly   See KELLY, SHANGHAI.

Shanghai Smoke

In the heyday of the San Francisco shanghaiers, various potions were used to knock out likely victims. Most, like the Miss Piggott Special, were concoctions of various whiskeys and brandies with a goodly amount of opium or laudanum added. It remained for the legendary Shanghai Kelly to come up with something really novel, in the form of a cigar known as the Shanghai Smoke, which he had specially made for him by a Chinese cigar maker. Heavily laced with opium, it rapidly dulled the senses of a potential victim to the point that he could be led into an alley and waylaid, eliminating the need to lure him into a saloon and thereby saving time. The Shanghai Smoke became very popular on the

Barbary Coast until cigars became so notorious that men would not accept a stogie unless the donor would smoke one also. Ultimately, the widespread wariness led to the Shanghai Smoke's decline in popularity.

shell game   swindle

The shell game—under which of the three shells is the pea?—is as old as America itself. Gambling authority John Scarne insists the first "thimble-rigger," as an operator of the shell game was called, arrived on these shores shortly after the *Mayflower*. The game itself is much older and was no doubt practiced by crooked gamblers in ancient Egypt and perhaps earlier in other places. Alciphron of Athens wrote an excellent description of the cups and balls, a forerunner of the shell game, in the second century A.D.

In its standard form the game can never be won by the sucker, since the pea is not under any of the shells when he is making his selection. After the operator clearly places the pea under one shell and starts shifting all three around, he gingerly lifts the shell so that the pea is stuck between the back of the shell and the table top (generally a felt surface). He then pops the pea out between his thumb and first finger, and when he takes his hand away, his finger is covering the pea. After the sucker makes his pick of the shells and loses, the operator pulls the other two shells back toward him as he turns them over, in the process slipping the pea under one of them and announcing, "If you'd picked this shell, you would have been a winner."

The principle of the shell game is never to allow the sucker to win even once, the theory being that a loser will become more desperate and bet even greater amounts in a futile effort to get even. The greatest thim-

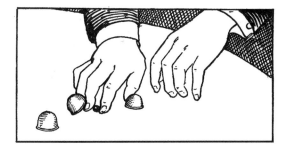

One of the oldest gambling scams, dating back at least to ancient Egypt, the shell game works on the simple principle that the pea is under none of the shells, being removed by deft finger manipulation.

ble-riggers were such 19th century gamblers as Canada Bill Jones ("Suckers have no business with money, anyway"), who is reputed to have won the deeds to several plantations with the shell game, and Soapy Smith, who made a fortune with the game before being shot dead by a vigilante in Alaska in 1898. There is only one recorded case where Smith lost at a shell game. A knowledgeable victim placed a gun on the little table, made a huge bet and announced he was wagering on which two shells the pea was not under. He turned them over himself and, naturally, found no pea. "I reckon there's no need to turn over the last shell," he said, taking his money. Smith folded up his table and left.

There have been numerous exposés of the shell game, the first by a reformed Mississippi gambler named Jonathan F. Green, who, beginning in 1843, wrote several books on cheating. Despite this exposure, the shell game has continued to prosper and can still be seen at carnivals, horse races and other sporting events and, in recent years, on the streets of major cities. The shell game is often played in New York's Wall Street area, especially on paydays.

See also: SOAPY SMITH.

shortchange artists

Shortchanging has long been a highly developed American swindle. As late as 1900 it was common among a number of small circuses traveling the country not to pay ticket sellers and in fact to charge them as much as $35 a week for the job because it gave them such a lucrative opportunity to shortchange the excited patrons. Police bunco squads have estimated there are as many as 5,000 professional shortchange artists who frequently take jobs as cashiers, ticket sellers, bartenders, checkout clerks and check cashiers simply because of the opportunities for stealing these jobs afford. However, probably an even more common form of shortchanging involves cheating clerks in stores.

The classic con of this type is the twenty and one. It calls for a gypster to make a purchase in a store for less than 50¢ and pay with a $20 bill. He starts talking about something: the weather, the news, anything. When the clerk puts the change down, it's usually in a standard form: a $10 bill, a five, four singles and a dollar in silver. The crook then makes another purchase of 10¢ or so, paying for it with a quarter from the silver change lying on the counter. He has made no effort to pick up the paper money. While this is going on, the slickster finds an apparently overlooked $1 bill in his pocket. He tells the clerk he's sorry for having forced him to change a twenty when he had the single. The customer then acts as though he is going to pick up the $10 bill from the paper money while putting down the single, but he does neither and continues talking.

Next, he shoves the $10 in bills across the counter and requests a $10 bill in exchange for the pile. When the clerk gives him the $10 bill, the con artist pretends he's going to leave. At this point the customer seemingly has been gypped out of $9. Most of the time the clerk doesn't even realize he or she is shorting the customer. And it makes no difference if they do or not, for at that moment the gyp pretends to have discovered the error. He asks the clerk to check on the money he has given him. The clerk does so and, red-faced, realizes the customer is right. Psychologically, the clerk has been put on the defensive, as the mistake is obvious. The gyp brushes off the matter but keeps up a steady flow of words to further confuse the clerk.

Now, he once more withdraws a dollar bill from his pocket and this time puts it on the bills on the counter and says: "Actually this whole mixup is my fault. I never should have given you the twenty in the first place. Here's twenty in change. You give me back the twenty and we'll be square." By this time the clerk, either still embarrassed or exasperated, is ready to do anything to be rid of the troublesome customer. He usually will hand over the twenty at this point, completely forgetting about the $10 the gyp has already picked up. Only a very alert clerk can keep up with such banter and not be talked out of the money. Even if the clerk does so, he does not accuse the customer of trying to swindle him, since the customer has already demonstrated his confused state of mind by almost getting gyped out of $9.

Despite the fact that security firms urge stores to educate employees to this most basic shortchanging racket, it remains perhaps the most successful of all such stings, with a success rate of far better than 50 percent. It accounts for a large amount of the estimated $500 million a year taken by all types of shortchangers.

Siegel, Benjamin "Bugsy" (1906–1947)
syndicate leader

"We only kill each other," the notorious Benjamin "Bugsy" Siegel once told construction tycoon Del Webb. Whether or not Webb took this assurance on the mores of syndicate gangsterism at full value is not known, but Siegel's own life and death certainly gives his statement some credence. Bugsy Siegel was simultaneously the most colorful, the most charming and the most fiery-tempered of all syndicate killers. As the saying went, he charmed the pants and panties off Hollywood, while at the same time functioning as a mob killer. It was an incredible act right up to the moment he got his head blown open by three 30.30 caliber bullets from a hit man's rifle.

Bugsy grew up on the crime-ridden Lower East Side and formed an early alliance with a runty little youth four years his senior, Meyer Lansky, already a criminal genius in his teens. By 1920 the Bug and Meyer Gang was running gambling games, stealing cars and getting into bootlegging. On occasion the gang hijacked booze shipments from other outfits until Lansky and Siegel realized it was a lot easier to hire out their gunmen as protectors for these shipments. They soon began working with rising young Italian gangsters such as Lucky Luciano, Joe Adonis, Frank Costello and Tommy Lucchese. The gang provided much of the muscle and, in Lansky's case, the brains for Luciano's big push to topple the old "Mustache Petes" of the Mafia: Giuseppe "Joe the Boss" Masseria and Salvatore Maranzano.

The emerging national crime syndicate assigned Siegel to carry out numerous murders aimed at gaining control of the important avenues of crime. He was so enthused about killing, he was called "Bugsy," but not in his presence. Face to face, he was just plain Ben.

Bugsy was sent to California to consolidate the syndicate's West Coast operations. There, in his quieter moments, he was a genuinely suave, entertaining sort, hobnobbing with Hollywood celebrities and becoming close friends with such personalities as Jean Harlow, George Raft, Clark Cable, Gary Cooper, Wendy Barrie, Cary Grant and many others, some of whom in-vested their money in his enterprises. Siegel sometimes left his "class" friends at a party to go on a murder mission, which he did one night in 1939 when he, Frankie Carbo, later the underworld's boss of boxing, and Murder, Inc. wheelman Allie Tannenbaum assassinated an errant criminal named Harry Greenberg, better known as Big Greenie.

Big Greenie had had the death sentence passed on him by the syndicate board in New York. When Greenie fled to Los Angeles, it was decided to "let Ben handle it." Siegel was happy to, doing the job personally, although he was only supposed to arrange matters. Los Angeles County Deputy District Attorney Arthur Veitch later explained why Siegel had to lend a hand personally: "In gangster parlance Siegel is what is known as a 'cowboy.' This is the way the boys have of describing a man who is not satisfied to frame a murder but actually has to be in on the kill in person."

Others would say Siegel's craziness explained his bizarre actions. For example, there was the time he and one of his mistresses, Countess Dorothy diFrasso, trekked to Italy to sell Benito Mussolini a revolutionary explosive device. While staying on the diFrasso estate, Siegel met top Nazi officials Hermann Goering and Joseph Goebbels. According to underworld legend, Bugsy took an instant dislike to the pair—for personal rather than political reasons—and planned to knock them both off, relenting only because of the countess' frantic pleas. When the explosive device fizzled, the Bug returned to Hollywood.

His main syndicate business was running the rackets and directing narcotics deals on the West Coast as well as overseeing the delivery of West Coast racing results to East Coast bookmakers. In the process Siegel dreamed up the idea of turning Las Vegas into a legal gambling paradise. He talked the syndicate into investing some $6 million in the construction of the first truly posh legal gambling establishment in the United States, the Flamingo (which was the nickname of Siegel's mistress, Virginia Hill). Unfortunately for Bugsy, he was a man ahead of his time, and the Flamingo proved to be a financial white elephant. Reportedly, the syndicate demanded he make good its losses, but Bugsy was guilty of more serious infractions than just losing the mob's money. He had skimmed off the Flamingo's construction funds and had been dipping into its gambling revenues.

The syndicate passed the death sentence on Siegel, the key vote being cast by Meyer Lansky, Bugsy's lifelong buddy ("I had no choice," Lansky reputedly said later). Lucky Luciano approved the decision at a 1947 conference in Havana, Cuba. On June 20 Siegel was sitting in the living room of the $500,000 Beverly Hills mansion of Virginia Hill, who had been sent on a syndicate mission to Europe, when a killer pumped nine shots through the window. Three hit Siegel in the head, killing him instantly.

See also: FLAMINGO HOTEL.

slot machines

With the end of Prohibition, gangsters who had engaged in bootlegging went into slot machines in a big way. These so-called one-armed bandits provided much of the revenue needed to hold criminal organizations together in the post-Prohibition era.

The American slot machine dates back to 1887, where a skilled German mechanic in San Francisco made a machine that took in and paid out nickels. It quickly became popular and was set up in saloons around the city. The house takeout was usually set at 25 percent. Since gambling devices could not be patented, the mechanic's idea was lifted freely. In Chicago, Herbert Mills began making machines for distribution throughout the country, and by 1906 he was known as Mr. Slot Machine. A slot machine is a very complicated mechanism, with over 600 parts, including one very reliable apparatus whose adjustment determines the house percentage.

The biggest Mafia operator of slot machines in the 1930s was Frank Costello, who saturated New York City with them. Each Costello machine sported a special sticker, which protected it wherever it was set up. If a freelancer tried to install machines without Costello stickers, the color of which changed regularly, they would be subject to attack by the mob or to police seizure. Police officers who made the mistake of interfering with the operation of Costello's machines could count on departmental harassment, such as transfer to the far reaches of Staten Island.

Costello's hold on the New York slot machine racket was secure during the administration of Mayor Jimmy Walker, but when reformer Fiorello H. La Guardia became mayor, an all-out war was launched against the machines. Costello used all his political pull to get a court injunction restraining La Guardia from interfering with the slots, but the Little Flower simply ignored the order and sent special squads of police around town to smash the machines. Costello did not know how to react to this "illegal" behavior by the mayor and eventually pulled his valuable machines out of the city. He found a new location for them—thanks to an invitation from Gov. Huey Long of Louisiana—and set up a slot machine empire in New Orleans. Years later, when an aggressive and ambitious young hood named Joe Gallo demanded, "Who the hell gave Frank Costello New Orleans?" the answer was, of course, "ole Huey did."

Today, slot machines are legal only in Nevada and Atlantic City, N.J. For some reason, a myth persists that the casinos pay off at 95 percent. The actual payoff is much nearer to 75 percent. What the casinos generally do is put one 95 percent payoff machine in a line to draw in the suckers. Sometimes a player will work three machines at once. What money he gets back from the middle one is quickly swallowed up by those on the left and right.

smack game   matching coin con

Among the most enduring of all con games is one called "smack." It involves two swindlers and a victim and is often worked at bus and train stations, airports and bars.

Con man A joins con man B, who has already lined up a victim, and suggests they pass the time matching coins for drinks or smokes. Soon, they are playing for money. The game calls for each to flip a coin with the odd coin the winner, such as one tails collects from two heads and so on. When con man A goes off to the men's room for a moment, con man B informs the victim how much he dislikes A and suggests they cheat him. Con man B says that whatever he calls, heads or tails, the sucker should call the opposite. That way A has to lose to one of them.

What happens, of course, is that A does lose each flip but most of the time B wins the money, especially on large bets, and thus collects not only from A but from the sucker as well. Suddenly, A gets suspicious and declares he thinks B and the sucker are cheating him. Both B and the sucker deny the charge, but A is not satisfied. If they aren't working together, he says, he would like them to leave in different directions. Con man B gives the sucker the high sign and whispers to him a place where they can meet nearby. The sucker goes off gleefully, looking forward to the division of the loot. Naturally, B never shows, and when the sucker returns to the scene of the swindle, A has disappeared as well. It is a great learning experience for most victims.

Smith, James Monroe "Jingle Money"
(1888–1949) college president and embezzler

A member of the Huey Long regime, Dr. James Monroe Smith, president of Louisiana State University, was credited by that state's press with making education profitable—for himself—and won the journalistic sobriquet Jingle Money Smith.

Born in Jackson Parish, La. in 1888, Smith served as dean of the College of Education at Southwest Louisiana Institute from 1920 to 1930 and as president of LSU from then until 1939. For part of his academic years, he was an adviser and lackey to Huey Long. As it developed after his tenure at LSU, Smith could have taught the state's political dictator a few things about making money. While serving at the university, Smith had become known as a rather wild liver and free spender.

In 1939 Dr. Smith resigned his post and fled the state as an investigation began delving into missing school finances. In due course, the sum was found to be extensive, and by the time Smith was found hiding out in Canada, he had been dubbed Jingle Money Smith. He was arrested on a charge of embezzling $100,000 in university funds and was indicted on 36 counts, which indicated the theft was far greater. Convicted on the $100,000 embezzlement charge, Smith was sent to the penitentiary. He was released in February 1946 in poor health and died on May 26, 1949.

Smith, Jefferson Randolph "Soapy"
(1860–1898) con man

An incorrigible con man and gambler, Jefferson "Soapy" Smith worked his trade—everything from three-card monte, the shell game and various other scams—throughout the West and in the goldfields of Alaska, areas where the suckers were plentiful but could prove unforgiving.

Soapy got his nickname from one of his famous cons. It involved selling soap to the hicks in the cow towns, where Smith would stand on a soap box and announce that several of the bars of soap he was selling had a $10 or $20 bill inside the wrapper. The suckers would rush to buy, especially after one buyer, one of Smith's shills, waved a $20 bill and yelled he had just pulled it out of a wrapper.

Soapy was in his early teens when he ran away from his Georgia home and ended up in Texas punching cows. He was separated from six months' pay by a shell game artist. Far from taking it badly, he decided to learn that con himself, eventually teaming up with a venerable old con man named V. Bullock-Taylor. When Bullock-Taylor died, Smith became the king of the con circuit throughout the West. He opened up a gambling hall in Denver that became famous for never giving a sucker an even break and recruited an organization that enabled him to control virtually all the city's con rackets, including gold brick swindles and phony mining stock. Later, he moved the center of his operations to Creede, Colo. to take advantage of the silver wealth pouring into that town. Smith took over most of the rackets there with only some opposition from saloon keeper Bob Ford, the assassin of Jesse James. Eventually, it was said, Soapy forced Ford to accept him as a secret partner. After Ford was killed by a man named O'Kelly, it was said that Smith had paid for the job.

Eventually, the silver ran out and Soapy and his gang headed for the Alaskan gold fields, setting up in Skagway to trim the miners just arriving and the big-strikers on the way home. Soapy's capers in Skagway became legendary. He trimmed suckers in his gambling saloon, robbing many of valuable claims. Too greedy to pass up any form of revenue, he set up a sign over a cabin that read "Telegraph Office" and charged $5 to send a telegram to anywhere and another $5 to receive a reply. Miners flocked to send out messages and paid their money for responses, never learning there were no telegraph wires out of Skagway.

Soapy also ran an "Information Office" to provide newcomers and travelers with whatever intelligence they needed. Inquirers imparted more information to Soapy's men than was wise and Skagway burglars and footpads became famous for their clairvoyance in locating sums of money. On some nights Skagway had as many as a dozen holdups, virtually all executed by Soapy's men. One of Soapy's most famous swindles involved a man of the cloth who was seeking funds to build a church. Smith was the first to contribute, giving the surprised clergyman $1,000. With the impetus from Soapy's contribution, the clergyman collected a total of $36,000, only to have it all stolen. Soapy thought 36 to one was a rather good return on his initial investment.

Efforts to control Smith's avarice were unavailing as he took control of the town, naming his own marshal and judges. A vigilance committee, called the Committee of 101, plastered up signs reading:

NOTICE
To all gamblers and bunco men:
We have resolved to run you out of town
and make Skagway a decent place to live in.
Take our advice and get out before
action is taken.

Soapy laughed at the warning and promptly formed his own Committee of 303 to indicate he had the power and was not about to relinquish it. The Committee of 101 quickly lost heart and failed to act. In July of 1898, however, Soapy's men robbed a miner of $2,500 in gold in a daylight mugging that sparked an instantaneous uprising. With the men of the Committee of 101 in the lead, hundreds of angry miners armed with picks and shotguns stormed into Soapy's saloon. Soapy tried to con his way out; the vigilantes listened for a while and then shot him to pieces. Most of Soapy's supporters were rounded up and what would have been Alaska's greatest lynching was prevented only by the arrival of U.S. infantry troops and the establishment of martial law.

With Soapy dead, the citizens enjoyed telling tales of his wild cons and observing how fitting it was that someone had ceremoniously tossed three shells and a pea into his grave as he was being lowered into it.

Smith, Thomas L. "Pegleg" (1801–1866)
mountaineer, thief and swindler

One of the legendary mountain men who roamed the American West a law unto themselves, Pegleg Smith could also be described as a slaver, thief, rustler and con man. William Caruthers in *Loafing Along Death Valley Trails* says:

> *Smith may be said to be the inventor of the Lost Mine, as a means of getting quick money. The credulous are still looking for mines that existed only in Pegleg's fine imagination. . . . [He] saw in man's lust for gold, ways to get it easier than the pick and shovel method. . . . When his money ran out he always had a piece of high-grade gold quartz to lure investment in his phantom mine.*

Born in Crab Orchard, Ky. on October 10, 1801, Smith ran away from home in his teens. After a stint of flatboating on the Mississippi, he headed for St. Louis, where he worked for a fur merchant and met such trappers and mountaineers as Jim Bridger, Kit Carson and Milton Sublette. When Alexander Le Grand made his first expedition to Santa Fe, Smith went along and got a taste of living in the wild, an experience he found most satisfying. He picked up several Indian tongues and, like the majority of mountain men, some Indian enemies. One shot him just below his right knee, which was how Smith acquired his peg leg. He remained as good a horseman as ever despite his handicap, and during most of the 1830s was one of the most successful of the fur trappers.

Near the end of the decade, the value of pelts dropped through the floor and Smith went into a more nefarious trade, stealing Indian children and selling them to wealthy Mexicans looking for slaves. In time, the Indians were on the lookout for this mysterious child stealer with a wooden leg; so Smith moved on to California, where for the next decade he became an accomplished horse thief, one time leading a group of 150 Utah Indians across the Sierra Nevada into California, where they stole several hundred horses. With two other famous mountaineer scouts, Old Bill Williams and Jim Beckwourth, Pegleg Smith formed one of the biggest horse-stealing rings California ever saw. In time, pressure from the law became so intense that they disbanded.

Following the discovery of gold in California, Smith developed his mining swindle, insisting that he had found rich samples of gold-bearing black quartz before he had to flee from vicious Indians somewhere in the Chocolate Mountains or the Santa Rosa Mountains or the Borego Badlands. The locale kept changing as Pegleg changed his story, but the gullible still listened; some staked him while others bought maps showing the alleged location of the gold. Even after Smith died in the county hospital in San Francisco in 1866, men kept searching for the Lost Pegleg Mine and they still do today, a lasting tribute to the old reprobate's snake-oil charm.

Spanish Prisoner Swindle

The Spanish Prisoner Swindle has been worked in America for at least 150 years. Most common now is a version initiated in a letter describing an alleged prisoner held captive in Mexico or Cuba. If he is a Cuban prisoner, he is in a Castro prison, a pity since he is a rich man who, before his incarceration, smuggled out of the country something like $250,000, which is now concealed in the false bottom of a trunk laying unclaimed in a U.S. customs house. The trunk can only be claimed by the writer of the letter, or perhaps his 18-year-old daughter. For a mere pittance, say $5,000 or $10,000, the prisoner could bribe his way out of prison and he and his daughter could escape Cuba to claim his fortune.

The letter also contains an offer that is difficult to refuse. If the recipient of the letter will send the bribe money to the address mentioned in the letter, generally a box number in Miami, not only will he get his money back within a month—when the prisoner gets to the United States—but he also will be rewarded by an additional $100,000 or so. Sometimes the letter is more pathetic. The prisoner writes that there is no way he can escape (the letter has been smuggled out at great risk) but by sending the bribe money, the recipient can enable the prisoner's young daughter to escape Cuba and claim the cache in the trunk.

Such letters are sent out by the hundreds and a large number of victims fall for the story. Of course, no money is sent to them, no prisoner escapes from Cuba and no trunk is claimed from customs. The Postal Service has issued constant warnings about the Spanish Prisoner Swindle without much success. Whatever the current situation, the confidence operators come up with a story to match it. In recent years the scam involved Mexican, Cuban or Turkish prisoners. During the 1930s it was Jewish prisoners in Nazi Germany. At least once, letters describing the plight of an "American prisoner" who had hidden $3 million in South America were sent to wealthy Latin Americans. In this particular case the operator employed six typists in New York to pound out letter after letter to be sent to Latin America.

sperm fraud   *preying on desperate would-be parents*

As technology marches on, blatant new crimes keep pace with the new advances, even in such unlikely matters as artificial insemination. In a shocking 1992 case, a Virginia fertility specialist, Cecil B. Jacobson, laid claim to having helped scores of desperate, infertile women by supplying them with an "extensive, carefully regulated donor program" involving physical, mental and social characteristics. The doctor always came up with the seemingly perfect donor, always the same one—Cecil B. Jacobson.

Dr. Jacobson had no need to screen donors or store sperm till the proper time. He produced the sperm in the privacy of his office bathroom before each patient arrived at his clinic. The flamboyant Jacobson referred to himself as "the baby maker" and boasted that "God doesn't give you babies—I do."

Some parents started finding out just how right he was. One couple testified in the 55-year-old doctor's trial that they became suspicious and shocked by their daughter's first baby pictures. "We pulled them out of the envelope and both went, 'Whoa, who does she look like?'" the mother said. "And we both had the same feeling—she looked a lot like Dr. Jacobson."

DNA testing proved that the doctor had fathered 15 children for his patients at fees of about $5,000 in many cases. Authorities estimated that some 75 more couples had been hoaxed by the "babymaker" but refused to submit to DNA testing to find out. A very standard response being "Please, we don't want to know."

However, at the time of Dr. Jacobson's conviction there were no laws on the books prohibiting a doctor from donating sperm to a patient or impregnating an unwitting woman with his sperm. Under those circumstances Dr. Jacobson could be convicted of no more than criminal fraud involving the use of telephones and the U.S. mails. He was sentenced to five years imprisonment.

Since this case more stringent rules have been passed concerning sperm donation.

Spiritualism

The birthplace of modern American Spiritualism, the belief that the dead can communicate with the living through physical phenomena, was Hydesville, N.Y.

In 1848, 15-year-old Margaret Fox developed the ability to snap her big toe so loudly that it resembled a sharp rap on wood. She and her younger sister Kate kept the ability a secret and decided to play a prank on their parents. One night they called their mother and father to their bedside and said they could not sleep because of some strange rappings. The girls said they were sure the sounds were being made by the ghost of the former owner of the house, who had been murdered. Kate shut her eyes and went into a sort of trance and asked if the ghost was in the room. Margaret answered yes by snapping her toe twice under the blankets (one snap meant no). Mr. and Mrs. Fox excitedly put more questions to the strange spirit and got answers via the girls. The parents concluded their daughters had supernatural powers.

News spread rapidly through the surrounding area and hundreds of people descended on the Fox home seeking to get in touch with deceased relatives. By now the hoax had gotten so big that the girls dared not confess. They ended up becoming famous mediums for the next 40 years. Meanwhile, other charlatans readily came up with various methods of producing rappings from the dead and the principles of Spiritualism became firmly imbedded in popular belief. Not even a confession by the Fox sisters in 1888 about their toe trick could stop the growth of this new racket.

Spiritualism caught on in America because it coincided with a loss of faith in authoritarian religious doctrine thanks to the profound impact of 19th-century science. Evidence became more and more a requirement and spiritualists seemed to satisfy that criteria through rappings, "spirit lights" and the "materialized spirit."

Some fakers carried off particularly bald-faced swindles. Typical of these charlatans was Mrs. Hannah Ross, the most popular medium in Boston during the 1880s. Her greatest trick was to make a long-dead baby materialize before her gullible victims' eyes. Eventually, Mrs. Ross' con was revealed by an enterprising reporter. She would seat herself in a cabinet in a dark room and allegedly go into a trance. Then she would expose one of her breasts through a slit in the curtain surrounding her and the dead baby would seemingly appear. On her breast she had painted the face of an infant.

Converts from around the world flocked to spiritualism in the late 19th and early 20th century. Among them were William Gladstone, Sir Arthur Conan Doyle, John Ruskin and Alfred Russel Wallace. In the late 19th century leading mediums became important international figures despite the fact that exposure of their frauds increased. Henry Slade, the slate-writing medium, was one of the most famous exposed.

Probably the greatest American Spiritualist was Daniel D. Home, who was one of the first to adopt the tapping trick of the Fox sisters. Leaving his home in Waterford, Conn. in 1850 at the age of 17, Home was one of the earliest swindlers to cash in on the spirit communication craze. He went to Europe in 1854 and, over the years, conducted thousands of seances, many by invitation in royal courts and the houses of nobility. At the court of Emperor Napoleon III of France, Home pulled off one of his most acclaimed performances. Knowing for a certainty that the empress would want to communicate with her departed father, Home smuggled in a rubber replica of the dead man's right hand. On touching it in the dark, the empress "recognized it at once" because of the missing third finger.

One of Home's greatest tricks, which convinced many of his supernatural powers, was having a chair he was sitting in rise and carry him around the room over the heads of his guests. Home retired in 1871 an extremely wealthy man. While all of his supposed psychic powers have been exposed as tricks, true believers in Spiritualism still celebrate him as the greatest medium of all time.

See also: HANNAH ROSS.

Star Route frauds

One of the greatest frauds in U.S. postal history involved the so-called Star Routes, roads built in the 19th century West for mail delivery via wagon and horseback. The situation was ripe for fraudulent claims and a combine of crooked Postal Department officials, contractors, subcontractors and politicians set up a vast conspiracy. The combination lobbied for congressional appropriations to start new and useless routes and upgrade old ones. One road was improved for faster travel at a cost of $50,000 despite the fact that its use brought in only $761 in postal income annually. A single fraudulent affidavit, unopposed by postal officials, netted one contractor $90,000. A later investigation of the road improvement claims made by another contractor, John M. Peck, revealed that to equal the distance he claimed could be traveled in a day a man would have to ride for 40 hours.

Probes by congressional investigators, special agents and Pinkerton detectives resulted in more than 25 indictments. Trials held in 1882 and 1883 uncovered frauds related to 93 routes. However, not a single conviction was obtained. It was estimated that the government had been defrauded out of at least $4 million.

television quiz show scandal

In 1959 the television broadcast industry was rocked by a quiz show scandal when it was established that many big-money winners had been provided with the answers to questions. Several recent highly acclaimed winners were exposed as frauds, perhaps the most shocking being Charles Van Doren, a 33-year-old Ph.D. who came from one of the nation's top intellectual families.

Van Doren, a $5,500-a-year instructor at Columbia University, had won $129,000 on NBC's "Twenty-One" after having been supplied with a trumped-up script in advance. Later, Van Doren said he had been convinced to take part in the quiz show because it would be a boon "to the intellectual life, to teachers, and to education in general." He added, "In fact, I think I have done a disservice to all of them."

On the basis of his new fame as a quiz winner, Van Doren got a $50,000-a-year post with NBC, but in the aftermath of the exposures he lost that position as well as his teaching job at Columbia.

In the ensuing investigation New York District Attorney Frank Hogan found that of 150 persons who had testified before a grand jury about the quiz fixes, about 100 had lied. From 1959 to 1962, 18 contestants who had "won" from $500 to $220,500 on now-defunct quiz shows pleaded guilty to perjury and were given suspended sentences, although they could have been fined and imprisoned for three years. The punishment seemed sufficient, considering the fact that nothing was done to the corporate sponsors, some of whom, according to confessions by the shows' producers, had decided whether a contestant would be bumped or allowed to survive as a contestant.

Abroad the scandal generally was viewed as demonstrating a failing in American life. France's *France-Soir* saw a parallel between Van Doren's confession and Vice President Nixon's campaign-fund confession and observed: "In America, more than anywhere, contrition is a form of redemption. A sinner who confesses is a sinner pardoned." Nixon would survive to be pardoned again, but Van Doren never returned to public life.

On-the-air photos of Charles Van Doren (top) and Herbert Stempel (below) show them going through the prearranged quiz show charade that made Van Doren for a time the most celebrated "egghead" in the nation.

Thiel, Alexander (1890–1956) forger

The bible of criminology, *Fundamentals of Criminal Investigation* by Charles E. O'Hara, labels Alexander Thiel "probably the most accomplished forger of modern times." It was an accolade few police authorities would dispute. From the 1920s to 1943 Thiel, known throughout the country as "Mr. X," was thought to be the head of the nation's most prolific gang of check forgers.

Only after he was apprehended did the police discover that Mr. X had no gang, that he was a loner who netted something like $600,000 to $1 million, in an era when a dollar was worth 5 to 10 times what it was in the 1990s.

What made the authorities sure they were dealing with a gang of criminals was the fact that Thiel was an expert at several different criminal crafts. The man who passed the checks, a dapper look-alike of actor John Barrymore, was a master forger capable of imitating a real signature from memory. Thus, whenever a bank teller requested that he sign the back of a withdrawal slip to verify his endorsement of a check, he always duplicated the signature down to the dotted i's. Certainly, the second-story man in the mob was a specialist who knew how to break into a business office without leaving a trace. Once inside, he would locate a blank check ledger and rip out a page from near the back of it. He would then stamp the stubs: "Defective Checks. Removed by Printer." Thus, even if the missing checks were noticed, the explanation was readily at hand. Generally, however, the missing checks weren't noticed until they were cashed and Mr. X and his "gang" were long gone. Thiel himself handled every step of the operation, including the second-story work. "Accomplices mean extra tongues that can wag," he told police, a philosophy that permitted him to avoid detection for almost a quarter of a century.

Thiel was born in Chicago in 1890, one of six children. When he was 14, his father, a reasonably successful architect, was wiped out in the bank crash of 1904. That experience was to shape Thiel's criminal future. As he later told the authorities, "Right then and there I decided banks and bankers were all a bunch of no-goods and someday I was going to get even with them." He was a delinquent in his teens and was sent to reform school after being caught in a burglary.

In his twenties he was a card dealer and croupier at illegal gambling joints, where he discovered his superior forging ability by sheer luck. A heavy gambler committed suicide; almost by impulse, Thiel hurriedly scrawled out an I.O.U. chit for $2,500, using as a model a marker the gambler had given him earlier in the evening. He tossed the chit into his money box and pocketed $2,500. His employers never suspected a thing, figuring the dead gambler had obviously killed himself because he had lost more than he could afford.

Thiel decided it would be a lot healthier to swindle banks than gambling-joint operators, who tended to be most unforgiving about such matters. He quit the job and went into the bad paper business.

In his first big caper Thiel managed to acquire some blank checks belonging to New York real estate millionaire Messmore Kendall. It was three weeks before Kendall and his bank realized the millionaire's account had been looted of $162,000. That haul set Thiel up in a style of living to which he was to remain accustomed for about 20 years, although he never again pulled a job on such a grand scale. He came to realize that passing checks of $50,000 or more was too dangerous. Thereafter, he kept his forged checks within a range of $5,000 to $15,000 and simply cashed more of them.

Thiel started living the good life and became a fixture in New York nightclub society. He was a regular at the Stork Club when it was still a speakeasy, where he was known by sight, if not by reputation, by host Sherman Billingsley. However, he had a strong drug habit, one that had started when he was a teenager in reform school, and needed to cash thousands of dollars worth of bad checks annually just to cover his addiction.

By the late 1930s Mr. X was being sought by police all over the country. Under the name of George Workmaster, a real stockbroker, Thiel cashed checks totaling $4,160; again, an alert went out for the John Barrymore look-alike. This time the police got their man—or at least thought they had after five witnesses identified Bertram Campbell as the forger. Campbell was sent to prison for five to ten years, despite his anguished claims of innocence. Alex Thiel read newspaper accounts of the supposed criminal career of Bertram Campbell with mixed feelings. It took the pressure off him but, at the same time, he felt sorry for the man.

Thiel wrote a letter to District Attorney Thomas E. Dewey, whose office had prosecuted Campbell, informing him an innocent man had been convicted. He also wrote several letters to newspapers. But, of course, Thiel was not about to come forward and the suspicion grew that a friend of Campbell was perpetrating a hoax in the hope of getting him off. Finally, Thiel tried another tack. He resumed pulling more of his Mr. X capers. Still, the authorities refused to believe they had the wrong man. They formed the theory that Campbell had merely been a front man for a "syndicate" of check forgers and that the gang was still in operation. No one person could pull so many jobs by himself, they maintained.

So, while Campbell rotted in jail, Thiel went on forging checks. He was finally caught, ironically, because of his drug addiction. In 1945 Thiel was "taking the cure" at the United States Hospital at Lexington, Ky. Two New York detectives visited the institution in search of wanted check passers, since drug addiction was recognized as common in that particular profession. Going through pictures of the inmates, they ran across a photo of a John Barrymore look-alike and remembered the Campbell case. Thiel was brought back to New York and confronted with the witnesses in the Campbell case, who admitted they had identified the wrong man. He then confessed to being Mr. X, and cleared Camp-

bell. When the two men were brought together, Thiel said, "I'm sorry for all the trouble I've caused you."

Campbell, in spite of his eight-year ordeal, showed no sign of anger. He simply replied, "I suppose you couldn't help it."

Within a few months, Campbell won a full pardon, and a short while later, he was awarded $115,000 for his wrongful conviction. Eighty-two days after getting the award, Campbell died.

Thiel drew jail terms totaling nine years. Freed in his mid-sixties, he went back to Chicago and, for a time, faded into obscurity. Then he forged a check for $100. When located by police, he was in bed near death. The master forger told the cops, "Give me a pen and a blank check and I'll square my bill with the undertaker now."

See also: CHECK PASSING.

three-card monte *gambling con game*

Three-card monte is a classic card gyp, whose history in America goes back to the early 1800s. Every few decades it enjoys a big revival because a new crop of suckers has grown up. Since the late 1970s, practitioners of the trade have been flooding most big American cities. On almost any weekday as many as a half-dozen street games may be in progress at one time, for example, on New York's fashionable West 57th Street from Fifth Avenue to Carnegie Hall, until determined block association campaigning got rid of them.

The idea in three-card monte is to guess which of three face-down cards is the red queen. It looks easy: the dealer shows the winning card, then he does a fast shuffle and places the three cards face down; pick a card and put your money on it. The average vic-

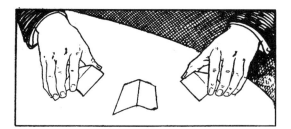

The lure of three-card monte is that because of the apparently stupid play of the shills it appears to be an easy game to beat. The scam artists follow one abiding rule, the sucker is never allowed to win a single bet.

tim will watch for a time and invariably spot the correct card every time. Other players try and win at times and lose at other times. These losing efforts are particularly exasperating to the potential victim who recognizes the correct card. Generally speaking, all these early players, winners and losers, are shills for the operation who try to coax outsiders to play. When an outsider does play, the dealer becomes extremely adept at his art and lays the cards out in a way that not only prevents the sucker from spotting the queen but makes another card appear to be the queen.

There are endless variations to the game. A victim may suddenly notice the corner of the queen is bent so that it can be easily identified. When the victim bets, the quick-fingered dealer will first straighten that corner and fold a losing card instead. Sometimes a victim will spot the correct card and try to put down say $50. One of the shills will quickly lay down $100 on a losing card and the dealer will take his bet and tell the victim, "Sorry, only one card can be bet a game." Should the victim protest his bet was down first, the other supposed bettor

will insist his was. The dealer will throw up his hands in disgust and say, "I don't know whose bet was down first, so all bets are off. New deal."

Tinker, Edward (?–1811) insurance swindler and murderer

The first captain of an American cargo ship known to have attempted insurance fraud by sinking his own vessel, Edward Tinker got caught up in his own plotting and finally had to resort to murder. Tinker sold off his cargo and then scuttled his schooner off Roanoke Island, Va., planning to claim the cargo had gone down with the ship. Two members of his crew, named Durand and Potts, readily joined his plot but a third, known as Edwards, expressed some trepidation. Tinker lured Edwards on a duck-hunting expedition and murdered him, weighting down the body with rocks and heaving it into the sea. The corpse, however, was carried back to shore by the tide, and Tinker, as the last person seen with the seaman, was arrested.

The captain then wrote a letter to his coconspirator Durand offering him money if he would testify that Potts had killed Edwards and had sunk the vessel earlier. Tinker explained to Durand that the worst that could happen to him if he was convicted of perjury was that a bit of his ear would be lopped off, the punishment for false swearing at the time. Durand, now terrified of Tinker's plots, feared that if he refused, Tinker would approach Potts with a plan to put the blame on him. The worried seaman solved his dilemma by revealing the letter to the authorities, and the scheming Tinker was convicted of murder and hanged at Cateret, N.C. in September 1811.

town-site fraud   19th-century swindle

One of the most prevalent rackets of the 19th century was the western town-site fraud, whereby gullible easterners were swindled by land sharks into investing their money in property glowingly described in phony prospectuses.

Typical was the Nininger swindle. The city of Nininger, Minnesota Territory in the 1850s, as depicted on large and beautifully engraved maps printed by one Ingenuous Doemly, was a well-built metropolis expected in due course to house some 10,000 people. It had a magnificent courthouse, no less than five churches and was jammed with warehouses and stores to service the surrounding area. Packet companies kept the levee loaded with freight. Here truly was a growth area in God's Country if ever there was one. And to still any remaining doubts, one only had to peruse the *Nininger Daily Bugle*. Of all the phony attributes of Nininger, at least the *Daily Bugle* did actually exist, although it appeared weekly or biweekly or triweekly depending on how energetic its publisher was at any particular moment. The paper was loaded with local advertising—dry goods stores, hardware stores, groceries, millinery shops, blacksmith shops, shoe stores, all obviously thriving. Each issue carried accounts of a new store opening, complete with a total of its receipts for the day. It was very impressive fiction. As a contemporary account put it: "Every name and every business was fictitious, coined in the fertile brain of this chief of all promoters. It was enough to deceive the very elect— and it did. When the Eastern man read that there were six or eight lots, lying just west of Smith & Jones's drygoods store, on West Prairie Street, that could be had at a thousand dollars per lot if taken quickly, and they were well worth twice that money on account of the advantageous situation, they were snapped up as a toad snaps flies on a summer day." In fact, some plain prairie land two miles from the river to which the anonymous promoters had not even bothered to obtain title, went for as high as $10,000 per acre. "If the editor or the proprietor had been found in Nininger in the following spring when the dupes began to appear, one or two of the jack oaks with which the city lots were plentifully clothed would have borne a larger fruit than acorns. Even the printer who set the type was forced to flee for his life."

An even more tragic swindle was the so-called Rolling Stone colony, also in Minnesota Territory. When some 400 purchasers, mostly from New York, arrived in Rolling Stone in the spring of 1852, they expected to find a thriving metropolis with library, lecture hall, a large greenhouse, a hotel, a large warehouse and a fine dock. That was how they had described the area to steamboat officers, who said they had never heard of such a place. The colonists, however, had produced maps supplied them by one William Haddock and from the maps the boatmen had pinpointed the location some three miles above Wabasha Prairie, on Sioux Indian land. Having insisted on being put ashore there, the colonists built sod houses for themselves or burrowed shelters in the riverbanks, but sickness came and many died through the summer and autumn. With the onset of winter, more died and the area was abandoned.

Waddell, Reed (1859–1895) *swindler*

Among the most successful American swindlers to operate both in this country and in Europe during the last century, Reed Waddell was an artful practitioner of the green goods racket and without doubt the greatest of all at the gold brick swindle.

Some historians erroneously credit Waddell with originating the gold brick game in New York in 1880, but there is ample evidence that the racket was pulled before that. It is known, for instance, that Wyatt Earp and Mysterious Dave Mather were selling "gold bricks" to gullible cowboys in 1878 in Mobeetie, Tex. Even though Waddell did not invent the game, he certainly made it pay off more than anyone else had.

The son of a very rich and respectable Springfield, Ill. family, Waddell refused to go into the family business and instead gravitated to gambling circles. In 1880 he turned up in New York with the first gold brick to be offered for sale there. The brick was actually a lead bar covered with three platings of gold and containing a slug of solid gold in the center. Waddell would tell a potential

sucker that he was forced to sell the brick. He would then guide the victim to an accomplice posing as an assayer, who would declare the brick pure gold. If the victim was still dubious, Waddell would impulsively dig out the slug of real gold in the center and insist the man take it to a jeweler himself for another test. When the assay turned out positive, the sucker was hooked. Waddell sold his first lead brick for $4,000, never got less than $3,500 and often made twice that price.

Another of Waddell's cons was the green goods swindle. In this scheme Waddell would show a sucker some real money, tell him it was counterfeit and then offer to sell him a large batch of the bills at bargain prices. Once the sucker was convinced the merchandise was absolutely undetectable, he would eagerly agree to make a big buy. At the time of the transaction he would again be shown real money, but at the last moment the package containing the bills would be switched for a similar-looking one in which there was nothing but cut-up pieces of green paper. From 1880 to 1890 Waddell took in more than a quarter of a million dollars with these two schemes before switching exclusively to gold bricks, a scam whose advantage was the great time lag before the victim realized he'd been taken. Waddell found Europe, especially Paris and London, an ideal locale for pulling the gold brick swindle. In March 1895 he was killed by another swindler named Tom O'Brien in a dispute over the split in one of their capers.

See also: GOLD BRICK SWINDLE, GREEN GOODS SWINDLE.

Wagner, John F. (1893–1950) embezzler

It has been said that the motives for most embezzlers are one or more of the three R's: rum, redheads and race horses. What made one of this country's greatest embezzlers so different was that he was motivated by none of the three.

John F. Wagner was the cashier of the First National Bank in the little coal town of Cecil, Pa. When the bank examiners came calling one Monday morning in 1950, they found Wagner sprawled dead on the floor next to the vault, a bullet in his head. Soon, they discovered why. The 57-year-old Wagner, a resident of Cecil all his life, was short the sum of $1,125,000.

But the motivation for the embezzlement remained a puzzle, since Wagner didn't wench, drink or gamble. In fact, he only owned two winter suits, one of which he was buried in. The examiners solved the puzzle when they found a note in Wagner's handwriting. "The reason for the shortage was because of paying checks that were not good." Appended to the note was a list of persons who had defaulted on their loans or had written scores of rubber checks. Townspeople had an explanation for Wagner's downfall: he was a complete soft touch who never could turn away a friend in need.

Authorities went about trying to make as many people as possible meet their debts. But for Wagner, it was too late.

See also: EMBEZZLEMENT.

watered stock swindle

"Watered stock" is the term used to describe a stock swindle in which the assets of a company, real or imagined, have been exaggerated to attract gullible investors.

The term is believed to have originated out of a time-honored tradition in cattle country. Unscrupulous stockmen would drive their animals to market while giving them all the dry feed stuff they could hold down. Just before reaching the selling yards, the cattle would be allowed to drink all the water they wanted. Since the animals were sold by weight, the watered stock brought in considerable extra profits.

We Boys Mob swindlers

One of the most audacious group of swindlers in America was the so-called We Boys Mob of the 1920s, who consistently hoodwinked the supposedly cynical and savvy journalists of the nation's newspapers. The gang, often no more than two fast talkers, would hit a newspaper city room with a sad tale about the death of some "old-time newspaperman," a story that was fictitious but profitable. The spiel would go something like: "We boys are getting together to see that he gets a decent burial and have something in the pot afterward for the widow, and knowing how all you guys feel about the boys in the business, we were sure all of you would like to make a small donation to build the kitty." There were just a few newsrooms exempt from such flimflams, which would only be discovered when the old reporter would one day saunter into the office. The racket died after newspapers ordered much closer checking of facts whenever the death of a journalist was reported.

Weil, Joseph "Yellow Kid" (1875?–1976)
con man

Joseph "Yellow Kid" Weil probably invented and practiced more swindles than any other confidence operator in the history of American crime and was most certainly the greatest con man of the 20th century. The only man to come close to him was Fred "the Deacon" Buckminster, who ironically started out in life as a plainclothes policeman in Chicago working on the vice and bunco squad.

In 1908 Buckminster had a warrant to pick up Weil after a waterproofing cover he had been paid to paint on some city buildings washed off with the first rains. As Buckminster was escorting Weil to the precinct house, his prisoner handed him a wad of bills. Buckminster counted $10,000. "How'd you get this?" he asked. Weil said from his swindles. Buckminster weighed the money in one hand and his badge in the other. He pocketed the money, tossed away the badge and shook hands with the Kid. They became partners in scams for the next quarter century.

Even in his twenties Weil could affect a most earnest and dignified appearance. At the turn of the century he and Colonel Jim Porter, a former riverboat gambler, carried off what became known as the Great Michigan "Free Land" Swindle. Weil introduced Porter around as an eccentric millionaire who was giving away free lots. The pair gave the lots to prostitutes, madams, bartenders, waiters and even Chicago policemen. The two then opened a sales office and showed the usual artist's concept of a huge vacationland

Yellow Kid Weil: "I never cheated an honest man...only rascals."

planned for the area, provided the supposed millionaire didn't give all the lots away before it was completed and ready for sale. Whenever Porter would give away some lots—which he and Weil had purchased at $1 an acre—Weil would sidle up to the sucker and beg him not to tell anyone else or everyone would be wanting free lots. He also advised the recipients of the land to make sure they had the transaction recorded at the county seat in Michigan. That was the key to the swindle. The recording fee was $30 and the recorder happened to be Porter's cousin. Previously, the fee was $2 but Porter's cousin had raised it with the understanding that $15 would go to Weil and Porter and he would keep the rest. Weil and Porter made just over $16,000 from this neat little flimflam.

In another of his great cons Weil posed as mining engineer Pope Yateman, who reportedly had garnered a fortune in Chile. Yateman was written up in *McClure's* magazine under the title "$100,000 A Year," together with a large picture of him. For a price a crooked printer who specialized in "first editions" of famous books agreed to substitute Weil's picture for Yateman's and reprint the required pages. Weil rebound the pages into actual copies of the magazine and then toured the Midwest trimming the gullible. He and a confederate would zero in on a rich man eager to invest in mining ventures and then Weil's confederate would mention the article in *McClure's*. Unfortunately, the confederate would say, he had no copies of the magazine, but "I'm sure you'll find one at the local library."

The swindlers had, of course, pinched the library copy and substituted a doctored one. The gullible victim would rush to the library, find the article with Weil's picture and be totally convinced. As soon as Weil milked a huge investment from the sucker, his confederate would retrieve the doctored copy of the magazine and return the original. As Weil often recalled later, "You can imagine the victim's amazement after being swindled, to go to the library and look up that article only to find that the picture did not resemble me at all!"

One of Weil and Buckminster's greatest coups was renting a vacant bank in Muncie, Ind., and stocking it with con men and their lady friends to act as depositors so that the pair could con financiers into investing in the bank.

Born in Chicago in 1875, Weil started hanging out in underworld dives early in life, almost always with a copy of the *New York Journal*, which contained his favorite comic strip, "Hogan's Alley and the Yellow Kid." Soon, all the crooks in town started calling Weil the Yellow Kid. He married young and had a devoted wife who spent most of her years trying to get him to go straight. Weil often tried for her sake, but even his honest efforts proved tainted. He once attempted to make a living selling a Catholic encyclopedia; using the name Daniel O'Connell, he told a priest in Flint, Mich. that the Holy Father, Pius X, had expressed the wish that at least 2,000 copies be placed in homes in Flint. The priest bought a set, and on the strength of that, Weil sold 80 more sets, earning $1,600 in commissions. Then the priest learned of Weil's imposture and canceled his order. Weil went back to his basic con rackets, selling phony stock and running phony boxing matches and horse races.

Although extremely glib, Weil, like other con men, was frequently arrested. Usually, he beat the rap because almost always his victim was put in a position of having been knowingly involved in a crooked scheme. "I never cheated an honest man," Weil often proclaimed, "only rascals." Still, he was convicted several times and did a number of stretches in prison. In 1934 Weil announced he had retired from the swindle game. Of course, he was lying. He had by then made some $8 million through his cons and was not about to give up the game.

Weil was always ready to lend a hand to a parish for a fund drive. One day he was walking down a Chicago street with a certain monsignor discussing a fund drive when a member of the police confidence squad stopped him and questioned him on his activities. Weil insisted he was on the level. The monsignor joined in to back him up, whereupon the detective turned on him and said, "You, aren't you ashamed to be wearing the cloth for a swindle?" The officer took both of them in and held them for questioning.

In 1948 the Kid decided to write his memoirs with Chicago journalist W. T. Brannon, once again announcing he was going straight. He proceeded to sell the movie rights to his autobiography to Brannon and then to a Hollywood studio.

One of his last attempted coups was to try to establish a little independent republic on a small island made of fill, somewhere in Lake Michigan. His object, he told Saul Bellow in a magazine interview, was to make himself eligible under the foreign aid program.

Weil died February 26, 1976. Newspapers listed his age as 100, a goal he often said he planned to attain. Quite a few printed records, however, indicated Weil was really born in 1877 rather than 1875, as he claimed in his later years.

See also: FRED BUCKMINSTER, GREAT MICHIGAN "FREE LAND" SWINDLE.

Wet Stock   stolen cattle

Many of today's great cattle fortunes were built by herds of "wet stock." The owner of a big spread would announce he was going to Mexico to buy cattle and his riders would be put on double or triple pay because of the "danger" involved. It was a shopping trip for which no money was needed, since the rancher would merely locate a large herd of cattle, stampede it away from its Mexican guards and drive the animals to the border, crossing the Rio Grande in the middle of the night. Mexican troops and cowboys might follow the rustlers' tracks to the river but

would hesitate to cross; the United States was intolerant of Mexicans retrieving their stolen property by force on the American side of the border. When the American rustlers felt there was a real chance that the Mexicans might continue the pursuit, the cattle would be driven straight to Kansas for sale. The profits would then be used to make legitimate purchase of American stock.

Occasionally, American rancher-rustlers would make an actual money offer to a Mexican owner. The price, of course, would be insultingly low, but the Mexican would look at the American army of cowboys and judge for himself whether it was prudent to accept some money or none at all.

white-collar crime

Despite America's growing concern about what is regarded as a surge in crime, one sort of criminal activity, easily the most pervasive and probably the one with the greatest impact on people's everyday life, is usually ignored. It is "white-collar crime," which can be defined as the criminal activities of middle- and upper-class citizens, generally college-educated, who steal in their occupational roles in government, the professions and business.

The crimes include embezzlements, antitrust violations, business swindles, graft taking, income tax evasion, stock frauds, defrauding the government, violations of pure food and drug laws, consumer frauds and union-management collusion. It is impossible to measure the actual extent of white-collar crime. For example, based on arrest records, well over 10,000 embezzlement cases are believed to occur each year. However, many experts are convinced that less than one embezzler in 10 is ever reported to the police or prosecuted. The President's Commission on Law Enforcement and Administration of Justice estimated that $200 million is embezzled each year, and embezzlement is a minor offense in the white-collar crime field.

President Lyndon B. Johnson commented in 1967, "The economic cost of white-collar crime—embezzlement, petty theft from business, consumer frauds, anti-trust violations, and the like—dwarfs that of all crimes of violence."

Edwin H. Sutherland, a sociologist who coined the term "white-collar crime," wrote in 1940:

> The financial cost of white-collar-crime is probably several times as great as the financial cost of all the crimes which are customarily regarded as the crime problem. An officer of a chain store in one year embezzled $600,000, which was 6 times as much as the annual losses from 500 burglaries and robberies of the stores in that chain. Public enemies numbered one to 6 secured $130,000 by burglary and robbery in 1938, while the sum stolen by Krueger is estimated at $250 million; or nearly 2,000 times as much.

Some major white-collar criminals who have been convicted and sentenced in recent years include Billie Sol Estes, who developed a multimillion dollar scheme to swindle money from farmers for nonexistent fertilizer tanks; Eddie Gilbert who fled to South America after stealing $1,953,000 from a company of which he had been president; and Tony DeAngelis, who raised $150 million by showing creditors fraudulent and forged warehouse receipts for vegetable oil that did not exist. In the field of influence peddling, Robert G. "Bobby" Baker went to prison for his illegal activities while secretary to the Democratic majority in the U. S. Senate under President Johnson. From 1955 until he resigned in 1963, Baker's net worth grew from $11,000 to $1.7 million. Other political influence cases have involved former New York City Water Commissioner James L. Marcus and former Democratic leader Carmine DeSapio. White-collar crime convictions even reached the office of the vice president when Spiro Agnew pleaded no contest to an income tax evasion charge after being forced to resign his vice presidency in 1973.

In addition, there is an almost endless amount of white-collar crime committed by officials of some of the biggest corporate entities in this country. Generally, their punishment is hardly commensurate with their offenses. Yet, while the effect of white-collar crime on the public purse is obviously enormous, very little demand for reform is heard from the public, especially the articulate middle and upper classes.

In *The Thief in the White Collar* by Norman Jaspan, an expert in the field of security, and Hillel Black, the authors cite a case that perhaps typifies the extent of the problem.

> In one suburban store recently we found 29 part-time employees involved in theft. Two were elementary school principals, one a parochial school principal, another a credit manager of a large company, another an insurance adjuster and so on.
>
> The merchandise they voluntarily returned exceeded $50,000. Total loss to the store—over $200,000. Most of the thieves held two jobs so they could afford to live in the new suburban area surrounding the store. The store carried items they needed in their new homes. As they helped each other steal, one would say to the other, "Be my guest."

Whitney, Richard F. (1888–1974) financial manipulator

Richard Whitney, former president of the New York Stock Exchange, earned himself two quite different nicknames during his checkered career. The epitome of conservative respectability, he was charged by the Bankers' Pool with handling the purchase of millions of dollars in stock on Black Thursday in 1929 in an effort to reinforce public confidence in the market; for his efforts he became known as the Strongman of Wall Street. In 1938 it was discovered that Whitney had misappropriated the securities of the clients of his bond company to cover his own losses. Renamed the Wolf of Wall Street, Whitney was sent to Sing Sing. He served three years and never returned to the Street, disappearing from sight for a time and then turning up as the manager of a fiber mill in Florida. He died in obscurity in 1974 at the age of 86.

PHOTO CREDITS

BIBLIOGRAPHY

Following is a bibliography of selected resources for further reading on frauds, deceptions and swindles as well as the history of crimes in America in general.

Adams, Ramon F. *Burs Under the Saddle*. Norman: University of Oklahoma Press, 1964.

Adler, Polly. *A House Is Not a Home*. New York: Popular Library, 1954.

Allen, Frederick Lewis. *Only Yesterday, An Informal History of the Nineteen Twenties*. New York: Harper & Bros., 1931.

———. *Since Yesterday*. New York: Harper & Bros., 1940.

Asbury, Herbert. *The Gangs of New York*. New York: Alfred A. Knopf, Inc., 1927.

———. *The Barbary Coast, An Informal History of the San Francisco Underworld*. Garden City, N.Y.: Garden City Publishing Company, Inc., 1933.

———. *Sucker's Progress*. New York: Dodd, Mead and Company, Inc., 1938.

———. *Gem of the Prairie*. New York: Alfred A. Knopf, Inc., 1940.

———. *The French Quarter, An Informal History of the New Orleans Underworld*. New York: Alfred A. Knopf, Inc., 1940.

———. *The Great Illusion: An Informal History of Prohibition*. New York: Doubleday & Co., 1950.

Berger, Meyer. *The Eighty Million*. New York: Simon & Schuster, 1942.

Block, Eugene B. *The Wizard of Berkeley*. New York: Coward-McCann, 1958.

———. *Great Train Robberies of the West*. New York: Coward-McCann, 1959.

———. *Great Stagecoach Robbers in the West*. New York: Doubleday & Co., Inc. 1962.

———. *Fifteen Clues*. Garden City, N.Y.: Doubleday & Co., Inc., 1968.

Bolitho, William. *Murder for Profit*. New York: Harper & Bros., 1926.

Bonanno, Joseph. *A Man of Honor, The Autobiography of Joseph Bonanno*. New York: Simon & Schuster, 1983.

Boswell, Charles, and Lewis Thompson. *The Girls in Nightmare House*. New York: Gold Medal, 1955.

———. *Practitioners of Murder*. New York: Collier, 1962.

Brynes, Thomas. *Professional Criminals in America*. New York: Chelsea House, 1969.

Burns, Walter Noble. *The One-Way Ride*. Garden City, N.Y.: Doubleday, Doran & Company, 1931.

Caesar, Gene. *Incredible Detective: The Biography of William J. Burns*. Englewood Clifs, N.J.: Prentice-Hall, 1968.

Chandler, David. *Brothers in Blood: The Rise of the Criminal Brotherhoods*. New York: Dutton, 1975.

Churchill, Allen. *A Pictorial History of American Crime*. New York: Holt, Rinehart & Winston,

1964.

Coates, Robert M. *The Outlaw Years: The History of the Land Pirates of the Natchez Trace.* New York: The Literary Guild of America, 1930.

Collins, Ted, ed. *New York Murders.* New York: Sloan & Pearce, 1944.

Crouse, Russell. *Murder Won't Out.* New York: Pennant Books, 1953.

Croy, Homer. *He Hanged Them High.* Duell, Sloan & Pearce, 1952.

DeFord, Miriam Allen. *Murders Sane & Mad.* New York: Abelard-Schuman, Ltd., 1965.

Demaris, Ovid. *Captive City.* New York: Lyle Stuart, Inc., 1969.

DeVol, George. *Forty Years a Gambler on the Mississippi.* New York: H. Holt & Company, 1926.

Drago, Harry Sinclair. *Outlaws on Horseback.* New York: Dodd, Mead & Company, 1964.

Eisenberg, Dennis; Uri Dan; and Eli Landau. *Meyer Lansky, Mogul of the Mob.* New York & London: Paddington Press Ltd., 1979.

Elman, Robert. *Fired in Anger.* Garden City, N.Y.: Doubleday & Company, Inc., 1968.

Emrich, Duncan. *It's an Old Wild West Custom.* New York: The Vanguard Press, Inc., 1949.

Emery, Edward Van. *Sins of New York.* New York: Frederick A. Stokes, 1930.

———. *Sins of America as "Exposed" by the Police Gazette.* New York, Fredrick A. Stokes Co., 1931.

Frank, Judge Jerome, and Barbara Frank. *Not Guilty.* Garden City, N.Y., Doubleday & Company, Inc., 1957.

Godwin, John. *Alcatraz 1868–1963.* New York: Doubleday & Co., 1963.

———. *Murder USA.* New York: Ballantine Books 1978.

Gosch, Martin A., and Richard Hammer. *The Last Testament of Lucky Luciano.* Boston: Little, Brown, 1975.

Hammer, Richard. *Playboy's Illustrated History of Organized Crime.* Chicago: Playboy Press, 1975.

Hecht, Ben. *A Child of the Century.* New York: Simon & Schuster, 1954.

———. *Charlie, The Improbable Life and Times of Charles MacArthur.* New York: Harper & Bros., 1957.

Horan, James D. *Desperate Men.* New York: G. P. Putnam Sons, 1949.

———. *Pictorial History of the Wild West.* New York: Crown Publishers, Inc. 1954.

———. *The Desperate Years.* New York: Crown Publishers, Inc., 1962.

———. *The Pinkertons, The Detective Dynasty That Made History.* New York: Crown Publishers, Inc. 1967.

Hynd, Alan. *Murder, Mayhem and Mystery.* New York: A. S. Barnes & Co., 1958.

Jackson, Joseph Henry. *San Francisco Murders.* New York: Duell, Sloan and Pearce, 1947.

Johnston, James A. *Alcatraz Island Prison.* New York: Charles Scribner's Sons, 1949.

Karpis, Alvin, with Bill Trent. *The Alvin Karpis Story.* New York: Coward McCann & Geoghegan, Inc., 1971.

Katcher, Leo. *The Big Bankroll, The Life and Times of Arnold Rothstein.* New York: Harper & Bros., 1959.

Katz, Leonard. *Uncle Frank: The Biography of Frank Costello.* New York: Drake, 1973.

Kefauver, Estes. *Crime in America.* New York: Doubleday & Co., 1951.

Kilgallen, Dorothy. *Murder One.* New York: Random House, 1967.

Klein, Alexander, ed. *Grand Deception.* New York: J. B. Lippincott & Company, 1955.

———. *The Double Dealers.* Philadelphia and New York: J. B. Lippincott & Company, 1958.

Kobler, John. *Capone.* New York: G. P. Putnam's Sons, 1971.

Kohn, George C. *Encyclopedia of American Scandal.* New York: Facts On File, 1989.

Lawes, Warden Lewis Edward. *Twenty Thousand Years in Sing Sing.* New York: R. Long & R. R. Smith, Inc., 1932.

Lewis, Alfred Henry. *The Apaches of New York.* New York: G. W. Dillingham Company, 1912.

———. *Nation-Famous New York Murders.* G. W. Dillingham Company, 1914.

McLoughlin, Denis. *Wild and Wooly.* Garden City, N.Y.: Doubleday & Company, Inc., 1975.

Maas, Peter. *The Valachi Papers.* New York: G. P. Putnam's Sons, 1968.

Messick, Hank. *Lansky.* New York: G. P. Putnam's Sons, 1971.

Morrel, Ed. *The Twenty-fifth Man.* Montclair, N.J.: New Era Publishing Co., 1924.

Murray, George. *The Legacy of Al Capone.* New York: G. P. Putnam's Sons, 1975.

Ness, Eliot, with Oscar Fraley. *The Untouchables.*

New York: Julian Messner, 1957.

Newton, Michael. *Hunting Humans.* New York: Avon Books, 1992.

Pearson, Edmund L. *Studies in Murder.* New York: MacMillan Company, 1926.

———. *More Studies in Murder.* New York: Harrison Smith & Robert Haas, Pub., 1936.

Peterson, Virgil. *Barbarians in Our Midst.* Little, Brown & Co., 1936.

———. *The Mob.* Ottawa, Illinois: Green Hill Publishers, Inc., 1983.

Radin, Edward D. *12 Against the Law.* New York: Bantam Books, 1952.

———. *12 Against Crime.* New York: Collier Books, 1961.

Reid, Ed. *Mafia.* New York: Random House, 1952.

———. *The Grim Reapers.* Chicago: Henry Regnery Co., 1969.

Reid, Ed, and Ovid Demaris. *The Green Felt Jungle.* New York: Trident Press, 1963.

Rodell, Marie F. *New York Murders.* New York: Duell, Sloan and Pearce, 1944.

Salerno, Ralph, and John Tompkins. *The Crime Confederation.* New York: Doubleday & Co., 1969.

Sann, Paul. *The Lawless Decade.* New York: Crown Publishers, Inc., 1957.

Scott, Gini Graham. *Homicide: 100 Years of Murder in America.* Lincolnwood, Illinois: Roxbury Park, 1998.

Smith, Alton. *Syndicate City.* Chicago: Henry Regnery Co., 1954.

Sondern, Frederic, Jr. *Brotherhood of Evil: The Mafia.* New York: Farrar, Straus & Cudahy, 1959.

Stone, Irving. *Clarence Darrow for the Defense.* New York: Doubleday & Co., 1941.

Tallant, Robert. *Ready to Hang.* New York: Harper & Bros., 1952.

Teresa, Vincent, with Thomas C. Renner. *My Life in the Mafia.* Garden City, New York, Doubleday & Company, 1973.

Teresa, Vincent. *Teresa's Mafia.* Garden City, New York: Doubleday & Company, Inc., 1975.

Toland, John. *The Dillinger Days.* New York: Random House, 1963.

Touhy, Roger, with Ray Brennan. *The Stolen Years.* Cleveland: Pennington Press, Inc., 1959.

Turkus, Burton B., and Sid Feder. *Murder, Inc.: The Story of the Syndicate.* Farrar, Straus & Young Co., 1951.

Turner, Wallace. *Gambler's Money.* Boston: Houghton Mifflin Co., 1965.

Wendt, Lloyd, and Herman Kogen. *Lords of the Levee.* New York: Bobbs-Merrill, 1943.

Wilson, Frank J., and Beth Day. *Special Agent.* New York: Holt, Rinehart & Winston, 1965.

Whitehead, Don. *The F.B.I. Story.* New York: Random House, 1956.

Wolf, Marvin J., and Katherine Mader. *L.A. Crime.* New York: Facts On File Publications, 1986.

Wooldridge, Clifton R. *Hands Up! In the World of Crime or Twelve Years a Detective.* Chicago: Police Publishing Co., 1901.

Index

Boldface page numbers indicate main headings.